MW01059704

B

THE POLITICAL CULTURE
OF LEADERSHIP

THE POLITICAL CULTURE OF LEADERSHIP IN THE UNITED ARAB EMIRATES

Andrea B. Rugh

THE POLITICAL CULTURE OF LEADERSHIP IN THE UNITED ARAB EMIRATES

First published in 2007 by
PALGRAVE MACMILLAN™
175 Fifth Avenue, New York, N.Y. 10010 and
Houndmills, Basingstoke, Hampshire, England RG21 6XS
Companies and representatives throughout the world.

PALGRAVE MACMILLAN is the global academic imprint of the Palgrave Macmillan division of St. Martin's Press, LLC and of Palgrave Macmillan Ltd. Macmillan® is a registered trademark in the United States, United Kingdom and other countries. Palgrave is a registered trademark in the European Union and other countries.

ISBN-13: 978–1–4039–7785–4
ISBN-10: 1–4039–7785–2

Library of Congress Cataloging-in-Publication Data

Rugh, Andrea B.
    The political culture of leadership in the United Arab Emirates / by Andrea B. Rugh.
        p.cm.
    Includes bibliographical references and index.
    ISBN 1–4039–7785–2 (alk. paper)
    1. United Arab Emirates—Politics and government. 2. Political culture—United Arab Emirates—History. 3. Tribal government—United Arab Emirates—History. 4. Leadership—United Arab Emirates—History. 5. United Arab Emirates—History. I. Title.

IQ1844.A58R84 2007
306.2095357—dc22   2006050666

A catalogue record for this book is available from the British Library.

Design by Newgen Imaging Systems (P) Ltd., Chennai, India.

First edition: March 2007

10 9 8 7 6 5 4 3 2 1

Printed in the United States of America.

To David, Douglas, and Nicholas

CONTENTS

PREFACE

This book examines the political culture of leadership in the United Arab Emirates (UAE) over the last two centuries—roughly between 1800 and 2006—as local states evolved from largely egalitarian societies into states with power in the hands of a few ruling families. Although the people of these seven emirates, Abu Dhabi, Dubai, Sharja, Ajman, Um al Qaiwain, Ras al Khaima, and Fujaira, shared a common culture, historically they occupied different niches in the complicated ecosystem of the Gulf, and therefore experienced political and economic pressures in unique ways. As a result, rulers differed in political objectives, even while drawing on similar strategic approaches.

Political culture consists of the shared values, norms, expectations, approaches, and conventions that shape political practice, and allow its meanings to be communicated to others of similar view. The approach used here to study political behavior relies on typical techniques of anthropology, personal observation, comparison during the same and different time periods, and holism—a perspective that examines any and all detail that sheds light on the subject matter. The anthropologist's job in this case is to identify the recurrent themes in political leadership and extrapolate back to conceptual frameworks that may have inspired them. The aim is to fill a middle ground in research between one that focuses on global forces shaping history and politics, and one that examines limited groups in restricted time frames. Both kinds of study are valuable, but it is also important to understand the "worldview" that informs the actions of leaders.[1]

Two conversations with Emiratis encouraged me to start this task. One was a discussion between an Emirati scholar and members of a delegation from a prestigious U.S. think-tank. The Americans were seeking academic cooperation and funds for a Gulf studies program. After listening to the particulars of the program, most of which involved studies of regional security and strategic oil interests, the Emirati scholar commented wryly, "But your analyses have nothing to do with the way politics work here." No one from the delegation responded, nor was it likely they understood what he meant. The second comment occurred in a discussion with an Emirati professor about the personal networks and connections that underlie Emirati politics. He concluded enthusiastically, "That's the way politics work but nobody writes about it."

Clifford Geertz once said that "In attempting to answer grand questions . . . the anthropologist is always inclined to turn toward the concrete, the particular, the microscopic . . . (hoping) to find in the little what eludes us in the large, to stumble upon general truths while sifting through special cases" (1968: 4). This study is no exception. Much of the interpretation is based on personal observation and interviews over the last 40 years, much of it spent in residence in Arab countries. The detailed historical information comes from British Foreign Office records, which lamentably are the main primary source for the period before 1972. There are difficulties in depending on these foreign sources. Most importantly, they are only glimpses of the complex social life that existed at the time and therefore do not provide the fertile data fields anthropologists enjoy when immersing themselves in local societies. More seriously, the view is through the eyes of outsiders who often do not understand local culture as well as they might. Critics have claimed quite rightly, that too much of the history of the UAE relies on foreign sources. This is undeniable, but even these critics recognize that there are few other accessible options. What makes the British records useful is that resident officers tried to record the actions of rulers as accurately as possible even when they themselves were not certain of what it was they were observing. This often forced them to delve into local relationships and motivations in trying to understand unfolding events. [2]

My information also comes from several careful histories written about the UAE by Muhammad Morsy Abdullah, Frauke Heard-Bey, Rosemarie Zahlan, HH Shaikh Sultan al Qassimi, Donald Hawley, B.J. Slot, and J.B. Kelly. These authors have drawn heavily on archival materials of the British, Dutch, and to lesser degree, other nations. There would be no point in trying to replicate their work. But I do refer to them frequently to report leaders' activities and the local contexts that shaped behavior during certain periods.

Theoretical inspiration comes from some of the great writers on tribal structures Lancaster writing on the Rwala, Madawi al Rashid writing on Saudi Arabia, Barth on the Pathans, and others. Metaphorical help comes from the creative thinker, Fuad Khuri, who brings to the description of Middle Eastern societies insights into their essential natures. And of course the great Arab sociologist Ibn Khaldun always provides cogent insights, many of which remain fresh even after seven centuries. The recently published work of Peter Lienhardt provides a model for what I consider useful insights into the workings of politics in the UAE. Closely in contact with the Abu Dhabi ruler, Shakhbut Nahyan, he draws nuanced conclusions from firsthand information.

Evidence for marriage patterns comes from genealogical information, the core of which is found in the genealogies published by the UAE documentation Center in Abu Dhabi. The problem with these genealogies from the perspective of understanding the role family plays in political culture is that females do not appear in the official record. As a result I spent a great deal of time trying to reconstruct marriage links and identifying female children who are part of the invisible record. This information was gathered painstakingly from several sources, including British Foreign Office documents. Though incomplete and sketchy, the information is reasonably accurate since the writers had no conceivable purpose other than to inform themselves about family members of public personalities. I also added recent wives and children from living people during my residence in the country. Overall I collected a large amount of genealogical data covering two and in some cases three centuries. But inevitably there are gaps. Often, too, there are contradictions in published works, and outright mistakes that cannot be resolved at this time. I recognize my limitations in this respect and consider this a work in progress that others will correct and build upon.

The details of royal marriages have significance since marriage was and remains an important tool that rulers use to promote their political interests. One cannot of course be certain that a particular leader chose a specific bride for a specific political reason, but if he furthered his interests at the time, it is likely that a political motive existed. Almost certainly his constituents assumed it did. These connections are sufficiently important to risk being wrong occasionally, since little other information exists to reliably inform us about what local people were thinking.

A final difficulty in obtaining information is local sensitivity on two points, first, reluctance by Emiratis to discuss past animosities among groups, including murders, tribal conflicts, and disloyalties, and second, an aversion to naming female family members.[3] These sensitivities have several implications. First, information of this kind is difficult to collect from many people, especially males who are the most reluctant to divulge such information. Second, historians writing about the UAE often consciously avoid any but the most occasional mention of these subjects, downplaying the considerable role women played in the country's history. Finally, the element of privacy and courtesy in writers' reticence raises the question of how to present crucial information. Should one avoid mentioning unpleasant aspects of tribal relations, such as the consequences to family branches that unsuccessfully challenged rulers? Should one omit naming women or the role they played in local politics? Would leaving out this information not support the myth that women are "invisible" in Arab society? In the end I concluded that the information in both cases is too important to omit, yet at the same time I regret any discomfort it causes Emiratis.[4]

A number of people have been helpful in answering questions about current and past ruling family members. I would like to acknowledge their assistance but due to the sensitivities mentioned above I will not include names. I want also to thank Rachel Navarre for help in computerizing the maps and genealogical trees, and the Middle East Institute for providing me with the status of Adjunct Scholar while I was completing the manuscript.

I do not pretend to know everything one would like to know about how political relationships work in the UAE—the culture is extremely and I believe intentionally, opaque and difficult to understand—but I do feel the time is ripe to publish the outlines of personal politics in this interesting region of the world. The definitive study will one day be written by an Emirati—but sensitivities are still such that it is too early for that to happen.

Note on usage and organization: I have simplified both the transliteration of Arab names and the use of titles. For the most part the shortest spellings are used that reasonably convey the Arabic sounds to an English reader. Thus "Nahayyan" becomes "Nahyan." "H" at the end of a word is dropped as in "Sharja" instead of "Sharjah," or "Fujaira" instead of "Fujairah." Rather than prefixing a title, such as "Shaikh" used in the UAE for male members of ruling families[5] to every mention of a ruler, as common politeness requires, I have often dropped the title. The term "ruler" did not technically apply to paramount leaders until the British recognized them as such. Therefore for much of the early period, the terms "paramount chief," "chief," "shaikh," and "leader" are more appropriate when referring to headmen of tribes. Even when "shaikh" became a common honorific for a ruler, there were still elders and ruling family members, even small boys of ruling families, addressed as "shaikh." The term has no real exclusionary meaning in the UAE but probably reveals what was once more true than now that chiefs were only "first among equals."

In naming people I have usually dropped the "*al*" meaning "the" to denote family or tribal collectivities. For simplicity I have also dropped the "*bin*" (son of) and "*bint*" (daughter of) that connects parts of names; for example Hussa bint Muhammad bin Khalifa becomes Hussa Muhammad Khalifa. Finally, for those not familiar with the way names are assigned in the Arabian peninsula, it is relatively simple to locate people on genealogical charts once full names are known since the names themselves give a full account of a person's patrilineal descent. Thus Zaid Sultan Zaid I Khalifa is Zaid, son of Sultan, grandson of Zaid I, and great grandson of Khalifa. When it is useful for the sake of clarity to refer to a person by more than one of his or her names I have done so. All these shortcuts may raise the eyebrows of purists but I believe they will make for a more readable text.

I have also used anthropological abbreviations to designate the relationships of people when it is important in understanding the context. The abbreviations are straightforward and easy to decipher, for example MoBr is mother's brother, FaBrSo is father's brother's son. The designations are important since the quality of relations with paternal and maternal kin is expected to be different.

I have found no satisfactory way of talking about the people of the interior of Arabia when, as frequently happened, they influenced events in the Trucial States. They can only correctly be called Saudis during the two periods when the Saud family were rulers of the Nejd from 1745 to 1881 and after Abdul Aziz Saud regained the rule from the Rashidi clan in the early-twentieth century. British records frequently refer to the people of the interior as Wahhabis after the religious reformer Muhammad ibn Abdul Wahhab (1703–1787). His followers in collaboration with the House of Saud mounted military activities to spread religion and the political ambitions of the Saud family. I have used the terms of my sources, even though in certain periods they are technically incorrect.

The book is organized in three parts The first introduces the topics covered by the book, suggests the reasons it is important to study them in the UAE context, and describes the factors that in lieu of government institutions, shape political actions, including the economic and political contexts, and the local culture or worldview. Three models are presented that describe people's expectations about the conduct of personal relations—in the tribe, the family, and with "outsiders." Although the models are "real" at an abstract level, it is important to see how they are used in the political context.

The second part consists of case studies of individual emirates, describing their leaders' political behaviors over two centuries. Material has been selected (to the extent it is available) to show the relationships of the chiefs with their kin, their constituents, other leaders, and the British. The details in the tradition of anthropology serve as the data—in effect as a "village," where we can observe and extract from leaders' behavior, the patterns of political culture. Each case concludes with a discussion of how a particular emirate's experience adds to our knowledge of political culture. The third and final part of the book draws conclusions about political culture and tribal leadership in the UAE, and suggests how they may be understood in terms of prevailing models of personal relations.

CHAPTER 1

THE ECONOMIC AND POLITICAL CONTEXT

History is a continuous chain of events. The present is only an extension of the past. He who does not know his past cannot make the best of his present and future, for it is from our past that we learn.

—Shaikh Zaid

During the twentieth century Middle Eastern tribal societies evolved into forms ranging from monarchies to republics. As they changed, they shared one feature—the tendency to concentrate power in a single ruler or president. In the fourteenth century, Ibn Khaldun (1967) wrote that it was in the nature of states to concentrate authority. Arab states in particular, he said, were founded on solidarities formed by the union of groups. When one group became more powerful than the rest, its leaders dominated other leaders.

Variation in modern Arab states is not just due to leaders' ability to dominate. Other factors including access to resources and the pressures brought about by external political and economic forces constrain their actions. Much has been written about British influence in the Gulf, the economic and political effects of tribal life, and about the discovery of oil. Important as these "external" events were in forming political structures, they constitute only one part of the story. Another part is the influence of less well-understood sociocultural factors affecting the way tribal leaders perceive their environments, and the relevance of options for meeting political challenges. Monarchy in England is not the same as monarchy in the Gulf, not so much because their institutional structures differ but because their people view the act of governing differently. We need to be careful though, not to assign too universal a framework to Arab worldviews.

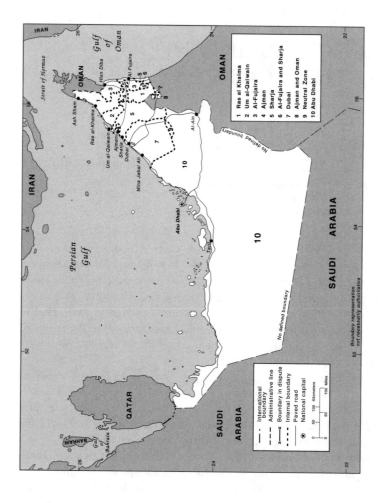

Source: http://lcweb2.loc.gov/frd/cs/united_arab_emirates/ae05_01a.pdf

Although similarities exist, views vary by geographic region, class, and time period, as well as within states.

Westerners are often said to approach history and politics through events and institutions while tribal societies focus on personalities and social networks. While the differences may not be as stark as this suggests, it underlines the importance of studying the personal aspects of leadership in tribal societies. This book examines the role of tribal leaders in the seven states of the United Arab Emirates (UAE) and looks at how their world-views intersected with local factors to shape their political agendas. The book asks four questions: "What is the political culture of leadership in a tribal society like the UAE?", "What were the external factors that transformed the shape of personal rule?", "Does a similar political culture still exist and if so how is it expressed?", and finally, "How did leaders adapt so quickly to new conditions in the Trucial States?" The analysis starts in this chapter with a short summary of the economic and political context.

Today, becoming a ruler in the UAE is comparatively straightforward—an already appointed crown prince takes over on the death of his predecessor. In the past, many aspirants only became rulers by actively seeking the position and many had their rules cut short when they failed to wield the instruments of power effectively. This poses additional questions about early regimes: What influenced tribal leaders' rise to power and how did they stay in power once there? To what extent did external forces affect politics and how did they influence the behavior of leaders? Did women have a role in what seems, on the surface, to be an exclusively male-dominated activity? If governance was organized around personalities rather than institutions, what took the place of institutions in sustaining the rule over time?

The UAE makes an excellent case example. Its seven emirates are governed by separate ruling families.[1] Considerable historic evidence shows how local rulers rose to power and maintained it over the last two centuries. The people of this small geographical area shared a common culture and until recently a similar livelihood, thus giving them a relatively similar way of perceiving and approaching the world. The individual emirates however experienced global economic and political pressures differently, partly because of their rulers' personal capabilities but also because of their different circumstances. Thus, early UAE chiefs shared similar socioeconomic conditions and viewpoints, and prospered to the extent that they ruled successfully when their circumstances changed.

The United Arab Emirates

The UAE is located on the southern coast of the Persian Gulf from Khaur Udaid in the west to Ras Musandam in the northeast. One state Fujaira is located on the Gulf of Oman. The country covers 32,300 square miles, about the size of the state of South Carolina. It was called Oman in the eighteenth century, the Trucial States during the nineteenth and early twentieth centuries, and became the United Arab Emirates in 1971 after the British withdrew from the Gulf. The entire population totaled about 100,000 at the beginning of the twentieth century and 500,000 by the time of its independence. Today the population is roughly 4 million, including approximately 80 percent who are temporary workers from South Asia, the Far East, and other Arab States. It is one of the richest countries in the world with a proven recoverable oil reserve of roughly 100 billion barrels or 10 percent of the world total and a per capita income estimated at around 16,500 dollars.

What was until the 1950s and 1960s, a region of small homogeneous settlements aggregated around protected inlets of the Persian Gulf, has now become a land of major contrasts. A drive up the coast reveals some of the differences. From the southwesterly state of Abu Dhabi, the road runs parallel to, but out of view of the sea through the main cities of Dubai, Sharja, Ajman, Um al Qaiwain (UAQ), and Ras al Khaima (RAK). From RAK, the road moves southeast through a largely unpopulated desert, until it loops eastward across the Hajar mountains to Fujaira, the only emirate located solely on the Gulf of Oman. The main distinction between the emirates is their varying levels of prosperity, with Abu Dhabi and Dubai the wealthiest at one end of the scale, and the small backwaters of Fujaira, RAK, and UAQ at the other. In the middle are Ajman and Sharja located close enough to Dubai to benefit from its modern amenities but with few resources of their own. Sharja, with some financial support from Saudi Arabia, has carved out a niche as the cultural, educational, and religious center of the Emirates with its multitude of museums, libraries, and universities.

Aerial photos of Abu Dhabi in the 1960s show a cluster of *barasti* (reed) huts surrounding a central fort in the midst of a desert landscape next to the sea. Now the city's skyscrapers rise out of palm-fringed gardens, flowering median strips, and luxurious malls. Sea-side walkways, fine restaurants, white and red sand beaches, and all the amenities of luxurious living make Abu Dhabi one of the most modern and livable cities in the world. Dubai has even more spectacular amenities built on its success as a world *entrepot* for the redistribution of goods within and outside the region. The people of Dubai with their multinational contacts form an open, sophisticated society, while by design, the people of Abu Dhabi see themselves as more tribal yet hospitable to foreigners. Abu Dhabi is visibly more conservative in business and social relations.

The smaller emirates of RAK, UAQ, and Fujaira still retain strong reminders of the not-so-remote past with their modest commercial centers, simple concrete residences, and towns that can be traversed in a matter of minutes. Visits I made to ruling families in these emirates in the 1990s were relaxed affairs, more like neighborly calls, with children brought down for viewing and social chatter about schooling, marriages, and births.

A metaphor for the rapid changes is the intergenerational differences among women in extended households. One prominent family in the interior city of Al Ain, for example, had three generation of women living in the same household. The thin wiry grandmother kept a herd of goats on the large family compound and each day swung her goatskin "churn" to make fresh butter for the family. She talked of her family's annual treks on camel taking days to reach the coast (a car now makes it in little more than an hour), and told me to punch her stomach to see how firm it was. Her daughter, in her forties, was seriously overweight and sedentary, and complained of medical problems including heart disease and diabetes. She was the first generation to move into palaces with imported servants to take care of basic household needs. Her daughters, in their teens and twenties, typified the modern generation with fluency in foreign languages, and an obsession with the latest fashions and diets. The grandmother was illiterate, the mother read basic religious texts, and the girls were enrolled in the local university where they would stay until they graduated.[2]

The Economic Context

During the nineteenth and most of the twentieth century, the people experienced a harsh and elemental existence that formed and sustained the tribal nature of society. Throughout this time the emirates were barely distinguishable from one another. Each had a main settlement along the coast, and auxiliary settlements in scattered oases of the hinterland where inhabitants cultivated dates and a few crops. The main seats of government were controlled by paramount chiefs and the smaller settlements by lesser chiefs loyal to them. The advantage of two-way access to sea and oases meant tribal members could engage in a mixed economy that included fishing, pearling, trade, and boat-building on the one side, and incipient agriculture and animal husbandry on the other. These interests fit conveniently into the seasons of the year, so that pearling was undertaken when the waters were warm between May and September, and herding took place in winter months when forage was abundant. In spring people cultivated the earth and in the fall they harvested the date crops. Herding required little manpower and therefore men were available in winter to join their shaikhs on military raids where in all likelihood they could add the spoils of warfare to their resources. Summer was sacrosanct, when able-bodied men wanted to be at the pearling banks and resisted their chiefs' requests to embark on military adventures. The shaikhs also depended on the revenues from the pearling boats and usually ceased their military activities before that season. In summer so many men were either pearling or tending inland date gardens that the coastal settlements with only women, children, and the elderly in residence, became vulnerable to attack. Not infrequently competitors took advantage of their vulnerability and launched attacks knowing that few men would be there to defend the towns.

The Bedouin of the region were mainly camel-herders but a few also kept sheep and goats. They augmented their income by selling firewood in the towns. Their chiefs often received sums from the paramount chiefs to ensure their loyalty. In summer they gathered around wells belonging to their tribes. Contrary to tradition elsewhere, the tribes of the Trucial States did not exclude other tribes from either their wells or their grazing areas, although there was somewhat more exclusivity among settled tribes in the north (Hawley 1970: 201). The traditional division between settlers and nomads was also not as distinct because of the mixed economy they pursued.

Only a portion of the country had enough rainfall or underground water to make agriculture possible. Extensive falaj (irrigation systems) were built in the eastern mountains to carry water to the crops. The main agricultural areas were located in the Hajar mountains to the north and west, the Shamaliya plains on the eastern Gulf of Oman, the oases of Liwa, Buraimi, and Dalma belonging to Abu Dhabi, Dhaid (Sharja), and Falaj al Mualla (UAQ). All the emirates had gardens in the interior where rulers extracted taxation on their production. Dates were the most important crop, but there was also some wheat and barley, and in the gardens of the Shamaliya fruit trees brought from India. Under a development scheme started in 1954 vegetables, including new varieties, were planted for local consumption (Hawley 1970: 202). By the end of the twentieth century investment in agriculture had made the UAE self-sufficient in dates and fish, almost sufficient in milk and vegetables, producing a third of its needs in eggs, and a quarter of its needs for meat and poultry (UAE Yearbook 2000/2001: 147). But during its history the diet of most inhabitants consisted mainly of dates, milk products, fish, and meat.

Throughout the period, trade was an important source of income. Seaman from the coastal areas of the Persian Gulf and the Gulf of Oman imported horses and dates from Basra and Bahrain, tobacco, carpets, sugar, and ghee from Persia and Makran in Baluchistan, rice, metal, and cloth from Bombay, coffee from Yemen, and slaves and spices from Zanzibar and other East African nations. The main exports were dates and dried fish used for food and fertilizer. Traders rode the northeast monsoons to Africa with dates and cloth from December through March and returned on the southwest monsoons between April and September (Hawley 1970: 199). Khaur Fakkan with the best natural harbor between Musandam and Muscat was the hub of these activities. The shaikhs received about a tenth of the value of all imported goods (Hawley 1970: 197).

One of the more lucrative trade commodities was slaves, with profits of as much as 20 to 50 percent (Hawley 1970: 198). They were brought from Zanzibar and other African towns to the Arabian Peninsula, Basra, and Persia. At its peak, about 12,000 slaves were traded in a year. With the Treaty of 1839, the British tried to ban slavery, but although the trade diminished in the Persian Gulf, the Bani Yas continued to trade slaves through Buraimi until the 1950s. For a time, slaves who reached British government offices in the Gulf were given their freedom.

Dubai became the main commercial port of the Trucial States for two reasons: one was its favorable location on the coast and the convenience of being able to sail up the Creek and off-load goods in the center of Dubai. More important however, was Dubai's economic climate. The precipitating event was the decline of Linga as a port on the Persian coast. In the nineteenth century, Linga was administered by an Arab governor and inhabited mainly by Arabs related to tribes in the Trucial States. But by the turn of the century the Persians took control of Linga and in 1902 established a Persian Customs Office. When they imposed high custom duties on vessels passing through the port, captains began to avoid the town and dock at Dubai instead. For the first half of the twentieth century Dubai grew at a slow but steady rate until in 1958 the rate of growth increased dramatically when it expanded its facilities. Since then it constructed a free-zone storage and industrial area, and created other amenities to attract businesses. In recent years, especially after Beirut's decline as the business capital of the Middle East, Dubai became the major *entrepot* for import and redistribution of commodities throughout the Middle East, South Asia, and the Far East. Its spectacular rise was facilitated by low customs duties, and the important role Dubai played in the gold market. Merchants would bring back gold from Europe to Dubai, and sell it legally to Indians and Pakistanis who would smuggle it into their own countries and sell it at much higher prices. The ruler in the late 1960s received customs duty of 4.52 percent on this trade (Hawley 1970: 200). Dubai also became a center for the boat-building industry.

Pearling was one of the most lucrative industries in the Gulf for hundreds of years. When piracy was suppressed in the nineteenth century, many of the sea-faring people turned to pearling as their main livelihood. The pearling banks were open to all inhabitants of the area and therefore anyone with a boat and gear could try their hand at the industry. In 1830, 3,000 boats took part in the pearling season, with roughly 350 boats from RAK and Sharja, and about the same number from Abu Dhabi and other coastal towns. A century later, the boats coming from the Trucial States numbered 1,215, with roughly equal numbers of boats run by Abu Dhabi (410), Sharja and RAK (360), and Dubai (335), and with a total of 22,000 men involved (Hawley 1970: 195). Several historians have written about the abuses associated with pearling, most of it involving the heavy debts and interest incurred by divers that made many little more than indentured slaves to boat owners. The merchants and the shaikhs earned the most from these operations, but divers who found an unusually excellent specimen could make their fortunes (Hawley 1970: 196). The market for natural pearls eventually collapsed in the late 1920s and 1930s with the Japanese invention of cultured pearls. This decline along with the world-wide depression caused many local residents to suffer serious hardship.

It was during this decline that oil discoveries first became a possibility. In 1935 the D'Arcy Exploration Company, a subsidiary of Anglo-Persian Oil Company, signed option agreements with all the Trucial States except UAQ and Kalba. These options were later assigned to Petroleum Concessions Ltd. (Hawley 1970: 209). After the hiatus caused by World War II and a number of unsuccessful drilling attempts on land, an offshore field in Abu Dhabi finally yielded oil in August 1958. By 1962 the first crude oil was exported from Das Island, followed in 1963 by oil found on Abu Dhabi's land concessions. Commercial quantities of oil were also found offshore in Dubai in 1955 but in smaller quantities than Abu Dhabi and after a peak in 1991, Dubai's oil production declined. By 2000 Abu Dhabi controlled 90 percent of the country's oil and more than 85 percent of its gas reserves. The country's proven oil reserves are 98.2 billion barrels or about 10 percent of global reserves (compared to about 22 billion barrels for the United States) and 5.8 trillion cubic meters of natural gas (www.uae.gov.ae/Government/oil_gas.htm). Sharja is the third largest hydrocarbon producer in the UAE with its offshore Mubarak field extending into Iranian territory. It shares production and revenues with Iran, and the remainder with UAQ (20 percent) and Ajman (10 percent). Sharja has about 5 percent of the country's gas reserves. RAK had estimated reserves of 400 million barrels but production ceased in 1998 (UAE Yearbook 2000/2001). No oil deposits were found in Fujaira, Ajman, or UAQ.

As a result of the changing economic situation in the Gulf over the last two centuries, the rulers' revenue sources varied both in kind and quantity.

At first their main sources of revenue came from customs, licenses, and the imposition of taxes. Although they exacted customs duties on trade goods of all kinds, with the exception of Dubai, these did not amount to much (Hawley 1970: 204). Abu Dhabi levied taxes on dates coming from its inland gardens, and licensed boats to fish off its shores. Rulers also levied taxes on pearling boats. Some collected *zakat* (an annual tax) from their constituents and neighboring tribes. From the mid-1930s, most rulers obtained some oil concession money, although it was only after the discovery and production of oil that large sums became available to Abu Dhabi and Dubai. Abu Dhabi's oil money, for example, increased from a few thousand pounds in 1963 to 63 million pounds in 1968 (Hawley 1970: 205). While the five other emirates continued to receive modest fees, by the late 1960s their main source of income was the sale of postage stamps to collectors (Hawley 1970: 204). In recent years Abu Dhabi offset some of the difference by forming the Trucial States Development Fund and supporting projects in the non-oil states.

There were thus three stages in the region's economy. The first, from roughly 1820 to the early twentieth century, saw aggressions at sea declining in favor of pearling and trade. It was a modestly prosperous time for the Trucial States. The second period, from the early to mid-twentieth century, was a time of deprivation resulting from a world depression and the collapse of the pearling industry. By the end of this time rulers began receiving limited oil concessionary fees. The third period, in the second half of the twentieth century, was a boom time for Abu Dhabi and Dubai with their massive oil incomes in one case and the expansion of commercial trade in the other. The changing circumstances throughout this period forced accommodations on local people as well as in the way tribal leaders conducted politics.

The Political Context

The forces affecting the economy were paralleled by forces shaping the political behavior of rulers. The key players in this transformation were the British. At the end of the eighteenth century, the polarities of power on the southern coast of the Persian Gulf were the maritime Qawasim family and the inland-focused Bani Yas confederation of tribes. The main political story of the nineteenth and twentieth centuries was the decline and fragmentation of the Qawasim empire in the northeast, and the expansion and consolidation of Bani Yas power in the southwest under the leadership of the paramount Nàhyan chiefs. By the end of the twentieth century the changes became accentuated with the discovery of huge quantities of oil in Abu Dhabi and insignificant amounts on Qawasim lands.

Britain's interference began with efforts to secure maritime peace in the Gulf in the early-nineteenth century. The British seemed unaware of how their actions gradually changed the structures that set limits on a local ruler's power, creating in their place new relationships and options. The British believed they were simply acting responsibly to protect maritime interests in the Gulf. As they stated again and again, it was their official policy not to meddle in the internal affairs of the local people. They continued to claim noninterference well past the time when it was evident to everyone that they were intensely involved. There were at least two reasons for their involvement. They had strong convictions about the way the emirates should be ruled, and conveyed these feelings when approving or disapproving actions of local leaders. Also as a consequence of the overwhelming power they brought to conflicts, they unknowingly stepped into a locally recognized role, albeit at a level never before seen in the area. This was the role of paramount chief whose power brokering became essential to the ambitions of lesser chiefs.

Before British involvement, politics in the shaikhdoms were organized around Ibn Khaldun's "alignment of solidarities to gain dominance." Shaikhs would line up strategic tribes to expand or defend their interests. The system involved creating personal loyalties and not defending land, although territorial benefits accompanied tribal loyalties. Enemies one day could become allies the next based on momentary interests.

A rough form of participatory politics was involved. Leaders were accessible and accountable. They defended their followers against aggressors so they could safely pursue their livelihoods. In return, the followers pledged their loyalty to their chiefs. Without their willing support, a chief could only pursue limited objectives, since his control over his followers even at the best of times was tenuous. Leaders were only "first among equals," and when they failed to perform satisfactorily, their follower could withdraw support by transferring their loyalties and territorial rights to other leaders. Most chiefs listened carefully to the discussions of elders who gathered in their *majlis*es (audiences), and tried not to demand more than their followers could support.

These *majlis*es took place at every level of tribal society from the extended family to confederations of tribes, with each level sending leaders to a more expansive level when matters concerned them. Although loosely organized, the system allowed anyone who needed to be heard to lay his case before others. Checks and balances, rather than appearing in documents and formal institutions, were embedded in social norms, including those that stressed loyalty to group and valued consensus, negotiation, and mediation. People's strong desire to maintain reputation (honor) served as a deterrent against violating tribal norms.

In a short period of time, governance changed from this egalitarian, participatory form of rule to one based largely on paternalism and the distribution of wealth. What hastened the change was a series of British actions. The first was suppression of the maritime activities of the Qawasim shaikhs. When demands to halt the raiding of commercial vessels failed to produce results, the British almost completely destroyed Qawasim fleets in 1819. The following year, the British concluded a general treaty "for the Cessation of Plunder and Piracy by Land and Sea" with local chiefs. And again in 1839, they concluded a Maritime Truce that was renewed a number of times until it was replaced in 1853 with the Treaty for Perpetual Peace. The British strictly enforced maritime peace but at first overlooked land-based aggressions not affecting shipping. Consequently over the next century, the Qawasim shaikhs were prevented from engaging enemies at sea where they held strategic advantage, and had to defend their territories by land where they were at a disadvantage. By the end of the nineteenth century, the Bani Yas with their great leader Zaid I Nahyan took advantage of their influence in the interior to expand their control over 85 percent of the territory of the Trucial States, and most certainly would have continued up the coast were it not for resistance from other states, supported by the British.

The second significant British action was to recognize a limited number of local shaikhs whom they concluded were capable of honoring agreements and enforcing fines for seized or damaged maritime property. Administratively it was convenient to deal with only a handful of leaders. Later they made this a cornerstone of their policy by strengthening the power of these shaikhs over tribes of the interior (Abdullah 1978: 293). The anthropologist Peter Lienhardt (2001) feels the British may have placed more confidence in the chiefs' abilities than was actually warranted, and in doing so made these chiefs more powerful than they could have become on their own. As the main channels to the British, the chiefs assumed an importance independent of their personal abilities to mobilize local tribes.

With the possibility of commercial quantities of oil, the British suddenly became more involved in the affairs of the states. From the 1920s on, the British wrote agreements with the Trucial chiefs about the possibility of oil discoveries.[3] And again, they took actions that proved significant in unanticipated ways. One was the creation of the Trucial Oman Levies in 1950. The Levies were a militia comprised of local troops under British command whose job was to suppress lawlessness in the interior, where travelers, including British representatives and oil exploration teams were often fired upon. With the establishment of the Levies the British expanded their role from control over maritime activities to control over the interior. The intent was primarily to protect oil exploration teams, but the British also noted that it prevented abductions for the purposes of slavery, a commerce that was still active in Buraimi. The Levies also brought the conflicts among the emirates to a halt. The last major military action—between Abu Dhabi and Dubai—occurred between 1945 and 1948 over territorial disputes, just before the establishment of the Levies. With inter-state conflicts suppressed, chiefs no longer needed strategic alignments with other rulers to accomplish their politico-military ambitions. Similarly they lost their important protection function, and thereafter had fewer ways to demonstrate their value to their constituents. Suddenly the personal relationships and networks they had taken pains to establish were no longer as crucial a part of maintaining power.

Another significant British action involved fixing the ownership of oil, and preventing disagreements with neighboring states (Saudi Arabia and Oman) over who had the right to grant exploration contracts. Although external boundaries had been established along the coast between the Trucial States and Oman as early as the beginning of the nineteenth century there had been little reason to mark the inland boundaries of states. Indeed until the possibility of oil in the 1930s, the concept of political boundaries was alien to the thinking of local people (Abdullah 1978: 291).[4] The size of a tribe's *dirah* (rightful territory) depended upon the extent to which tribes aggressively expanded their acreage or submitted to aggressions from other tribes. The *dirah*s of tribes submitting to a ruler at any given time constituted the extent of that ruler's influence. When tribal loyalties shifted, as they frequently did, "boundaries" also changed.

By the mid-1930s, the British needed assurances that rulers who gave them exploration rights had jurisdiction over the territories they claimed. The shaikhs scrambled to claim as much territory as possible even in the wastelands of the interior that previously held little value. However with British encroachment on their internal affairs, the rulers' power had been seriously weakened and several tribes took advantage of the situation to harass oil exploration teams on lands they claimed as their own. One oil company suggested giving gifts to local chiefs but British officials refused believing it might undermine the authority of the rulers and set a costly precedent (Abdullah 1978: 293).

By 1935 the rulers could see the advantages of stable boundaries, not only to control oil concessions but for relief against their opponents (Abdulla 1978: 291). The British urged them to identify tribal groups loyal to them in order to define their boundaries. When there was disagreement, the British tried to ascertain which tribes paid *zakat* (taxes) to which rulers. The issues became so complex that it was not until the 1950s when oil exploration increased, that a British team decided to draft a map of the region's internal boundaries. This draft was not finalized until 1963 and even then there were many areas still in contention, including the boundaries between Abu Dhabi and Dubai, and those between Saudi Arabia on one side and Abu Dhabi and Oman on the other where they converged in Buraimi. Most of the emirates still possess enclaves surrounded by territories of other states.

Creating permanent boundaries had implications for the local political system beyond the matter of oil rights. Boundaries essentially froze tribal relationships at the point the maps were finalized and further removed the rationale for many past tests of leadership. Leaders no longer engaged enemies or expanded their influence in ways they found useful when boundaries were fluid and tribal groups independent. When territorial boundaries and populations became fixed, there was no need to court supporters to access territory, nor account to them to prevent them from shifting their loyalties to other chiefs. Land and tribes were essentially assigned to chiefs, giving them a personal control that was theirs to exploit. No longer "first among equals," chiefs had become "pinnacles" of power, and their constituents had lost the leverage to transfer loyalties elsewhere. As the cases show, this act of defining state boundaries along with the acquisition of wealth at a level never seen before, eroded the close and intimate relations rulers and their supporters had enjoyed. However, Lienhardt warns that although the demarcation of land boundaries and the Levies made rulers more powerful, they were only powerful as long as their interests coincided with the British (2001: 12). Ultimately, he says these British actions made them responsible for the subsequent changes in rulers' styles of governance (Lienhardt 2001: 14).

Another pivotal action set the precedent that revenues earned from natural resources belonged to rulers. Earlier tribal tradition assigned natural resources like water wells, fishing areas and grazing lands to the communal use of tribal members, or to residents of specified areas, as in offshore fishing along the Abu Dhabi coast. The British however paid oil revenues directly to the rulers in whose lands the oil was found. The sudden acquisition of vast wealth, like the demarcation of boundaries, further transformed rulers' relationships with their people. They no longer needed tribute nor their constituents' active support. Rather the people depended on their rulers to share the wealth. In the 1950s and early 1960s, when Shaikh Shakhbut refused to share his revenues with either his family or the tribes, the outraged British supported his brother in deposing him. Shaikh Zaid proved to be a generous ruler, but the system remained discretionary based on the goodwill of rulers. Oil in the end proved a major factor in changing the social order through the accident of its distribution, and because, in securing its exploitation, the British undercut many traditional functions of chiefs while simultaneously raising them to unassailable positions of power.

Finally, the British increasingly refused to recognize rulers who overthrew or assassinated their predecessors, thereby suppressing a means by which tribes rid themselves of unsatisfactory leaders. Previous incumbents stayed in power by actively proving their worth, while later they became virtually immune to challenge. Rulers today continue to rule through many of the old customs—public audiences, assigning influence, and providing generously for their people. But they now act within a framework that puts them beyond any formal accountability other than a desire to be viewed favorably by their citizens. Although influences introduced from the outside provoked fundamental realignments in social relations and livelihoods, an important stabilizing factor during this time was the cultural perspectives of the people that helped them cope with the changes. The next chapter looks at these characteristic ways of perceiving and approaching the world, and suggests how they may have influenced rulers in their use of power.

CHAPTER 2

THE CULTURAL CONTEXT

The companionship of a hunting trip on the desert permits . . . (people) . . . to speak freely . . . and allows the one responsible to acquaint himself with the wishes of his people, to know their problems and perceive their views accurately, and thus to be in a position to help . . .

—Shaikh Zaid

This chapter examines the main concern of the book, the cultural perspectives that informed the views, approaches, and ultimately the outcomes of regional politics. Culture shaped leaders' behaviors as much, if not more, than the economic and political influences that changed their local environments.

Culture here means the shared framework of norms, values, and expectations shaping the way people perceive and react to the world. This framework includes expectations about how people of a culture should interact with others. It is essentially a "worldview" affecting how people behave and rationalize their actions. People learn culture as they learn language from the consistent behaviors of those around them[1] until it becomes so internalized that they act upon its rules automatically. The cultural grammar rules—norms, beliefs, values—feel so naturally correct that people rarely examine them critically.

If there are *purposes* in culture, they may be similar to those of language. Culture lets people pass on to succeeding generations, ways of coping with a particular environment. Practically speaking, culture narrows the options believed to lead to a good result, while making behavior understandable to others without lengthy explanation. Observers of culture may not always be correct in their understandings but, right or wrong, they usually apply a cultural lens to what they see.

Culture is *invisible* and therefore more difficult to discern than historical events or material resources. This book assumes that, with patience, cultural principles can be extracted from consistent patterns in human behavior. People on the whole conform to the norms of the society, and when they break the rules, may be seeking the shock value their behavior produces. Both consistent and contradictory behaviors can derive from the same mental templates. As in language, culture's grammar rules generate behavior but do not guarantee specific actions. People who ignore the rules sow confusion, much in the way scrambled sentences that ignore syntax do.

Political culture is similar to general culture, with the added element that it focuses on explaining political behavior. It may draw on the same norms, practices, or expectations applying generally to social behavior if these affect political outcomes. Relevant questions include: How do cultural expectations shape leaders' perceptions of the world, and define the strategies they use? Are there different expectations for rulers beyond those expected of commoners?, What happens when leaders violate norms?, How do leaders adapt to changes in the local political and economic environments?

The hardest part of understanding culture is determining what it is. It requires, as Geertz says "sifting through the particular to find what eludes us in the large"(1968: 4). Fortunately scholars have done much of this work for tribal societies, whether or not they labeled their findings as culture. This conventional wisdom provides background for a nuanced look at political culture in the case studies. But first, we need to look at some mind-sets, influenced by historic experience, which affected political behavior in the Gulf.

Regional Identities

Anthropologists have noted that human societies where people interact in defined areas such as communities, associations, or geographic spaces, tend to form opposing groups.[2] They base their opposition on criteria that range from place of origin and ethnic characteristics, to religious or political affiliation. These distinctions help groups coalesce.[3]

Some organizational advantages of opposition relate to leadership: (1) Leaders dominate groups more easily when they can exploit differences with outsiders; (2) Groups within a faction form more powerful units when coalescing around affinities; (3) Factional leaders can stabilize their interactions with one another by formalizing their contacts (e.g. sending delegations for purposes such as congratulatory visits). While two groups simplify organization in multi-unit societies, three or more groups tend to complicate it. In the Gulf, small states or tribes used their third party status to side with one or another larger state, gaining influence they would not otherwise have.

Oppositional groups help clarify identities. Groups may, for example, highlight occupational niches or stress moral superiority ("we are more hard working," or "more noble" or "more religious"), thereby helping to solidify in-groups. The Gulf tribes juxtaposed themselves as nomads against the *hadr* (settled people). Nomads saw the *hadr* as less honorable because they engaged in commerce rather than the noble pastime of camel-raising. The *hadr* in turn saw themselves as more sophisticated than the nomads. These distinctions were never clear-cut in reality, since tribes tend to be social rather than ecological groups. There are tribal nomads, tribal peasants, and tribal urban people (Khuri 1990: 128). Still, mental constructs often survive a shift in reality. Today the *hadr*-tribal distinctions translate into *medani* (technocrats and merchants) versus tribals, the distinguishing feature of tribal no longer being camel-raising, but rather the importance of a known and lengthy genealogy (tribal) against a virtually unknown and undistinguished ancestry (*medani*) (Khuri 1990: 128).

Belief in the nobility of tribal life caused those who identified as tribal, especially in the most tribal emirate of Abu Dhabi, to distinguish among modern activities. Tribals disdained commerce but engaged in buying and selling property. They avoided manual labor but acted as managers. They refused to carry loads but acted as drivers of loads.

Other oppositions arose in the Trucial States. One was the polarization of tribes around the maritime Qawasim on one side and the more interior-focused Bani Yas on the other. The Qawasim dominated the northern Gulf coast around Linga and the southern coast from Sharja to RAK as well as several towns on the Gulf of Oman and in the Hajar mountains. The tribes of the Bani Yas with their paramount chiefs from the Bu Falah,[4] controlled the interior, first from their center in Liwa and later from Abu Dhabi after moving there in the eighteenth century.

The rivalry between the two powers was reinforced by other oppositions. They sided with different political factions in Oman as far back as the eighteenth century.[5] The Qawasim supported Oman's Bani Ghafir faction, while the Bani Yas supported the Bani Hina faction. The Hinawi candidate won and ruled Oman ever since, putting the Bani Yas on the side of the ruling family of Oman.[6] The Qawasim became their rivals because of their support for the Ghafiris and because they clashed as neighbors and rival sea-faring powers. The Ghafiri-Hinawi divide had geographical as well as social implications. Tribes north of Dubai were mainly Ghafiri, and those south of Dubai and in parts of the Shamaliya, mainly Hinawi. A few Ghafiri pockets resided in Hinawi territory and vice versa, giving them strategic advantage with larger neighbors. The Ghafiri-Hinawi distinction persisted, becoming one of the factors that weighed into decisions about which tribes made comfortable allies[7] (Heard-Bey 1996 edition: 273–277).

Another opposition deepened the differences between the Qawasim and the Bani Yas. When the tribes of central Arabia conquered eastern Arabia in the eighteenth century, they converted the Qawasim to the puritanical creed of Wahhabism.[8] This conversion came in the late eighteenth century when Qawasim political influence was waning in the Gulf, and the region reverted to inter-Arab warfare.[9] The Wahhabi connection proved useful when the Qawasim sought support against other Trucial States, or wanted to raise British anxieties about their contacts with their Arabian neighbors.

The differences between the Qawasim and the Bani Yas, were consequently accentuated by their leanings toward Ghafiri or Hinawi persuasions, and Wahhabi or moderate interpretations of Islam. The Qawasim felt a greater affinity to the rulers of Arabia, while the Bani Yas felt closer to Oman. Their leaders did not always act on these distinctions, but the tendency to side with one group or another continued as a factor in the politics of the region until the mid-twentieth century. Even now most Emiratis know which group they belong to.

The rest of this chapter describes models for personal relations in Arab society.[10] Since much of political behavior involves leaders' modes of relating to others, the description necessarily focuses on the way people view and interact with various categories of "other": their families, tribes, and nonkin outsiders. The discussion enlarges on Ibn Khaldun's idea that creating "group spirit" is key to the political process.

The Tribal Model

Political leadership in the Gulf after the Arab conquests was organized around the tribal traditions of the northern Arab conquerors to which the Prophet Muhammad belonged (Crone 2004: 51). A major feature was that all adult males participated in decision-making and little was accomplished without general consensus. People believed power and resources should be shared through consultation, generosity, accessibility to the chiefs, and close familiarity between the chiefs and their followers (Crone 2004: 52). There was no state apparatus and indeed the mindset was to resist authority while strongly affiliating with kin and tribal groups. Crone says ". . . the tribal tradition was not just libertarian, in the sense of opposed to overweening rulers, but also communitarian . . . in the sense of (being) strongly attached to communal unity and solidarity" (2004: 51). The prevailing attitude was that barring flagrant acts of misbehavior, families as the smallest practical unit of society should be accorded equal respect and dignity. Even when paramount families provided leaders from their ranks, they occupied a position only slightly elevated from other tribal members.

The anthropological literature describes tribal society as a loosely organized system of segmental units with their configuration depending on ecological and other factors. A kin group might link up with other congenial groups on annual migrations, based on the numbers in their herds and the capacity of the land to support them. Larger groups of mostly related persons settled near wells in off-seasons when forage was poor. The larger groups usually had interests in common: protection of their land rights and water wells, expansion of their livelihoods, and defense against enemy incursions.

The tribal system was therefore an outgrowth of the nomadic environment where the low carrying capacity of desert pasturelands forced human populations to spread out in low-density settlements. In physical terms, this meant erecting tents at some distance from one another and calibrating the number of tents in terms of local resources. A minimal social unit was the occupants of a tent, or at the next level of inclusiveness, the cluster of tents whose members habitually traveled together. Mostly the unit was self-sufficient but when conditions required it, units become part of a complex community.

What was good for desert resources was not always good for defense, and that meant leaders often needed to mobilize groups quickly for raids or defense. The critical issue[11] for a scattered community was who would heed the call for help. The classic answer was that, all else being equal, the closer the kin relationship, the more people felt the responsibility to defend, avenge, or protect one another. Although brothers competed in every day life, they united in conflicts against cousins, and cousins and brothers joined against more distantly related kin or outsider enemies. Seeing reality as a series of discrete units, combining or fragmenting in pursuit of political goals, was a keystone of tribal politics.

Khuri gives some interesting insights into tribal society. He says tribesmen see society as a community of brothers[12] following a leader, rather than a state with a graded authority system (1990: 21). The discrete units of the society—some with automatic and some with voluntary membership—are composed of members trying to dominate others or acknowledging their domination. People join groups[13] where they risk being dominated because they fear being alone and vulnerable (Khuri 1990: 14).

Khuri compares the process of mobilizing/dominating others with the strategies of backgammon. For him, this game more than chess represents

Arab tribal ideals. At the throw of the dice, a token moves a designated number of places forward. It finds protection if it stops on a space where other teammates are congregated, while it is vulnerable to being taken if it lands on an empty space. As the token moves on, the first alignment of protectors loses importance until needed to ensure the safety of other team tokens. Safety requires "strength at one's back." By analogy, leaders mobilize support before they make political moves, and the alignment of supporters changes as leaders' aims change. The game is to dominate equals and the measure of differentiation is dominance or power (Khuri 1990: 107). Ibn Khaldun (1967) warns however that a time ultimately comes when a loose collectivity transforms itself from an egalitarian nomadic status into a ruling elite. The egalitarian ethic, he says, is doomed when transformed into a hierarchical state. The strategies of backgammon for example do not work in chess.

Four principles of organization are implied by the tribal view of politics. People have a nonpyramidal image of reality, feel vulnerable if isolated, seek protection in groups, and believe tactics are more important than office in achieving political objectives. These constitute ideological constraints on tribal communities, believed true without need for validation (Khuri 1990: 11).

How does an aspiring leader come to power in a nonhierarchical system? He starts by becoming the "first among equals" in a group that surrounds him. He establishes relationships with each member of the group and wins them over to his candidacy. In kin groups he appeals to people's sense of kin obligation, and in nonkin groups he evokes a kin-like relationship. After dominating the small group (e.g. family), he goes on to dominate a group of extended relatives, then the subsection of the tribe, and then the tribe itself. The "first among equals" in the core group, becomes "first leader among equal leaders" in each more inclusive field of supporters. All else being equal[14] he dominates to the level of his ambition, creating the same kind of personal relationships he established in the first group. The result is a set of relationships uniquely linked to himself. When he dies this network of personalized relations collapses, and a new person comes to power with a new network (Khuri 1990: 13).

This process is congenial to personal leadership. Groups at each level consist of limited numbers of players, thus making face to face personal interaction possible. Once a leader dominates a group, he possesses the nearly unconditional capacity to deliver their loyalty, tribute, or military support. That is implicit in the act of dominating. As he dominates more groups he also increases his capacity to dominate new groups through his growing reputation. The risk is that he becomes vulnerable to challenges from his core supporters whom he has neglected by broadening his focus.

Personal relations are hard to sustain at a distance. He must convince his base of the benefits of his expanding influence.

This process of co-opting groups applies somewhat differently to members of paramount families whose backgrounds give them only two main constituencies to convince: their kin (who may also be potential rivals), and leaders of groups traditionally supporting rulers of their states. Being from a paramount family is a necessary but not sufficient condition for becoming ruler. Contenders must also prove themselves.

On a personal level how do tribal leaders manipulate relationships to achieve their aims? One way is through "the strategic manipulation of custom"—the tone of voice, gestures, positioning of hands and body, verbal expressions, and seating arrangements—that have the potential for asserting dominance (Khuri 1990:12). Hospitality shows how ritual control is exerted. Kanafani speaking about the UAE, writes about the importance of visiting where people "affirm and confirm the status and prestige of individuals and groups" and develop client-patron relationships. Visits are also arenas in which people can improve their status through a show of hospitality (1983: 107). The guest and the host essentially compete to ". . . increase or decrease their prestige and esteem in the community or reinforce their original status" (1983: 93). Both attempt to assert their dominance over the other (1983: 98).

How is this accomplished? First the threshold of the home is the boundary initiating the competition. Some of the guest's personal power is removed by having him take off his shoes and sit on the floor. He is then compelled to take part in the rituals the host has arranged. The host controls where they sit and what and when they eat. He "satisfies all the guest's needs, rendering him helpless to serve himself, choose when to be served or when to terminate the visit." Social distance between host and guest is minimized if the host offers the meat, cuts the fruit, and circulates the coffee, and distance is increased if a servant takes on these functions. By providing all the elements of hospitality the host honors the guest, who in turn is expected to accept them graciously. If he refuses any part he insults his host (Kanafani 1983: 99). Kanafani concludes that despite the many changes in the UAE today, the society still adheres to traditional forms of social relations (1983: 104).

To achieve power then, essentially means that one person succeeds in controlling or influencing the behavior of others. This suggests the importance of visible, public demonstrations of power, for otherwise there is no way of knowing a person's relative dominance over another. For example, it is important for rulers to mount aggressive raids against enemies or react strongly to raids mounted against them. These military engagements are not random events as they sometimes appear but calculated happenings with ritualistic overtones. The more formidable the enemy he routs, the more the ruler demonstrates his ability and convinces others to support his causes.

Another way leaders manipulate custom is by controlling endogenous (confined to the group) practice. They restrict marriage, residence, official positions, and other types of association to a defined in-group. For years Shaikh Zaid controlled the distribution of land in Abu Dhabi by assigning plots on the basis of tribal affiliation, since he assumed these groups would prefer to live among their own extended relatives. Parts of the city are still identified by the names of tribes that first settled there. The system broke down when differences in wealth encouraged rich members of tribes to seek large tracts of land among wealthy neighbors of mixed tribal origin (Boot nd: 45). Another endogenous practice is the tendency to reuse given names in families so that, although there is overlap, names often identify a given family.[15]

Endogenous practice can be extended to form more expansive solidarities. The Nahyan contracted marriages with loyal Dhawahir and Manasir tribes to establish them as part of their in-group. An endogamous solidarity was also formed when the Bani Sultan and the Bani Muhammad Nahyans intermarried and generally supported one another against other kin lineages. Khuri notes that allegiances within solidarities often last a long time because they are built on enduring commitments such as family obligations, fealty ties, or common property, while alliances among separate solidarities tend to change with political circumstance because they are built on shifting interests (Khuri 1990: 120).

Another way of expressing dominance is through "ritually stratified systems of communication" where the higher the rank, the more rigid the means of communicating (Khuri 1990: 109). An example is seen in a dialogue between two sons of the late ruler of Abu Dhabi. Although meeting regularly on a social basis, they prefer the buffer of intermediaries to conduct business. A prominent local man asked the younger Shaikh to help get his son into Al Ain University, and the Shaikh, wanting to help, felt his older brother had more influence in university circles. He therefore asked an intermediary to, "Give my greetings to the Shaikh and ask if he can help this prominent person." If the brother answered, "It will be done, send my regards to my brother," the favor was likely to be granted, but if he said, "Send my regards, and God willing, it will be done" it might not happen. By using this "tactful" means of communicating, the younger Shaikh avoided the semblance of ordering his elder brother to do something, and the possibility that an embarrassing refusal might disrupt their social relations. He also showed deference for his elder brother's authority.

Leaders establish a personal closeness with those they want to dominate. Since family relations are the ideal, a leader approaches others as though they are family, using kinship terms to generate positive attitudes toward himself and create behaviors associated with kin relations—loyalty, trust-worthiness, and an assumption of mutual interests. With more prominent people, he is likely to use status terms generally applied to older and more authoritarian members of society. The kinship terms establish closeness and equality in a situation, while the status terms imply differentiation and distance.[16] The person accepting the imputed relationship tacitly allows the other person to set the stage for action (Khuri 1990: 29).

A common way to rework relationships is through genealogies. Genealogies constitute maps of relationships going back generations and defining how one group relates to others. As Khuri says, genealogies are "the cultural expression of corporate actions manipulated by leaders" (1990: 100). Over time genealogical ambiguity develops about how groups are linked to a distant eponymous forefather. The extent to which a leader wants to expand his support is the extent to which he casts his genealogical net broadly to include more people among those he considers his relatives (Khuri 1990: 102). This is essentially what the paramount Bu Falah family did when imputing kinship links to the Bani Yas tribes who probably did not have any true blood connection. Thus they created a large group of loyal supporters. A leader can also narrow the number of effective kin by naming his lineage after a predecessor that excludes collateral branches of the family. This was what happened when the Al Bu Falah paramount family became the Nahyans.

Official trees like those in the Documentation Center in Abu Dhabi make political statements as much in what they do not show as in what they show. They are not inclusive of all living members nor do they reveal the degrees of emotional closeness or estrangement that are inherent in relations among family branches. They show no female members, nor the linkages of marriage that might reveal which groups enjoy a greater share of influence. Consequently they do not distinguish between sons of differ-ent mothers, lumping them all under the father. Although fathers theoret-ically bind their children in a mutuality of shared interests, this often does not happen, especially when children grow up in the separate households of their mothers. These genealogies leave many gaps in the political story, and as political history reflect the way people would like things to seem rather than how they actually are.

Khuri's backgammon metaphor works well at a general level for describing tribal strategy, but it does not give the full complexity of tribal relations in the nineteenth and early-twentieth centuries. A ruler not only had to manipulate tribal relationships effectively but he had to deal with a full range of other relationships, drawing some persons closer and distancing himself from others. Altogether this complexity led to an exciting and dynamic society where a leader's skills in personal relations often had life or death consequences for himself and his followers. Some rulers, like Zaid I Nahyan and his grandson, Zaid Sultan, proved highly effective in these matters while others failed miserably. Those who failed invariably violated expectations about how personal relations should be conducted.

The Family Model[17]

The previous section underlines the importance of kinship in the tribal worldview. Not only do kin form the most basic social group but kin relations represent the ideal for close and intimate personal relations. The aim, if it can be called that, of these relations is to coalesce family members into supporting one another throughout their lifetimes. This purpose works well in an environment of scant resources where people at one time or another need to depend on others who feel a sense of mutual commitment.

Unlike the tribal model that stresses horizontal, egalitarian relations, the family model sees relationships in a hierarchical, vertical form. At a minimum there are four expectations for family relations.[18] They should be fixed, unbalanced, enduring, and required. They are fixed in the sense that each family member is expected to meet obligations toward other members relative to their age, sex, vested authority, and role. As spouses, parents, children, siblings, et cetera, people know roughly what their obligations are. For example children should always obey parents, and parents should provide children the necessities of life. If there is any doubt about specific obligations, people can consult religious texts, everyday moralistic sayings, or watch how others behave.

Family relations are unbalanced in that, no member of the household has exactly the same obligation to any other member because of age, gender, and role expectations. An older brother is responsible for the care and protection of his younger brother, while the younger brother should be respectful and obedient to his older brother. A sister serves her brother food while he protects her from dangers in public. Parents hold children responsible for their actions by what is reasonable for their age and sex. Each person has unique sets of responsibilities in the family and is expected to fulfill them.

A corollary of being unbalanced is that family roles extend to other kin members. Nurturing and authority roles are so important that their defining behaviors extend to maternal and paternal relatives—aunts, uncles, and grandparents. Maternal relatives (including men) should be warm and nurturing just as mothers are, while paternal relatives (including women) should hold children to high standards just as their fathers would. In fulfilling these personal responsibilities, people practice being warm in some relations and disciplinarian in others, deferring to higher authority in some and assuming authority in others. This forces people to develop complex social personalities where they practice being leaders or followers depending on the circumstances.

Kin relations should be enduring. They cannot be discarded even when left inactive for some time. In theory, family members should always be loyal and supportive of one another. Finally, family relationships are required because there is no discretion in whether to intensify or dismiss the responsibilities. People should always implement them in roughly the form described. The system is socially conservative since it depends on all members fulfilling family responsibilities over a lifetime and across a range of kin before fairness is achieved. The greater deference required of younger people is balanced by the greater authority people acquire in old age. Convention approves behaviors that conform to expectations and is unforgiving of people who opt out of their responsibilities.

How do these features promote cohesiveness of family groups? When each person's responsibilities are fixed, it weakens internal debate over who owes what to whom. When obligations are unequal, people can not use equal treatment as the measure of fairness. When family relations are expected to endure, even when neglected, they can be restored. Finally, when family responsibilities are required, there is no agonizing over whether to intensify or abandon them. In short, this way of seeing family relations makes clear how every person is expected to behave with every other person. Consequently the strands of family relationship become so densely interwoven that even when a rupture occurs, others are there to fill the vacuum. It is those who neglect their duties that suffer the vulnerability of isolation.

An important feature of this model is its stress on people's obligations to one another, rather than on their entitlements. Relating to people in terms of what one owes them rather than what they owe gives a qualitatively different character to relationships. Mayer (1999) notes that many Arabs believe responsibilities derive directly or indirectly from divine sources, and that people who meet their responsibilities are, in effect, fulfilling God's Will. Rights are man-made concepts without the same moral authority. These beliefs are important in understanding the sense of responsibility that rulers like Shaikh Zaid feel for their citizens, and their comparatively modest feelings of entitlement.[19]

Men and women experience this model of family relations differently. They climb different authority ladders and fulfill different functions in their lifetimes. Both assume positions of deference, authority, and control, but often, not in the same activities or physical spaces. In practice, while males exert ostensible authority over household members, their control is limited by lack of access to areas where women's activities take place. The literature tends to emphasize where women's access is limited while ignoring the limitations on men. In fact, women exert a great deal of control over matters important to the society, and to rulers in particular: honor, marriage, sex, children, and nurturance, and their cooperation has to be sought by men in these areas if they want to achieve their ambitions.

Kinship, like tribal organization, has a segmental nature that allows it to coalesce or fragment to create a preferred reality. An aspiring leader may challenge an established leader of his own family by refusing to support him during a crisis, criticizing him in public, or responding to him on the basis of strict reciprocity. He may eliminate his family's established leader, and become leader himself, or he may take his followers and split off from the main family group. If the situation continues for two or three generations, the cleavage becomes permanent. The more prosperous the members, the more politically splintered and genealogically proliferated they are likely to become (Khuri 1990: 99–101). These points are important in the Emirates where genealogical splintering within paramount families has been common throughout its history.

The Outsider Model

Almost as important as kin, from a ruler's point of view are nonkin outsiders. Commoners can confine most of their activities to family groups, but leaders have to expand relations with outsiders if they are to be effective. The outsider model gives them a way to include or exclude others. Expectations about outsider relations are the direct opposites of those for kin, largely because it is desirable to draw a clear distinction between kin and nonkin. In tribal society, outsiders are unknown quantities, even potential enemies, with their own group interests at heart. People fear the potential harm outsiders may cause if allowed access to their in-groups.

Relations with outsiders are typically undefined, balanced, temporary, and discretionary. They are undefined in that, behavior is not specified *a priori* for relations between two unrelated people, outside of normal politeness, protection, and hospitality in certain situations. People decide what they want to make of these relationships.

Relations with outsiders should be balanced, or else there are consequences.[20] If the outsider offers a gift, favor, hospitality, et cetera, the recipient must give something of at least equal value so as not to lose face. If this does not happen and goods and hospitality flow in one direction only, the giver establishes dominance over the recipient and the latter becomes his client. The client continues to be obligated until the debt is paid. Equal exchanges, on the other hand, leave the relationship without obligation on either side. If the intention is to keep the relationship cordial but distant, the recipient can return a comparable gift at once, thereby maintaining a correct posture, or he or she can wait a while and let the relationship cool. During the waiting period the original gift-giver possesses banked assets in anticipation of a return. Some gift-givers intentionally amass credit that they can call on when needed. This is useful for a ruler who wants banked assets available when he needs them. At the same time he does not want to incur debts that might force him to support the political goals of others. This is one reason Gulf chiefs receive lesser status people but do not return the visits.

Relations with outsiders are temporary since they can be broken off at any time. They are discretionary in that, the concerned parties have a range of options, from balancing their exchanges, increasing them to become closer, drawing them out to make the relationship less friendly, or breaking them off entirely.

As noted earlier, there is some flexibility in how boundaries are drawn between kin and nonkin outsiders. One draws outsiders closer by invoking the terms of address and behaviors that establish a kin-like relationship. One can reverse this and treat true kin as outsiders by ignoring the obligations of kinship. A ruler indicates by his actions, whether he is treating outsiders like kin, or kin like outsiders. While the latter is not as common, history provides examples where rulers cut kin off entirely when they committed egregious acts such as assassinating or deposing their successors. The most famous case is the family of Saqr Nahyan who assassinated the ruler of Abu Dhabi, Sultan Nahyan in 1926. When Sultan's son, Shakhbut, succeeded, Saqr's family was exiled and still does not have normal relations with the rest of the Nahyan family. Leaders and their followers are acutely attuned to the nuances of relationship and the messages being communicated on both sides.

A leader would have difficulty establishing kin-like relations with all the people he wants to co-opt into supporting him. To do so, would leave him vulnerable to potentially excessive demands. He can however establish closer relations by providing open hospitality to people who want to declare their loyalty. By eating at his table they publicly acknowledge their support, and he banks their loyalty until he needs it.[21] Kanafani says the host does not operate under as many constraints when guests are outsiders, as he does when guests are from his own kin group. Strangers are more dangerous than powerful. Their potential for harm comes when insiders communicate private secrets to them. Consequently the host must treat close relatives and friends with careful "consideration to neutralize their potential power" (Kanafani 1983: 104).

A chief tries to maintain a position of equality with other chiefs, but he does not lose face if he takes a subordinate role when another chief is unquestionably stronger—indeed he would be foolish not to seek the protection of a strong chief. This was the way most Trucial chiefs viewed British power.

The Marriage Option

An important option for drawing others—kin and nonkin—into closer, more enduring relationship is marriage. A characteristic of tribal groupings is that they enforce endogamy (Khuri 1990: 51). The preferred marriage is between paternal cousins (FaBrCh) where power and resources are contained within the extended family. By marrying their children, brothers form a complete social unit without linking to any external group (1990: 51). The relationships that exist among family members before marriage continue undisturbed as the bride moves into her paternal uncle's house and her husband stays near his mother. Both partners have interests in the same extended household so there is little to divide them.[22] Thus paternal-cousin marriage keeps blood and lineage goals intact without introducing the danger implied by marriage to outsiders (Khuri 1990: 52–53). The stress on the private domain in cousin marriage means that the public domain is given only secondary moral value (Khuri 1990: 127). For commoners this endogamous marriage produces an inwardness that satisfies most of their needs.

Rulers' interests are also often advanced by endogamous marriages. They help rulers co-opt brother-challengers or by extension uncle/cousin-challengers. When a ruler's power is virtually absolute, these marriages ensure that power and influence stays in his patri-lineage. They also increase the chances of producing a male heir with the converging bloodlines of two closely related lineages. Finally these marriages are politically correct in that, they ensure more opportunities for royal women to marry (discussed later). The down side is that, these marriages may create jealousies among excluded family members. Why, they will ask, did the ruler establish closer links with one brother's lineage and not another?

Rulers have broader interests that in many cases are better served by exogamous (outsider) marriages. These marriages can link them with other chiefs to encourage their support. They can be used to reward long-term loyalists (such as Nahyan marriages with the Manasir and the Dhawahir). They can diffuse kin challenges by expanding outsider support. They can fill gaps in resources and manpower. They can solidify peace with enemies. All these benefits depend on the wide-spread assumption that marriage creates long-term commitments between families.

The down side of exogamous unions is the risk of bringing outsiders and their conflicted loyalties into family circles where they have access to private information. Since women traditionally go to their husbands' households, it is outsider brides who create the most risk. Despite these concerns, rulers feel more comfortable marrying their sons to outsider women than they do their daughters to outsider men. Parents want certain guarantees before they are willing to give their daughters to outsiders. The main one is that women should marry men from families of similar or higher status backgrounds so the daughters enjoy the same standards of comfort they are accustomed to. Men by contrast can marry down since children carry their names and benefit from their backgrounds. If a woman marries into an inferior family, she appears to be deficient in some way since her parents are so eager to marry her. If her marriage to an outsider fails, she loses her children to her husband's family. If a falling-out occurs between her family and the groom's family, she bears the brunt of her in-laws' anger, or if she and her husband do not get along, their problems may spill over into relations between the two families. If women are mistreated their families feel obliged to avenge the insult. Families are most vulnerable through their women and therefore want their daughters settled into families that can be entrusted with their welfare. Most of these difficulties with outsider marriages for daughters, parents feel, can be avoided with paternal cousin marriage.[23]

The implication for rulers is that it is safer to arrange exogamous political marriages for males of their families since the issues surrounding daughters' marriages are usually too complex to use them as political pawns, except under special circumstances. An unintended consequence of males marrying outsiders however, is to reduce the number of appropriate marriage candidates left for royal women.

This section has looked at the most common types of endogamous and exogamous marriages and the benefits each bring to the political arena. Rulers, of course, also marry maternal kin, more distant kin, and foreigners (Arab and non-Arab) where the political benefits, if they do exist, are usually unique to specific marriages. Although incomplete, the discussion shows expectations associated with various marriage decisions. As with any set of idealized expectations these are what people believe will happen. The ideology constrains their behavior and in the end often shapes what actually does happen. A local person, knowing these expectations, looks for political advantages in royal marriages, whether or not they are intended. Like other deeply embedded values, the implications of marriage choices constitute well-established truths to culture members.

This chapter began with a definition of culture showing how norms, values, customary practices, and expectations shape the way people perceive and respond to the world. People conform to grammars of culture to establish their personal networks and increase the chances that their actions will be understood and approved. The chapter showed how regional identities caused fault lines in the way people of the Trucial States perceived themselves and others. The text described three models for personal relations in Arab societies with seemingly contradictory implications. The first for tribal relations is based on an ethos of egalitarianism that on the surface avoids hierarchy and domination. The second for family relations stressed hierarchical authority based on age, role and gender characteristics. Finally the most flexible model, for personal relations with outsiders, offers options to create closeness through fictive kin strategies, to dominate with patron-client strategies, or to distance oneself through formal status strategies. One sees the complexities for rulers. As tribal leaders they need to dominate others; as family members they need to fit into authority hierarchies; as efficient leaders they need to draw outsiders into support for their goals, while distancing themselves from others who might be a burden. Depending on the circumstances, rulers may find these expectations useful in drawing distinct boundaries between themselves and other groups, or in blurring the boundaries when they want to be more inclusive. Marriage provides a unique opportunity to draw some groups closer on a semi-permanent basis. The next section looks at the actions of historic leaders to see whether and how they used this cultural tool kit to achieve their political ambitions.

CHAPTER 3

EARLY LEADERS OF ABU DHABI

Early Founders and Rulers of Abu Dhabi

- Yas — Eponymous founding ancestor
- Falah — Perhaps early-eighteenth century
- Nahyan Falah — Circa early to mid-eighteenth century; eldest son of predecessor
- Isa Nahyan — Circa mid-eighteenth century; eldest son; first recognized Nahyan leader
- Diab Isa — Before 1761 to 1793; the first ruler to live in Abu Dhabi; killed
- Shakhbut Diab — 1793–1816; son of predecessor; (Lorimer says son of Isa (1986)); deposed
- Muhammad Shakhbut — 1816–1818; eldest son of predecessor, deposed
- Tahnun Shakhbut — 1818–1833; brother of predecessor; killed
- Khalifa Shakhbut — 1833–1845; brother of predecessor; killed
- (Isa Khalid) — 1845; great-grandson of Nahyan's brother, Khalid; ruled for 2 months; killed
- Said Tahnun — 1845–1855; son of an earlier ruler; killed while attempting to regain rule

Abu Dhabi is the largest of the Emirates. Since the eighteenth century, the Nahyan, a subsection of the Bu Falah, have been the recognized paramount family of the Bani Yas federation of tribes, providing all but one of its rulers. The first written reference to the Bani Yas is found in an

32

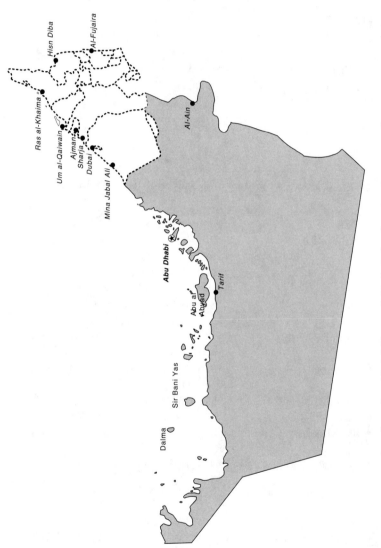

Source: http://lcweb2.loc.gov/frd/cs/united_arab_emirates/ae05_01a.pdf

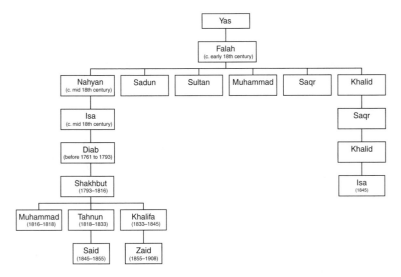

Figure 3.1   Early Bani Yas Chiefs and Rulers in Abu Dhabi

Omani manuscript in 1633 (Tamman 1983: 24). It says the Imam of Oman called for a jihad to drive the Portuguese out of Julfar, a settlement near present RAK, and that the Bani Yas with other tribes joined the Omanis in expelling the invaders. From that time on—the report continues—the two main forces in the Gulf were the Qawasim on the sea and the Bani Yas on the coast as far as Udaid (Tammam 1983: 22) with an inland base in Liwa. The Portuguese retook Liwa and it was not until 1666 that the local population drove them out. A hundred years later Omani forces destroyed Liwa, forcing the Bani Yas into two groups, one that remained inland and one that relocated to the coast.

The Bani Yas tribes came originally from the Najd in the interior of the Arabian Peninsula to settle in areas from Bidda to Buraimi. Most were Bedouin tending herds but those who lost their livelihood settled on the coast between Dubai and the area near where Abu Dhabi now stands (Rush 1991: 29–30). The accidental discovery of fresh water on Abu Dhabi Island in 1761 made it possible for the Bani Yas to establish a settlement of 20 *barasti* (reed) houses there at a time when Omani and Wahhabi forces were making frequent attacks on their base in Liwa (Rush 1991: xix). Within two years the Bani Yas built 400 houses, and in 1790 established a fort for the defense of the settlement. Soon the Bani Yas were settled in many of the 200 offshore islands including the important pearl diving center of Dalma (Tammam 1983: 32).

The Bani Yas are a confederation of tribes that include among others, the Bu Falah, the Sudan, the Hawamil, the Gumsan, the Muharaba, the Qubaisat, the Muzari, the Sabais, the Rumaithat, and the Bu Falasa. They varied in the extent to which they relied on sea livelihoods or nomadism, but all mixed together in Liwa and Abu Dhabi, intermarried, and had close relations. The ruler depended on their support and they relied on the ruler to take up their causes. A Bani Yas practice that gained them allies was the custom of letting others use their traditional grazing lands, wells, and fishing and pearling areas (Heard-Bey 1996: 34).

The Bani Yas tribes claim common descent from Yas bin Amr Qais bin Nizar,[1] a link they use to explain their long and close relation. Two independent tribes, the Manasir and the Dhawahir, also roamed the area of Abu Dhabi and maintained a long-term loyalty to its rulers. The Manasir were largely nomadic while the Dhawahir lived mainly in villages of Buraimi. Other tribes of the area such as the Awamir, the Bu Shamis, the Naim, and the Bani Qitab sometimes supported Abu Dhabi but often used their strategic locations to support chiefs opposing Abu Dhabi.

Four leaders dominated the Nahyan succession from the beginning of the eighteenth to the end of the twentieth century, making it possible to arbitrarily divide the succession into four periods, each dominated by a major leader and his sons and grandsons. They include: (1) The Falah period during most of the eighteenth century; (2) The Shakhbut Diab period lasting about 60 years to the middle of the nineteenth century; (3) The Zaid the Great period lasting about 100 years to the middle of the twentieth century; and (4) The Zaid Sultan period lasting from the middle of the twentieth century to the present. These last two periods were dominated by the two great Zaids, the first, consolidating Nahyan rule over most of the territory now comprising Abu Dhabi, and the second, overseeing the transformation of the emirate from a little known traditional society to one of the most modern nations in the world.

The Falah Period

Well before the end of the eighteenth century[2] Falah and his sons, established themselves as the paramount family of the Bani Yas. They claimed descent from the Anazah tribe through Falah of the Dawasir who two centuries before migrated from the Najd in central Arabia to the southeast coast of the Persian Gulf.[3] Falah had six sons, four of whom formed the major sublineages of the Bu Falah. The four were Inihyan or Nahyan,

Saadun, Muhammad, and Sultan. The descendents of the eldest, Nahyan, secured the rule, thereafter using Nahyan to name the branch[4] that provided all but one of the Bani Yas rulers in the ensuing centuries. The exception was a descendent of Nahyan's youngest brother, Khalid.

It is likely Falah was a strong chief, given the time he appears to have remained in office and his legacy that prompted such bitter rivalries. It is likely too, that he married more than once as was a common practice among chiefs trying to consolidate the loyalties of their followers. The number of his sons suggests this in an age when infant survival rates were low. The strength of his sons' antagonisms toward one another also suggests half brothers. Four of Falah's sons, including Nahyan, carried on an extended competition to become chief. After three of them died, their sons, Isa Nahyan,[5] Zaid Muhammad, and Sultan Saadun continued the fight. Isa Nahyan became chief, later followed by his son Diab around the mid-nineteenth century. When Diab discovered that Bani Yas support was coalescing around his uncle, Zaid Muhammad, Diab killed him to preserve his position. Diab ruled peacefully for a time until his victim's son, Hazza, set out to avenge his father. Learning of the plot, Diab exiled Hazza and his family from Abu Dhabi in 1793, but Hazza returned and killed Diab.

The Bani Yas split into two groups, one supporting the usurper Hazza[6] and the other Diab's son, Shakhbut. Shakhbut was so angered by his father's murder that he ordered the death of several people who had stood by without helping Diab. This show of force caused Hazza to flee Abu Dhabi in 1793 leaving Shakhbut undisputed chief (Rush 1991, *Buraimi Memorial*).

Over more than a century—from the mid-eighteenth to the mid-nineteenth—Nahyan's descendents continued to fend off sporadic challenges from their uncles and cousins. Even though the succession seem to pass in an orderly fashion from father to eldest son: from Falah, to Nahyan, to Isa, to Diab, and finally to Shakhbut, the details show that the order of succession was anything but peaceful. Paramount families originate so far back in history that there are no detailed accounts of how they came into being but the efforts to establish Nahyan hegemony are probably as good an example as any. At the point when they defined themselves as Nahyan, they effectively cut off other lineages and made their dominance permanent.

The Shakhbut Period

The reigns of Shakhbut, his three sons, and one grandson constitute the second major period of the Nahyan dynasty that lasted more than 60 years before another grandson, Zaid I, began a remarkable career that deserves special attention in a third period. Although the details of Shakhbut's descent are contested (whether he was the son of Diab or Isa), it is uncontested that he was a direct descendent of the lineage founder, Nahyan Falah. Three of Shakhbut's sons succeeded to the rule—Muhammad, Tahnun, and Khalifa—-in contrast to the previous period when eldest sons succeeded one another. With the exception of Muhammad who was deposed the others succumbed to violent deaths.

After the murderous conflicts of Diab's reign, the Bani Yas were ready for a quieter period under Shakhbut. After his early show of force eliminated his main competitor in 1793, Shakhbut appears to have shaken free of family opposition. Between 1800 and 1814 he led the Bani Yas in fighting off Saudi incursions with a bravery that earned the respect of officials in Muscat. When the Saudi State eventually fell in 1818, Muscat regained control of Buraimi, even though the tribes residing there were split between the Naim who were Ghafiri/Shafi and the Dhawahir, who were Hinawi/Wahhabi.[7] Shakhbut made a point of forging close relations with the Dhawahir in order to extend his influence into Buraimi. In 1818 after the Saudi withdrawal, he built a fortress at Muraijib, near the village of Qattara in Al Ain, the first step in strengthening Nahyan influence there.

Shakhbut took up permanent residence in Abu Dhabi and in 1795 fortified the tower that the early settlers had built near the fresh water spring. The move to Abu Dhabi Island meant more tribesmen spent time in seacoast pursuits while others continued to exploit their traditional inland livelihoods. Voluntary summer truces made it possible for pearling and summer pastimes to take place and eventually these were extended by the British in 1835 when they abolished war at sea altogether (Rush 1991) (Lienhardt 2001:5). The pearling industry was organized around profit sharing and loans rather than wages, leading to a patron–client relation between the owners of boats and their workers. The townspeople who owned boats had major economic advantages that counterbalanced the power of the tribal chiefs. After the decline of pearling in the 1930s the influence of these groups disappeared (Lienhardt 2001: 16). A factor contributing to Shakhbut's sons' interest in the chieftainship was the new lines of revenue opened by the move to the coast. The chief drew income from pearling taxes, custom duties, *zakat* (taxes on a proportion of income) on dates in Liwa and Buraimi, water taxes in Buraimi, and fishing rights off the coast (Maitra 2001: 22).

Shakhbut ruled for 23 years in relative stability before his sons were old enough to become active in politics. Starting then, they succeeded in cutting short the rule of every incumbent in the first half of the nineteenth century. The first challenge came from Shakhbut's eldest son, Muhammad, who in an unusual show of filial disloyalty, deposed his father in 1816 and assumed the chieftainship. Two years later, with sympathetic help from the Bani Yas and financial support from Muscat, Shakhbut assisted his second son, Tahnun, regain the rule and expel Muhammad from Abu Dhabi.[8] For a while father and son ruled together until gradually Tahnun's influence eclipsed that of Shakhbut. Shakhbut continued to live in Abu Dhabi where he occasionally took on administrative tasks for his son, and mediated between the British and RAK when their difficulties deepened during 1819–1820 (Rush 1991: 30). Shakhbut signed the General Treaty of 1820 between the Maritime chiefs and the British to suppress piracy. Up until this time the Bani Yas had been on good terms with the Qawasim but as a result of the financial support provided to Tahnun by the Imam of Muscat and other incidents, the Qawasim became less friendly and eventually bitter enemies of the Bani Yas (Rush 1991: 31).

One incident, occurring about this time, shows the difficulties the chiefs were having with one another and with the deepening involvement of the British in local politics. It concerned a peace agreement mediated by the British between the Imam of Muscat and the Nahyan and Qawasim chiefs. At issue was the occupation of the Dera fort by Abu Dhabi's allies from the Sudan tribe. Most settlements possessed similar forts for the protection of inhabitants when they came under attack. The forts represented tribal juris-diction and consequently establishing or capturing a fort amounted to control over a settlement. The Dera fort was located strategically between Dubai and Sharja in an area normally controlled by the Qawasim. For Abu Dhabi's ally suddenly to take over a fort from which they might mount an attack was viewed as a major provocation.

Shaikh Tahnun by then was using every means possible to extend his influence up the coast, and saw an opportunity in supporting the Sudan. The Qawasim rightly recognized the move as a threat. The main condition of the agreement brokered by the British was that the fort of Dera should be destroyed. But the Sudan would neither withdraw nor destroy the fort and when the Qassimi Shaikh violated the truce by attacking, hostilities flared. In 1825, the Imam in Muscat, brokered a new peace agreement where again the condition was that the Dera fort should be destroyed and Abu Dhabi's allies leave Qawasim territories. This time a contingent of troops from Dubai under an officer of the Imam was sent to secure the agreement. Tahnun however continued to support the Sudan who remained such a source of annoyance to the neighboring tribes that they declared themselves ready to go to war over the issue. Finally, the British, asked the Imam to prevent Abu Dhabi from sending support by sea to the Sudan, and the Qawasim from sending supplies by land (Rush 1991: 33).

In 1827 the Imam demolished the Dera fort with his fleet. This did not however end the problems between Tahnun and the Qawasim. In June of 1829 they concluded a peace agreement, largely because it was not economically feasible to carry on hostilities during the pearling season. This controversy was typical of how incidents in one area could galvanize parties from all over the region to prevent the aggressions of other chiefs.

Although he acted as directed by the British, the Imam of Muscat was reluctant to see a reconciliation between Abu Dhabi and the Qawasim that might threaten his own future (Rush 1991: 34–35). The situation however remained peaceful for several years until incidents involving support for the Imam—including commandeered boats and stolen properties—again threw relations between Abu Dhabi and the Qawasim into turmoil (Rush 1991: 36).

Meanwhile in Abu Dhabi, the aging Shakhbut was encouraging his son, Tahnun, to reconcile with his younger brothers, Khalifa and Sultan. They had earlier earned Tahnun's wrath by supporting their deposed brother Muhammad's efforts to regain his position as chief. Tahnun reluctantly agreed to let them return from exile provided they did not meddle in government affairs or carry arms. But he discovered in April 1833 that they were plotting to overthrow him with the help of some of the principal elders of the tribe. He summoned them, whereupon Khalifa drew out a pistol and shot Tahnun in the side, while Sultan finished him off with his dagger (Rush 1991: 38) (Lorimer 1986: 765).

Overall Tahnun had been a weak leader both in his external and domestic relations. The breach in relations with the Qawasim started over issues related to Abu Dhabi's allies in Muscat (Lorimer 1986: 763). Efforts to expand into Qawasim territory merely added to the problems. He was equally unsuccessful with kin who challenged his rule as much because he excluded them from the centers of power as from the fact that their father, Shakhbut, proved incapable of controlling his sons. Tahnun's inability to forge stable relations with his Wahhabi neighbors in the south also led to a series of uprisings in their areas of control. When Tahnun's brothers finally replaced him, their first act was to pay tribute to the Wahhabi Emir, Turki bin Saud, in return for his protection (Rush 1991: 38).

After Tahnun's assassination, Khalifa and Sultan ruled Abu Dhabi jointly until the elder of the two, Khalifa, became more prominent. However, his weak position resulting from the opposition of his relatives required continued dependence upon the Wahhabi emirs to protect his southern flank (Lorimer 1986: 765). Immediately upon assuming the rule Khalifa uncovered a plot to kill him on behalf of a first cousin. He immediately killed the ringleaders and expelled the others to Sharja (Lorimer 1986: 765).

When the Bu Falasa and Rumsha sections of the Bani Yas tribes learned that Khalifa, whom they had not supported, would become ruler, they decided to leave Abu Dhabi to set up permanent residence in Dubai. Lorimer (1986) estimated that they comprised about one-fifth of the population of Abu Dhabi at a time when the combined settlements of Abu Dhabi, Sharja, and RAK were only estimated to be between 2,000 and 3,500 houses.[9] Consequently the group that moved to Dubai was a serious loss to Abu Dhabi. By then Abu Dhabi was a substantial settlement, able to mount 600 boats with 7 to 15 men each in the pearling season. Its island site, however, was vulnerable to blockades since it depended on provisions from the mainland (Rush 1991: 29).

The flight of the Bu Falasa delighted the Qassimi Shaikh in nearby Sharja who immediately gathered his men to help the defectors attack Abu Dhabi. On September 7, 1833, the Dubai fleet set sail with 700 men of the Bu Falasa and Rumsha tribes in 80 boats, assisted by 520 men in 22 boats under the command of Shaikh Sultan Saqr of Sharja and Hussein Rahma. Three days later they over-nighted a few miles from Abu Dhabi before attacking their enemies. In the meantime Shaikh Khalifa in Abu Dhabi quickly resolved his differences with his brother and father and mobilized a force of 3,500 Bani Yas and Manasir tribesmen to rout Shaikh Sultan and his men (Rush 1991: 39).

The Qawasim continued to blockade Abu Dhabi, although a small number of Abu Dhabi boats broke through and attacked the Sharja boats. Khalifa countered by launching an attack against the inland tribes that were helping Dubai cut off his supplies. He proved so successful that he continued killing and robbing the people wherever he went. This so alarmed the tribes that they refused further assistance to Dubai. He continued the attacks on Qawasim ships at sea, however, until pressured by his own people over the loss of pearling revenues, he sent his father to Sharja to conclude a peace agreement. This time he stipulated that the Qawasim take responsibility for preventing further attacks on him by the Bu Falasa in Dubai (Rush 1991: 40). It seemed an acknowledgment that Abu Dhabi would not try to recover the breakaway groups.

Late in that eventful year of 1833 Shakhbut died of natural causes. His death received little notice since in his final months he had spent most of his time among his allies, the Dhawahir in Buraimi.. In later years Nahyan influence would grow in the oasis until by the late-twentieth century the family was identified with the town of Al Ain more than with their previous center at Liwa.

The following year in 1834, Shaikh Khalifa launched attacks on local and British boats and refused to submit to fines and restrictions imposed as a result of those attacks. The British sent ships of war to intercept his "piratical" fleets. In the first engagement a British ship damaged one of Abu Dhabi's boats while the rest got away (Rush 1991: 42). The British then detained his boats as compensation for "the outrages committed by the Bani Yas on the peaceable Arabs of the Persian Gulf" (Rush 1991: 43). A number of citizens left Abu Dhabi to avoid the fines demanded by the British (Rush 1991: 44). Among them were the Qubaisat who, under their leader Khadim Nahman, fled to Khaur Udaid near Qatar (Lorimer 1986: 766) leaving behind debts including fines for some Abu Dhabi fishing boats they plundered. This defection was a problem for Khalifa since the Qubaisat were one of the larger tribes of the Bani Yas. Their flight suggests that the British overestimated the abilities of chiefs to enforce maritime infractions. The chiefs increasingly found themselves caught between the forceful demands of the British and their desire to maintain the loyalty of their tribes.

Unlike the case of the Bu Falasa, Khalifa could not tolerate the defection of such an important group and yet was prevented by the maritime truce from forcibly bringing them back to Abu Dhabi. He appealed to the British saying Abu Dhabi would be depopulated if residents found refuge under the jurisdiction of other chiefs. The British eventually agreed and began discouraging other chiefs from harboring Abu Dhabi citizens trying to avoid British fines. But the Qubaisat refused to return and Udaid and Wukra continued to provide refuge for those evading fines. The situation deteriorated when residents of these towns started systematically plundering boats that ventured along their shores. The "only course left" to the British Political Resident was to hold the chiefs of Bidda, Wukra, and Udaid responsible for the acts of their residents (Rush 1991: 45). They followed up by moving British vessels to nearby waters so shallow the inhabitants thought them unapproachable by large ships. Under pressure, the governors agreed to seize the boats of the renegades (Rush 1991: 46).

Still Khalifa wanted his citizens back and in an unusually vicious act to assert his leadership sent men to destroy Udaid in 1837, killing 50 men and making the place uninhabitable by destroying houses and throwing bodies down the wells. Simultaneously, he offered such favorable terms to the remaining Qubaisat that most returned to Abu Dhabi. The following year, other defectors in Wukra also returned to avoid the Shaikh of Bahrain's increasing efforts to control the coastal areas (Rush 1991: 47, Lorimer 1986: 766).

Once the Qubaisat rebellion was quelled, the earlier desertion of the Bu Falasa to Dubai began to rankle and in May 1838, Khalifa retaliated by destroying their date groves and taking possession of their poorly defended fort. At the time most residents were out pearling, but they quickly returned and with the help of the Qawasim Shaikh of Sharja dislodged the Bani Yas after only three days (Rush 1991: 47). For a short time each side continued to mount incursions on the other's boats but eventually slaves and plundered properties were returned and both sides went back to pearling (Rush 1991: 47–48).

The following year the British assembled the Trucial Chiefs to discuss Egyptian aggressions in the interior of Arabia. Khalifa promised the British to oppose the Egyptians but soon communicated with the Egyptian agent offering to attack the Naim in Buraimi. The Naim put up a stiff resistance and when Khalifa proposed peace they refused, knowing he was trying to avoid retaliation by the Bedouins who helped him. The British insisted that Khalifa conclude a peace with the Naim and restore camels stolen from the Qawasim and the Bu Falasa or they would fine him 1000 German Crowns. The Naim finally produced a letter of reconciliation, conditional on Khalifa's behaving properly with regard to Buraimi and the Egyptians (Rush 1991: 48).

Khalifa embarked on a more peaceful course in 1840 and 1841. The British felt encouraged by his efforts to restore seized property and to discipline Bani Yas tribesmen who plundered property of "respectable" people living near Bahrain. These hopeful signs encouraged the British to believe their policies were finally paying off (Rush 1991: 49–50). In 1842 and 1843, efforts to conclude a peace were mounted when Shaikh Maktum of Dubai sent his cousin to Abu Dhabi and Shaikh Khalifa countered by sending a relative Diab Isa[10] to Dubai. The final peace excluded Dubai's ally, the Qassimi Chief, who knew the price of his involvement would be to stop attacks on the Imam of Muscat. The British commentator noted wryly that although Dubai offered to act as intermediary between Abu Dhabi and the Qawasim, it was in Dubai's interest that they remain at odds so that Dubai would hold the balance of power. Thereafter the choice between peace and war often rested with Dubai, for each side needed its support to oppose the other (Rush 1991: 51).

No sooner had Abu Dhabi and Dubai concluded their peace than Khalifa sent his brother, Sultan, on a plundering raid against the Bani Qitab who were allies of the Qawasim and thus vulnerable because of the Qawasim's exclusion from the peace agreement (Rush 1991: 51). Dubai's Shaikh Maktum managed to bring the two enemies to agreement in July 1843. But almost immediately Khalifa collected a force from Abu Dhabi's traditional allies, the Manasir and Mazari, to plunder the Bani Qitab, the Ghufla, and the Naim, all traditional allies of the Qawasim. When the Qawasim complained, Khalifa promised to restore their property even though he had no intention of fulfilling his promise (Rush 1991: 52). During his reign he frequently took advantage of the feud between the Naim and the Dhawahir to evict the Naim from areas of Buraimi (Heard-Bey 1996: 49).

At the end of 1843 Khalifa set out on a tour of the tribes whom he plundered asking them to abandon their support for the Qawasim and ally with him. He succeeded in convincing them to conclude alliances with him (Rush 1991: 53). Consequently his influence over the tribes increased during the 1840s at the expense of the Qassimi Shaikh. By 1844 the British Residency Agent in Sharja reported that he was not opposed by a single Bedouin tribe in the interior (Kelly 1964: 95ff). He had managed to move Abu Dhabi's expansionist aims forward.

Despite the numerous problems he caused them and the dislike he engendered in his own tribesmen, British records state that in the 12 years that he ruled as Chief of Abu Dhabi, Khalifa was able to make Abu Dhabi one of the most powerful states of the Persian Gulf. The British lauded his good relations with the British government and said he was usually successful at keeping his followers from committing maritime infractions (Rush 1991: 54). Obviously what impressed the British most were his efforts to preserve British interests.

The events that brought Khalifa's rule to a close constitute a bizarre anomaly in the annals of Nahyan successions. In July 1845 a distant relative Isa Khalid took the opportunity of a feast, to which the unsuspecting Khalid and Sultan were invited, to move against them. Most of the inhabitants were away working in the date groves of Liwa or on the pearling banks. Isa met the brothers on the beach, and after watching an entertainment staged in the shade of a *buteel* (a local type of boat) killed them with the help of his sons and accomplices (Rush 1991: 55).

This is the only case where the claimant's legitimacy was not immediately apparent. Lienhardt quotes Thesiger as saying there was no apparent reason for Isa Khalid's attempt on the chieftainship and he himself offers no explanation (2001:176). The challenge came well after the Nahyan lineage was established as the paramount family of the Bani Yas for over a half-century. But a closer look at the record hints at family links that may have emboldened Isa.

Isa was a descendent of Falah's younger son Khalid,[11] and a brother or half brother of the Nahyan whose name identifies the lineage of the paramount family. By the time of the assassinations Isa was too distant in the family lineage to be an obvious challenger and therefore could not have had many supporters. History suggests two avenues for his sense of entitlement. On one side he was a generation closer to the founding patri-lineal ancestor Falah than his victims, Khalifa and Sultan, and therefore may have felt he retained some legitimacy. On the other, his mother was sister to Shakhbut, the father of the victims, and thus he was closely related (MoBrSo) to them. Indeed his maternal grandfather, Diab, had been a ruler in direct Nahyan descent, making Isa the product of two branches of the ruling family. Under normal circumstances, the marriage of Isa's father to Shakhbut's sister, would have been seen as a way to mollify an excluded family branch by giving them access to influence, and they in return would be expected to support Shakhbut's family.

Claims to the rulership through maternal links, of course, would have carried little weight in local society, But Isa's access through his mother to his ruling maternal uncle and cousins would give him an idea of what he was missing and, at the very least, would have facilitated the physical access that made the murders possible. He may also have been encouraged by the tumultuous rules of Shakhbut's sons who were not greatly liked by their subjects.

Isa ruled for only two months before he was killed along with his son, Khalid, on orders of Said Tahnun Shakhbut. Said was the nephew of the victims Khalifa and Sultan, and son of their ruler–brother, Tahnun, whom Khalifa and Sultan had killed to gain the chieftainship. In theory Said should have been pleased to see his father's death "avenged" by Isa. But a more pressing concern was to regain the chieftainship for Shakhbut's lineage. As noted earlier kinsmen whose history puts them in opposition, often join in this way to fend off the threat of more distant kinsmen—in this case Isa. An alternative version of the story claims Isa was assassinated by a first cousin of Khalifa named Diab Isa,[12] who was then killed by Isa's son Khalid in 1845. According to this story, after avenging his father's death, Khalid fled to Sharja where his family lived in exile. Later Khalid's brother tried to capture the Abu Dhabi fort but was prevented from doing so by two Bani Yas leaders acting for Said. Whichever story is true, Said Tahnun became ruler of Abu Dhabi in 1845.

At the time Said was considered by both the British and the Bani Yas to be the most eligible of Shakhbut's descendents to assume the rulership (Lorimer 1986: 767). Shortly after he acceded, the Shaikh of Sharja asked if he would form an alliance against Shaikh Maktum of Dubai and his allies in Ajman and UAQ. Said agreed and this alliance held for two years until 1847 when a dispute over a proposed attack on Dubai caused its collapse. By that time Said had managed to isolate himself from most of his neighbors, much as his predecessor Khalifa had done a decade before. He was deserted by the Qawasim, made enemies with the Maktum of Dubai, and angered the deputy of the Wahhabi Emir by attacking a village under the

Emir's protection. His position became untenable, leaving him no recourse but to seek an agreement with Shaikh Maktum in Dubai and with the Qawasim. The Qawasim concluded an agreement with Dubai in March 1847 but refused to do so with Said because of the latter's insistence on including the Bani Qitab[13] among the parties to the agreement. The situation remained unresolved until January 1848 when the Qassimi Shaikh attacked the fort of Ajman, and Dubai's chief proposed a general peace that Abu Dhabi and the other maritime chiefs accepted. This time the Qawasim were isolated (Rush 1991: 56).

It was not long before Said disregarded the agreement and decided to expel the Wahhabi Lieutenant from Buraimi. He mobilized help from the Sohar tribe in Oman, and the Naim Chief's son, Saif Humud, who although customarily at odds with Abu Dhabi, this time united with him against the Wahhabis. Their efforts succeeded and both forts, at Subauh and Khunduk, fell with little resistance (Rush 1991: 57). The rest of the maritime chiefs, although pleased with the rout of the Wahhabis, were becoming uneasy with Abu Dhabi's growing power, and formed a coalition to remove Said's men from Buraimi. He held out against the combined forces of the Najdi, Qawasim, Dubai, and Ajmani Chiefs, but when Muscat sent no forces to relieve him, concluded a peace in February 1849 that restored Buraimi to its position before the hostilities.

Upon his return to Abu Dhabi, Said found that, at the end of the pearling season, the disgruntled Qubaisat subsection of the Bani Yas had departed Abu Dhabi again, this time seeking refuge in Bidda on the Qatari coast. The Shaikhs of Sharja and Dubai, not unhappy that Said was having trouble with his followers, encouraged the Qubaisat by telling them that the Wahhabi Emir, Bin Saud, would rebuild their center at Udaid that Abu Dhabi had earlier destroyed. Said acted quickly to seize the chiefs of the Qubaisat who remained in Abu Dhabi and told those who left that they would be welcomed back. However, when they returned, he removed the masts and rudders from their boats and urged anyone with a debt against them to ask for immediate payment (Rush 1991: 59). In the end they sold their boats and goods to pay their debts.

In 1849 and 1850, attempts and counterattacks to control the oasis of Buraimi pitted Said against the combined forces of the Qawasim, Dubai, UAQ, and Ajman with little success on either side. Several serious breaches of the Maritime Truce occurred when Abu Dhabi and Dubai seized each other's slaves and boats, and when Abu Dhabi seized a Hamriya boat, killing two Qawasim crew members. The British brought a warship into the harbor of Abu Dhabi to back demands for indemnification and the return of the Hamriya boat and its goods (Rush 1991: 61).

The year 1851 saw continued shifting alliances and incursions. Said concluded a peace with the Qassimi Shaikh in Sharja, despite the Shaikh of Dubai's efforts to prevent it. He then supported the Bahraini Shaikhs in their conflicts with the Wahhabis until in July he arranged an agreement between them. He also supported the Sultan of Muscat and the Shaikh of Dubai's battle with the Chief of Sohar (Rush 1991: 62).

During 1852 and 1853 the British continued to report incidents involving Abu Dhabi at sea and in the interior at Buraimi where Said was receiving an allowance to protect the Sultan's territory (Heard-Bey 1996: 50). Said raised such strong objections with the Political Resident over Wahhabi plans to invade the coastal areas of Oman that the Wahhabis abandoned the project, and settled for increasing the tribute from the local residents. In 1852 Said supported Said Butti's efforts to replace his brother Maktum as Shaikh of Dubai but when his claims were challenged by Maktum's sons and he sought refuge with the Qawasim in Sharja, Said dropped his support. In May the same year Said signed the new British-sponsored Treaty of Peace committing the Maritime Chiefs to cessation of hostilities at sea forever (Rush 1991: 63).

By 1854 Abu Dhabi was the major power in the region with a military force of 5,000 fighting men, compared with 1,000 men in Dubai, 2,000 in Sharja, 1,000 in RAK, 600 in Ajman, and 1,000 in UAQ. Abu Dhabi's local revenues, mainly from pearling, amounted to about 6,000 rials, a sum only matched by the Qawasim from their various sources of income (Rush 1991: 6–8).

Said's rule in Abu Dhabi ended in 1855 over a dispute with his subjects. A tribal elder committed what people felt was the justifiable murder of his brother, and Said promised he would forgive the killer. But when the man was brought before him, Said stabbed him to death. When his subjects heard he had killed a person under their protection, they rose up against him and he fled to the Persian island of Qais. To gain sympathy, he told the British Resident he had been expelled because he tried to punish piracies committed by the Hawamil and Mahairba sections of the Bani Yas (Rush 1991: 81). Said was slain a year later trying to make a comeback with the help of the Shaikh of Sharja (Lorimer 1986: 768). In the end he turned to his long-time enemies for help and the Qawasim willingly supported an effort that might weaken Abu Dhabi.

After Said's flight, the Bani Yas elected his first cousin, Zaid Khalifa, to succeed (Rush 1991: 67–68). Neither Said nor his two brothers had sons, nor did Muhammad, the eldest son of Shakhbut. Consequently the only obvious candidates were the sons of Hilal Shakhbut (who is little heard of and may have been dead by that time) or the sons of Khalifa Shakhbut.

Zaid was the older of Khalifa's two sons and from all accounts the obvious choice based on his reputation and leadership qualities. His rule begins the third period of Nahyan rule (see chapter 4).

Discussion

The eighteenth and early-nineteenth centuries provide a basic primer of leaders' political relationships before the transformative changes of the twentieth century. From this period we see the kinds of solidarities Abu Dhabi chiefs were building, solidarities that both Ibn Khaldun (1967) and Khuri (1990) say are essential in creating a power base. Three types of solidarity are apparent: (1) family blocks that supported or challenged a chief's leadership; (2) long term allegiances built around traditional tribal loyalties; and (3) short-lived alliances forged with independent chiefs. Some relationships seem more fragile than one would expect given the "cultural ideology" that encourages family and tribal solidarities.

Alliances among chiefs were the least permanent of the relationships, with the nature of the enemy and geography playing crucial roles in alignments. Recurring adversaries were often neighbors trying to expand into one another's territories. To offset these aggressions, chiefs recruited strategically located groups to expand their forces or open new fronts against their enemies The main regional players were Muscat/Oman to the east, the Nahyan/Bani Yas to the south and midsections, and the Qawasim roughly in-between. From Shaikh Tahnun's time, the Nahyan and the Qawasim who had been friendly began a long-term rivalry encouraged by Muscat's favoritism toward the Nahyan and British suppression of the Qawasim. At times, Muscat cultivated the Nahyan to offset encroachments of the Qawasim and, less frequently, allied with the Qawasim when the Nahyan became too powerful. Occasionally the Nahyan and the Qawasim joined forces to support Muscat against its neighbor, Sohar. When the Bu Falasa broke away from Abu Dhabi to settle in Dubai, they found themselves conveniently positioned to play off their Nahyan and Qawasim neighbors on either side. Independent tribes roaming the interior, such as the Bani Qitab, the Bu Shamis, and the Naim, took similar advantage of their locations to effect a disproportionate political influence. Those who allied in one season frequently became enemies in the next.

The advantage in short-lived arrangements is that their impermanence conserves energies otherwise needed to maintain long-term relationships. Chiefs recognized the fragility of agreements and were not unduly concerned when they were broken. Only the British characterized broken agreements as duplicity. Duplicity in this case gave chiefs breathing space before they resumed their offensives.

The shifting alliances served another function as well. In the absence of "office," chiefs manifest their power and tested the loyalty of their supporters through political engagements. Realistically speaking, with their limited resources, chiefs found it difficult to sustain high levels of loyalty among such dispersed groups. In this period, chiefs proved themselves powerful to the extent they persuaded others to join their military adventures. The chiefs of smaller tribes on the other hand survived by forging alliances with powerful groups that offset aggressions against them. These less powerful chiefs reciprocated with material and moral support, mediation services, and strategic locations from which the more powerful chiefs could launch attacks.

The hallmark of power was aggressive activity, since passivity only invited incursions. Thus the major chiefs continually expanded their influence and weakened their opponents by every means possible. We see them employing various strategies: co-opting tribes previously aligned to other chiefs; using surrogates to move into new territories (Egypt used Abu Dhabi, Abu Dhabi used the Sudan, the British used Oman); joining the battles of allied chiefs to gain influence over additional tribes; and using the symbolism of fort construction to signal their long-term intentions. They weakened opponents by undermining their agreements, by demanding conditions their enemies could not accept, by taking in their enemies' exiles and refugees, and by striking at their peripheries to open new fronts. Once any major confrontation started, most chiefs were drawn into taking sides. But if one group suddenly became too powerful, the others would quickly form a coalition to oppose them.

The second type of solidarity was with long-term allies. These allegiances were considerably more durable than fleeting alliances with short-term allies, since defections had consequences. The Bani Yas were the most reliable Nahyan supporters. Others like the independent tribes of the Manasir, the Sudan, and the Dhawahir normally supported Abu Dhabi. Both types of allies expected special consideration for their long-term loyalty and, as we shall see later, the Nahyan took care to cultivate relations with the independent tribes whose support was more tenuous than the Bani Yas. The elders of these tribes were involved in decisions on issues of importance such as succession, and they intermarried their children with the Nahyan. In tribal parlance, they were given a place in the inner circle. It was not they but full-fledged Bani Yas groups, the Qubaisat and Bu Falasa, who defected. After the Qubaisat were forcibly brought back, the ruler paid them more attention. In practice rulers often seemed more preoccupied with distantly connected supporters than close kin, in part from fear of their defection.

What is interesting is the rarity with which defections occurred. The Nahyan were so firmly established as the paramount family that there was virtually no challenge to their rule. The story of how families achieve paramount status as noted above is likely to have been similar to the way Nahyan and his progeny fought off the claims of other kin over several generations. Once established, close relatives of the incumbent would possess the resources and prestige that made it easier for them to retain the rulership in the future.

The third and most contentious solidarity in this period was kin groups. These formed around ruler incumbents and their sons, or the kin seeking to overthrow them. In the eighteenth and early-nineteenth centuries the chief was synonymous with the chieftainship and the easiest way to achieve power was to depose or kill him. In most cases the usurper would claim the rule himself. If his candidacy was contested, he tried to convince tribal elders that he had sufficient support to confirm him. The British grew alarmed over the frequency with which chiefs met violent ends and attempted to put a halt to the practice, but it was not until the last quarter of the twentieth century that it ceased. During the period covered by this chapter, nine individuals served as chiefs starting with Nahyan. Four met violent deaths at the hands of relatives, two were deposed by relatives, and two died of unknown causes. Only Shakhbut died a natural death. Four opponents were killed and others went into exile.

Ibn Khaldun (1967) says blood is the strongest basis for forming solidarities. In the early Nahyan record, close kin often supported one another. But they could not be counted upon as a single solidarity to back a chief. In fact it was kin in every case who challenged the sitting chief, and often kin divided on which candidate to support. Indeed, the chiefs' trust in kin loyalty may have lowered their guard enough to make it easier to overthrow them. Lienhardt explains kin divisions by saying that the main principle at play is that those who are closer in blood relation defend those who are more distant, with the exception of when they are one another's main competitors (2001: 22). A shaikh may overthrow his brother with the help of another brother, but will not usually help a cousin overthrow his brother.

The intense competition for the chieftainship throughout this period suggests it was a coveted position even under the harsh conditions of the time. What intensified the competition was the lack of a clear protocol for succession other than the understanding that the candidate would come from the paramount family. Lienhardt notes only a slight tendency toward primogeniture. He says a shaikh comes to power because of the strength of his supporters (2001:184–185). Evidence suggests however that age lends strength to claims, but personality and leadership may overcome birth order. The main contenders were rulers' sons and rulers' brothers, and by extension their uncles and nephews. If a ruler's sons were not old enough at his death, his next eldest brother would usually succeed. But if the sons were old enough, the ruler would probably secure their succession before he died. Fathers naturally prefer their sons over their brothers because of the long-term implications for their lineages. The brothers seeing the reign being secured for an incumbent's sons often made last ditch effort to wrest power before the opportunity slipped away. Lienhardt points out that the chance of a bypassed kin member (son or brother) becoming ruler fades quickly as other candidates press their claims. After two or more generations of not becoming rulers, members of a lineage are no longer viewed as legitimate candidates. Lienhardt blames the intense infighting among ruling family members on their quickly diminishing opportunities to gain power (2001: 188). The pressures build a predictable progression: Brothers of the chief fear his longevity will deprive them of their chance to reign. They may attempt an overthrow while the ruler's sons are young and he is vulnerable. As the sons mature, the brothers see their opportunities fade. Finally when the older generation of the chief and his brothers is gone, the competition shifts to paternal cousins in a last effort to seize the chieftainship. If the cousins lose, it is rare for any further claimant in their lineage to challenge the incumbent. The lineage disappears from the annals of power and often from the genealogical tables.

To offset these tensions, rulers sometimes sought to mollify kin by sharing power and resources with them while their sons were immature, usually by giving the kin allowances or responsibilities that gave them visibility—in the way Khalifa used his brother Sultan to conduct business for him. Later we will see how marriages helped to defuse the competition with relatives.

All else being equal the eldest son of a ruler was the favored successor. This helped reduce competition among other brothers who still had a chance at the position. Kin theory suggests the authority of an eldest brother would keep younger brothers in line. Age was equally a factor in inclining brothers to overthrow a ruler. Family challengers were usually the next oldest candidates in line. Age and immediate links to a deceased ruler heightened the sense of entitlement. Brothers were more likely to overthrow one another than sons overthrowing a father. Shakhbut's overthrow by his eldest son was an exception. He seems to have been unusual in his inability to control his sons and form a cohesive kin group. The excuse that half brothers are inclined to be more competitive did not hold in Shakhbut's case since he was reported to have had only one wife. Even though their competition was intense, at times the brothers reconciled long enough to cooperate when challenged by outsiders. Kin cohesiveness—an ideal in commoner society—is overlaid in paramount families by conditions that make kin who should be close—brothers and paternal kin—the most serious of competitors.

By the time Shakhbut's grandson Said Tahnun fled into exile, the Bani Yas needed a strong leader to unite the fractious paramount family and consolidate the affiliated tribes. The Qawasim were weakening, and the Nahyans had established ties with the Omanis and Wahhabis that gave them a freer hand in the interior. They were on reasonably good terms with the British. As a result they were in a position to expand their influence under a skilled leader. They found that leader in Zaid I.

CHAPTER 4

ZAID THE GREAT AND THE CONSOLIDATION OF ABU DHABI

Nahyan Rulers in the Middle Years

- Zaid Khalifa   1855–1909; called Zaid or Zaid the Great; natural death
- Tahnun Zaid   1909–1912; son of predecessor; natural death
- Hamdan Zaid   1912–1922; brother of predecessor; killed by brother Sultan
- Sultan Zaid   1922–1926; brother of predecessor; killed by brother Saqr
- Saqr Zaid   1926–1928; brother of predecessor; killed by brother Khalifa and Khalifa's son

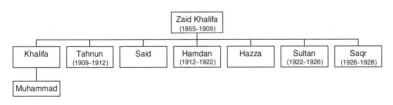

Figure 4.1   Later (1855–1928) Nahyan Rulers in Abu Dhabi

This chapter describes the third Nahyan period dominated by Zaid Khalifa (known as Zaid I or Zaid the Great).[1] By the end of his reign he had consolidated Nahyan rule over most of the territory now comprising Abu Dhabi, or roughly 85 percent of the UAE. This chapter looks at his responses to political challenges and shows how he used marriage to link himself with important allies. By this time there is sufficient information to see the important, albeit backstage, influence women exerted on politics. After Zaid's death, his sons began a series of bloody conflicts to succeed him. One son's lineage, the Bani Saqr, became outcasts as a result.

Rule of Zaid (1855–1909)

Zaid Khalifa was born around 1833 in the year his grandfather, Shakhbut, and his uncle, Tahnun, died, and his father, Khalifa, became ruler. Zaid was the eldest son. His mother was from the Sudan tribe that had long been loyal to the Bani Yas. When Zaid was about 12 years old his father was killed by the surprise contender, Isa Khalid, who ruled for two months before Zaid's cousin, Said Tahnun, became ruler. When he fled Abu Dhabi over a dispute with tribal elders in 1855, the elders appointed Zaid to replace him. Zaid was in his early 20s, but because he was considered courageous, wise, and well behaved, both the Bani Yas and the British believed him an ideal candidate.

Zaid began his rule by appointing his brother Diab as deputy. This was a customary practice among the Bani Yas but after a short time the deputy is no longer heard from (Lorimer 1986: 768). It helps to co-opt a relative with the most obvious claims to the rule.

Zaid's first major challenge came in 1856 when Said Tahnun tried to regain his position as ruler. The attack failed and Said was killed. After this, internal relations in Abu Dhabi were uneventful with no further challenges from within the Nahyan family. Zaid faced three main problems during his more than 50-year rule: (1) Defections by Bani Yas subsections; (2) Resistance from Wahhabis and local tribes to his influence in Buraimi; and (3) Disagreements with Sharja over his efforts to expand into Qawasim-claimed territories. A brief history of these events shows how Zaid pursued his expansionist aims while staying in the good graces of the British.

The first issue involved defection by a tribe of the Bani Yas Federation. In the mid-1830s during his father's rule, the Qubaisat fled to Udaid to avoid maritime fines. Khalifa's men destroyed Udaid. Again in 1869, the Qubaisat, under Butti Khadim (the son of the leader of the former revolt), left Abu Dhabi for Udaid for similar reasons. Two years later when they had not returned, Zaid complained to the British that Abu Dhabi's prosperity was suffering because the Thani rulers in Qatar provided refuge to its debtors. Hoping to resolve the issue, the Political Agent arbitrarily declared that Udaid belonged to Abu Dhabi. The Udaid settlers reacted by declaring their independence and saying they would seek Turkish protection if challenged. The British decided not to pursue the issue since Abu Dhabi had not been directly attacked. By 1873 with the problem yet unresolved, Zaid asked for permission to attack Udaid by sea, since a land expedition was impractical. He repeated his request again in 1874. The people of Udaid countered by flying Trucial or Turkish flags depending on which was most advantageous to their case (Lorimer 1986: 769).

The British organized reconciliation talks between Abu Dhabi and the defectors after Murra tribesmen in Udaid launched raids on ships in 1876 and 1877. When these talks failed, Abu Dhabi attacked but the refugees simply moved to Doha in 1879. A year later Zaid sent his son Khalifa to negotiate their return. After the treachery of Zaid's father, the Qubaisat were understandably reluctant to return but Zaid kept his word and gave them back their confiscated property. From that time on Udaid no longer played a significant role in the affairs of Abu Dhabi (Lorimer 1907: 770). This episode demonstrates the vastly different leadership styles of father and son. Khalifa cruelly forced the return of the Qubaisat and confiscated their property, while Zaid resolved the problem through negotiation and the return of their property. By sending his son to accompany them, he signaled his desire to resolve their differences peaceably.

A second issue occupying Zaid sporadically after 1875 was the Buraimi situation. The Bani Yas traditionally roamed the vast Dhafra area southwest of Abu Dhabi Island to Liwa. The discovery of sweet water on Abu Dhabi Island encouraged some sections to settle there by 1793 (Maitra and Al-Hajji 2001: 16). When a thriving trade developed between Abu Dhabi and the gardens of Buraimi, the oasis took on importance for the Bani Yas. The two major tribes of Buraimi were the Naim and the Dhawahir. The Naim were dominant before the nineteenth century, but were weakened by their split into two feuding sections, the Bu Shamis and the Bu Khuraiban whose chief was Wali of the Sultan of Oman. In the early-nineteenth century Zaid's grandfather Shakhbut started buying property in Buraimi and in 1839 his father Khalifa took advantage of disputes between the Naim and the Dhawahir to help oust the former. Khalifa claimed he held the date gardens in common with the Dhawahir (Heard-Bey 1996: 49). The British intervened and by 1844 Khalifa had made peace agreements with all the tribes in and around Buraimi including the Manasir, Qitab, Naim, and Dhawahir. His successor, Said Tahnun, successfully mobilized the tribes to fend off Wahhabi attacks on Buraimi so that by 1850 aggressions from the interior ceased (Heard-Bey 1996: 48–50).

By 1875, Zaid was again at war with the Naim assisted by his allies the Manasir and the Bani Hajir Bedouin (Rush1991: 84). Eventually he brought Buraimi into the undisputed possession of the Bani Yas, and he and his sons began buying property and water rights from the Dhawahir. When their interest in possessing the oasis became clear, the Dhawahir resisted. In 1887 Zaid went to war against them, with help from the Manasir and eventually subdued them. But by 1891 the Dhawahir were restive and Zaid, with the assistance of Dubai, returned and took the village of Al Ain (previously Ain al Dhawahir) where he completed a fort in 1897. Sometime between 1891 and 1897 Zaid married the daughter of the Naim Shaikh holding the Buraimi fort (Maitra et al. 2001: 181). In a conciliatory gesture in 1896 he appointed the Chief of the Dhawahir, Ahmad Muhammad Hilal, Wali in Buraimi to collect taxes from Dhawahir villages. From that time on the Nahyan maintained good relations with the Dhawahir (Boot n.d.: 38). His son Tahnun married the granddaughter of the Dhawahir Shaikh, Muhammad Surur, and other marriages linked the families. Dhawahir still hold important positions in the government.

The Naim who occupied villages in Buraimi received subsidies from the Sultan of Muscat, and their Headman of the Bu Kharaiban,[2] Sultan Muhammad Hamuda, was the Sultan's Wali in Naim areas. He needed Zaid's support to offset the split in the Naim that weakened his control. Zaid signified his support by marrying his daughter (Heard-Bey 1996: 52–53; Lorimer 1986: 770).

By allying himself with both sides, Zaid extended his influence throughout Buraimi and in 1888, the Sultan of Muscat turned the administration over to Zaid with a subsidy to look after the Bedouin tribes and settled groups of the Dhahira, as well as Sohar (Heard-Bey 1996: 53). Thus a large part of Buraimi came under Zaid's authority (Heard-Bey 1996: 38), a fact that became important when the British defined Abu Dhabi's borders with Saudi Arabia in the 1950s.

The third challenge to Zaid's leadership was a crisis at Zura. This event was reminiscent of Tahnun Shakhbut's support for Sudan construction of a fort at Dera. This time Zaid's ambition to become leader of all the Trucial Coast tribes led him to encourage his father-in-law, Sultan Nasir Suwaidi to establish a settlement on Zura Island off Ajman in 1897. They were opposed by all the Ghafiri sheikhs including the neighboring Qassimi Ruler of Sharja and the Ruler of Ajman. As in the previous attempt, Zaid's efforts came to nothing (Heard-Bey 1996: 33).

These challenges illustrate Zaid's relationships with three groups: a rebellious section of the Bani Yas, local chiefs resisting his expansion in Buraimi, and independent chiefs in the northeast resisting his moves up the coast. Zaid was a master at exploiting weakness in his adversary and then if victorious offering them generous face-saving concessions. He secured longer-term support by marrying his adversaries' daughters. Even when the marriages failed, people understood his intention had been good.

Through his marriages Zaid affirmed long-term connections with tribes loyal to the Nahyan and established closer relations with those opposing him. This was an achievement considering the complicated nature of marriage negotiation, the fact that appropriate women might not be available, and that he probably did not exceed the Islamic limit of four wives at a time.[3] He also needed to support the women in a style they were accustomed to or he would risk offending the families he was trying to win over. As his sons and daughters came to maturity he similarly arranged their marriages to promote Nahyan family ambitions.

The evidence that his marriages were politically motivated is circumstantial—the likelihood that there was a link between the benefits of specific marriages and events occurring at the time. His marriage dates estimated here are based on knowledge of the approximate birth dates of his sons;[4] and an assumption that children were usually born within a year or two after marriage. This would put the marriage at least a year or two before the birth of sons, assuming that the eldest was a boy and not a girl for whom dates would not be available. The margin of error may be high in some cases, but these assumptions probably give a rough time frame. Historic events are then matched to the dates to see if there might be a political relationship.

Even without these assumptions, a list of Zaid marriages constitutes a catalog of groups playing important roles in his political career.[5] Accounts differ about the number of marriages, but he had at least six reported wives (Heard-Bey 1996: 148) and several more appear in various sources.[6] His marriages were of four kinds: (1) With women from tribes with long-term loyalties to the Nahyan, (2) With women from among his blood relatives, (3) With women from tribes influential in Buraimi, and finally (4) With women from families of other Trucial State rulers. He later married some of his sons to women from merchant families.

The marriages involving the independent tribes included Zaid's marriage to Maitha Salmin of the Manasir (Heard-Bey 1996: 33). A story tells of how Zaid visited a Manasir village to discipline residents and found many of them absent on a hunting trip. A young man approached Zaid and answered his complaint by saying, "Would a wolf eat its own paws?," meaning "Would Zaid punish those who are so loyal they are an inseparable part?" The young man turned out to be the Shaikh's daughter Maitha dressed as a man. Her courage so impressed him that he returned later and married her.

Maitha bore Zaid's eldest son Khalifa in 1856, which puts their marriage around 1854 or 1855, shortly before he assumed office (1855) and after (in 1848) the Manasir had been helpful in ridding Buraimi of Wahhabi occupation (Heard-Bey 1996: 50). Although usually loyal, the Manasir had a history of occasionally taking sides with enemies of the Bani Yas. Zaid's marriage to the Chief's daughter would have reaffirmed the relationship when their support was wavering. It would not be unusual for a romantic story to be used to obscure political motivations.

Another tribal marriage was to the daughter of Sultan Nasir Suwaidi, a paramount shaikh of the Sudan tribe. The Sudan resided mainly in port towns, with strong concentrations in Abu Dhabi and along the Batina coast. As noted earlier, Sultan Nasir, with support from Abu Dhabi, tried to settle the island of Zura near Ajman in 1897 (Heard-Bey 1996: 33). Zaid's Suwaidi mother (with Naim ties) may have encouraged his marriage to a woman of her own tribe. Some sources claim the Sudan had been paramount chiefs before the Bu Falah and if so these marriages would signify their unity.

The second type of marriage was to Bu Falah women. One, Miriam, was the daughter of Muhammad Saif Falahi, a distant paternal cousin of Zaid who led many of his expeditions and was one of his most trusted advisors (Maitra and Al-Hajji. 2001: 106). Another was to Latifa, daughter of Said Tahnun, his paternal cousin (FaBrSo) and predecessor (Lienhardt 2001: 178) who fled into exile and was killed in 1856 trying to reclaim his position. She was the only wife who as a close paternal cousin fit the culturally preferred ideal. That she was not his first wife as would have been ideal if a "full-blooded" Nahyan heir were to be produced suggests a marriage contracted not so much for ideological reasons as to heal the breach between two branches of the family. Zaid characteristically made such gestures to those he bested in political competition. Latifa bore Zaid's second son, Tahnun, in 1857 a year after her father was killed (in 1856). From the date of this birth, Zaid may either have married her in a goodwill gesture shortly after her father fled Abu Dhabi in 1855 or after his death in battle in 1856. Either time would have been opportune to assuage a family that might later challenge him. Said himself had no sons but had two brothers who might want to rule.

During Zaid's reign, Buraimi was a major focus. A third category of wives consolidated his interests there. Zaid married daughters of both major shaikhs of Buraimi who, much of the time opposed one another and sometimes his own efforts. He probably married the Dhahiri wife in the mid-1850s when he was still peacefully purchasing Dhawahir property at Al Ain (Heard-Bey 1996: 51),[7] and the daughter of the Naim Shaikh holding the Buraimi fort (Heard-Bey 1996: 52) in the 1890s. The latter marriage to the daughter of Sultan Muhammad Hamuda, Chief of the Bu Kharaiban was additionally significant in that, this lineage traditionally provided the *tamima* (chief authority) for the Bu Shamis, the Bu Khuraiban, and the Khawatir sections of the Naim. The chief was also related to the ruling family of Ajman. Her father accepted a reduction in status when he assumed authority over the Naim tribe in the Dhahira (Kelly 1964: 164–165), and it may have been Zaid's marriage to his daughter that allowed him to accept the inferior position. After Zaid's death, he replaced him as the Sultan of Muscat's representative in Buraimi (Abdullah 1978: 304, Heard-Bey 1996: 38, 52). The Naim wife bore Zaid a single child who died young and consequently there is little further mention of her in the records. (Heard-Bey 1996: 149). A final Buraimi group was indirectly connected into Zaid's network when his governor there, Ahmad Muhammad Hilal (1897–1936) married a Bu Shamis (Abdullah 1978: 304).

A fourth category of marriages was to daughters of ruling families in other Trucial States. They included the daughters of the Qawasim Rulers of RAK and Sharja, and a daughter of the Bu Falasa ruling family in Dubai. Upon the death of the Qawasim patriarch, Sultan Saqr in 1866, power increasingly shifted from the Qawasim to the Nahyan. One reason was the protracted conflict waged by Sultan's sons that weakened the family and by 1869 caused Sharja and RAK to become separate principalities (Butti 1992: 103). Zaid may have taken advantage of the family split to marry from both sides in the late 1890s. It could also have been an act of reconciliation after the rebuff on Zura Island.

The marriage to the Bu Falasa wife from Dubai seems to have been more complicated. She bore Zaid's third son, Saqr, in 1874 or 1877 (reports differ), putting the likely date of marriage a year or more before these dates, or around 1873 or 1876. Abu Dhabi and Dubai had a disagreement in 1871 on the issue of runaway debtors, but by "1873 Abu Dhabi and Dubai were once again reconciled and their alliance was then directed against Sharjah" (Maitra and Al-Hajji 2001: 179). Thus a marriage in 1873 would have reconciled the neighbors and confirmed their intent to go after a mutual enemy. If the marriage occurred at the later date, it would have fallen within a period (1875 and 1878) when Zaid waged war with the Naim shaikhs in Buraimi and drew Dubai into the conflict on his side (Maitra and Al-Hajji 2001: 178). It is possible at either time to make a case for a marriage that cemented the relationship between Zaid and the Dubai sheikhs. In addition Dubai probably welcomed a marriage that acknowledged Abu Dhabi's acceptance of their independent status. Through these several marriages Zaid connected himself directly or indirectly with the ruling families of four emirates: Dubai, Sharja, RAK, and Ajman.

One would like to know how he dealt with the divorces that were an inevitable part of adding more wives. To stay within the Islamic tradition of no more than four wives at a time, Zaid had to dissolve some marriages before contracting others. Not much is known about how wives were selected for divorce, or whether the tribes maintained their influence with Zaid after their daughters were no longer married to him. Heard-Bey believes death probably ended more marriages than divorce because of the high rates of mortality in childbirth (1996: 148). Looking at the numbers of children born and the time span over which they were born, only two wives could have remained married to Zaid for an extended period. One was Zaid's "love marriage" to Maitha Mansuri who bore Zaid's first son and eight girls. The other was Miriam, the daughter of Zaid's trusted advisor and kinsman, Muhammad Falahi with whom it would have been awkward to have a divorce. She produced four (Hazza ca.1879, Said ca. 1880, Hamdan b. 1881 and Sultan ca. 1882) of his eight sons (Lienhardt 2001: 178) and perhaps one or more daughters.

Several wives produced only one son each, suggesting short marriages with Zaid.[8] If this was true, then the short-lived marriages were to the daughter of his predecessor, Said Tahnun, and the daughters of the Dubai and RAK ruling families. The Suwaidi, Dhahiri, and Naimi wives produced no known children and probably returned home or died early. These "fragile marriages" may have been politically useful at the time but their usefulness may have faded as Zaid's political interests changed. Indeed in certain situations "outsider" wives were thought to be a liability through their intimate knowledge of the ruler's household. There were degrees of "outsiderness" however even among outsider wives. For example, Zaid's mother was from the Sudan and he probably married a Suwaidi woman as a result. Tribes like the Sudan and the Manasir were long-term Nahyan allies and therefore not "outsiders" in the same sense that long-term adversaries like the Qawasim were. Aside from the personal elements that might have led to short-lived marriages, there is a structural element that may also apply. The fragile marriages, like short-lived alliances, fit the outsider rules of relationship (see chapter 2) where the parties decide whether to continue or dissolve them when their usefulness is over. As an ambitious politician, Zaid took many outsider wives for himself and his sons, rather than adhering to the culturally preferred marriage to kinswomen. This differentiates him as a leader from those who only consolidate their holdings with kin.

Al Rasheed, in talking about Ibn Saud in Arabia, rejects the idea that rulers who marry frequently and terminate marriages after a short period achieve long-term political ends. She says there are four preconditions for relationships to be enduring: (1) The husband and wife need to come from groups that are roughly equal in power; (2) The unions need to be monogamous, or rivalries are created among the wives' groups; (3) Divorce should not be easily achieved after a short period; and (4) There should be a reciprocity between wife-givers and wife-takers. She feels dominant groups that are only wife-takers and not wife-givers cannot expect loyalty from lower status groups (2002: 78). While it is true relationships created by marriages are not necessarily enduring or equal, they do seem to accomplish short-term goals of reconciling warring parties and rewarding allies. Likewise loyalty is not always a product of equal relationships; it may also occur where clients feel it is in their best interest to maintain long-term connections with strong patrons. Most local people probably coveted the privilege of being close to someone as powerful as Zaid even for short periods. The wife-giving shaikhs surely understood the symbolic value of the marriages, and knew they were unlikely to survive long with a leader as politically active as Zaid. They could still build long-term connections to Zaid based on a mutual interest in grandchildren that were born.

An important additional point comes from the discrepancy in names and numbers of Zaid's wives reported by various historians. Even careful observers like Lorimer and Lienhardt who wanted to document important females in the ruling families, worked with genealogies that recorded male members only. Thus although they could connect mothers to known males, they had difficulty finding a place for women who either bore no children or had only girls. These women's links to the family were invisible until they bore sons. The historians probably followed local custom and ignored women with no links to the charts.

The marriages of Zaid's sons also proved important in showing his political thinking. As patriarch, he played an active role in arranging these marriages, using them as he did his own, to consolidate old relationships and extend his influence to new groups. The new development during his children's time was the increasing importance of marriages to merchant families. One of these families was the Utaibas, a wealthy Sunni Arab merchant family. Some Utaibas claim to have come from the Arabs who migrated to Dubai from Persia in the 1880s after the Persians replaced Arab with Persian officials. Others claim, origins from the Utaiba tribes of Saudi Arabia (Boot n.d: 32). Supporters of the Persian claim say it would be highly unusual for Saudi Bedouin to engage in commerce (Boot n.d.: 35). The Abu Dhabi sheikhs frequently requested Utaiba financing for their military expeditions, and the British suspected they acted as agents for

Ibn Saud in Abu Dhabi (Boot n.d.: 31). Some Utaibas claimed to have intermarried with the Marar tribe thereby connecting themselves to the Bani Yas (Boot n.d.: 33). Marriage connections would have been advantageous to both groups and could perhaps have been justified, if needed, in terms of the Utaibas' claims to Bani Yas membership. The advantage to Zaid would be access to Utaiba wealth, and for the Utaibas the protection of the Abu Dhabi rulers.

Zaid's eldest son Khalifa predated this innovation when he married, probably in the late 1870s, a Mansuri, Shaikha Muhammad Salimin (MoBrDa), his mother's niece. Conventional, wisdom believes maternal-relative marriage enhances the power of women at the expense of their husbands. Everything we know about the Mansuri women suggests they were strong personalities. Both Maitha and Shaikha reportedly discouraged their sons/husbands from becoming rulers, even though by birth order they were natural candidates. Khalifa undoubtedly spent time as a child in his maternal relatives' household (her family) and his bride likewise in his household with her maternal aunt. There would have been a high level of comfort in this relationship. Khalifa's mother probably encouraged this marriage, but it was also politically expedient for Zaid to maintain close ties with the Manasir who were his chief allies in fighting the Naim in Buraimi. Later Zaid's grandson, Muhammad, born to the couple in 1880, drew on the support of his mother's tribe to remove his usurper uncle, Saqr, and return the rule to the sons of Sultan Zaid. At that time, in 1928 Muhammad was married to his victim's daughter (who was also his paternal cousin), a fact that did not deter him from organizing the death of his father-in-law. Muhammad also had two more wives, Muza Ahmad Utaiba, from the merchant family described above and Miriam, his paternal cousin and the only daughter of Sultan, whose children he restored to the throne.

Zaid's second son, Tahnun, by the daughter of his predecessor, married Shaikha Sultan Muhammad Surur. whose grandfather was Dhawahir chief in Buraimi. They were probably married in the 1890s when Zaid was establishing closer ties with the Dhawahir. No son was produced from this marriage and she remains one of the invisible wives. After Tahnun died, she married his half brother.

Zaid's third son Saqr, murderer of his brother Sultan is discussed below. He was the first of Zaid's children to marry into the merchant families. His connections in Dubai became an important escape-valve for his descendents after his assassination.

The four sons of Miriam (Zaid's Falahi wife whose marriage endured), are known to have had several wives. Said married and had a daughter Miriam (and/or Salama) but her mother is not recorded. The third son

Hamdan married three wives: Shamsa Sultan Mujrin (related to the Dubai Bu Falasa) with several female relatives married into the Dubai ruling family (Lienhardt 2001: 179). She had two children, one, Latifa, became the wife of Rashid Said, Ruler of Dubai. Shamsa's other child, a son, Hamdan, was born after his father was killed and she fled to Dubai. Hamdan's second wife was also Shamsa, daughter of Ahmad Khalifa from the Sudan tribe.[9] Her daughter Miriam married Hazza Sultan, the son of her father's murderer (Lienhardt 2001: 174), perhaps in a gesture of Nahyan reconciliation. Miriam and Hazza had a particularly close relation and remained married even though she bore no children.[10] Hamdan also married his half brother Tahnun's widow from the Dhawahir but she had no children. Around the turn of the century Miriam's fourth son, Sultan, married Salama Butti of the Qubaisat. The events surrounding this son will be discussed in the next chapter.

Zaid also had daughters, reportedly at least nine in number. Of the eight from his Mansuri wife six remained unmarried and two married the sons, Muhammad and Shakhbut, of Zaid's only brother Diab. Zaid rigorously adhered to the custom of marrying women to their paternal cousins. After the first two daughters married the only eligible candidates, the rest remained unmarried. For Zaid it seemed a point of honor not to use his daughters as political pawns.

Marriages to paternal cousins also held political significance, even though Zaid may not have viewed it as primary. Property would be conserved in his close patri-lineage, and more importantly, Zaid signaled his closeness to his brother, Diab. As Zaid's only brother, Diab was the most obvious person to challenge him. Giving his daughters to Diab's sons consolidated their relationship while avoiding marriages with outsiders that might have created tension between them. So even the marriages of two of his daughters, contracted with much honor, turned out to have political advantage. As for the fate of the other daughters, Zaid probably was reluctant to elevate other family branches, or simply may not have trusted others to provide adequately for them.

Zaid died quietly from natural causes on May 19, 1909, some reports say at age 90 but more likely in his mid 70s by the Western calendar if he was born around 1833. During his reign of more than half-a-century, he established Abu Dhabi as a major power in the Gulf, and his rule was often described as a model for effective leadership in the pre-oil period. During his lifetime, he increased the influence of the Bani Yas to unprecedented levels by consolidating the loyalties of tribes that had been on-again, off-again allies up until that time. He surrounded himself with prominent citizens who were known for their intelligence, including Ahmed Hilal

Dhahiri who served all the rulers from the end of the nineteenth century until his death in 1936, and others from the Yasi, the Mansuri, Dhahiri, and Amri tribes. He reestablished friendly relations with the Qawasim of Sharja/RAK and the Maktums of Dubai, consolidated his authority in Buraimi, and forged close relations with the rulers in Muscat. He understood the art of negotiation and of showing generosity to those he defeated, fulfilling the cultural ideal of healing divisions once fighting was over. Groups such as the Qubaisat and the Naim and at times, the Dhawahir, when they opposed him were given generous terms to reconcile their differences. He ended the Qubaisat revolt by returning their properties and urging them to come home, and brought them closer through marriage.

In 1901, the Political Agent in Muscat said that Zaid enjoyed an immense authority up until the last day of his life, and indeed in the last 30 years of his rule was unchallenged in the region. He felt it was an authority that none of his predecessors or any other shaikh of the coast enjoyed before him. After the Exclusive Treaty of 1892 preventing the Trucial rulers from developing economic interests with any state but the British and their surrogates (mainly Indians), the economy of the Trucial States rested almost entirely on a flourishing trade in pearling with lucrative markets in Europe and India. Abu Dhabi controlled the majority of the pearling banks, and possessed more divers and boats than any other emirate. Zaid also promoted agriculture by cleaning and restoring the neglected *falaj* (irrigation) system in Jahili near al Ain where in 1898 he constructed a fort.

The Rule of Zaid's Sons (1909–1928)

After Zaid's death, conflict soon erupted. The succession started peacefully with the ascension of Zaid's second son Tahnun. With the agreement of his other sons, Zaid designated Tahnun his successor before his death, hoping to secure a trouble-free transition. It is not clear why Zaid's oldest son Khalifa[11] refused the position but reports say his mother, Zaid's Mansuri wife, was so sickened by the violent overthrow of many previous rulers that she asked her son not to seek the rulership. What lends credence to these reports is that later when Khalifa's son Muhammad was the logical candidate for the position, he too declined and supported others.

Tahnun was an invalid who had lost the use of his limbs (Rush 1991: 92) possibly through contracting polio. He ruled three years before dying of natural causes in October 1912,[12] the only one of four brothers becoming ruler to die peacefully. He had three daughters but no son to carry on his line, and therefore the issue of succession appeared again.

Khalifa again declined (Tammam 1983: 41), and so the elders selected Zaid's sixth son Hamdan (1912–22).[13] His selection meant skipping over an elder half brother, Saqr, and two full brothers by the same Bu Falah mother. Hamdan turned out to be a strong ruler who kept firm order but was disliked at first because of his frequent conflicts with the Bedouin.[14] British political agents accused him of dabbling in arms traffic, to which he replied that he needed to protect himself from the Wahhabi, Ibn Saud, after he conquered the eastern areas. In 1913, Hamdan negotiated a truce between the Omani Sultan and rebellious chiefs of the interior (Rush1991: 123).

Hamdan ruled for ten years until he was murdered in 1922 by his younger brother, Sultan (Zaid's seventh son), with the help of a half brother Saqr (the third son). They claimed that Hamdan had not paid customary allowances to ruling family members, had oppressed the people, had stopped traders from visiting Abu Dhabi with their goods, and had alienated the Bedouin by subduing them. Lienhardt (2001) believes that the real reasons for the disagreement were not those stated by Sultan, but a jealousy between their two wives, Hamdan's Mugrin wife and Sultan's Qubaisi wife over the subsidies they received from Hamdan and the fact that Sultan's several sons spent more time with Hamdan than with their own father. Hamdan was reputed to be generous, giving away most of what he had to those in need, and therefore he was not as wealthy as his brother and his brother's wife assumed from observing his generosity. When Sultan discovered after Hamdan's death that there was no money in the treasury, he is reported to have wept (Lienhardt 2001: 180). Evidence for the wives' involvement was seen in the fact that after his death, Hamdan's wife Shamsa from the Sudan, married Sultan's wife's brother, Hamid Butti Hamed. Observers saw this as collusion between the two rivals of Hamdan's Mugrin wife.

Sultan's half brother, Khalifa and Khalifa's son, Muhammad, both disapproved of Hamdan's murder (Zahlan 1978: 43; Rush1991: 127) but by September 1922, Sultan had made peace with them and gained the acceptance of the people of Abu Dhabi (Rush1991: 131). Four years later, many of the issues raised about Hamdan's rule were now being raised about Sultan's rule. On August 4, 1926, Saqr, the brother who had assisted in Hamdan's murder, invited Sultan and one of his sons Khalid, to dinner. Saqr greeted Sultan and killed him while his sons stabbed Khalid waiting for his father elsewhere. Khalid was wounded but escaped to his maternal uncles who were chiefs of the Qubaisat.

Saqr supported or engaged in the murder of two of his half brothers before becoming ruler. Local people ascribed his actions to pure ambition (Lienhardt 2001: 180) but he may also have held a grievance at being bypassed for ruler by both Hamdan and Sultan. According to birth order, he should have succeeded Tahnun. Although not a hard and fast rule that older sons take precedence, it was a respectful thing to do. Why did it happen? One reason may have been that his half brothers who were rulers, Tahnun, Hamdan, and Sultan, all had mothers from the Nahyan family. Saqr's mother and wife were related to Dubai's Bu Falasa ruling family (Lienhardt 2001: 180). Whatever were Zaid's earlier reasons for contracting these Bu Falasa marriages, they resulted in making it difficult for Saqr to come to power at a time when considerable rancor remained between the Bu Falah and the Bu Falasa.

Khalifa did not like Saqr and was upset by the murder of Sultan. When he learned Saqr had made several attempts to murder him and his son Muhammad in December 1927 (Rush 1991: 158), he told Sultan's widow Salama to take her sons to Sharja for safekeeping. He also asked them to send him a Baluchi servant. When the servant arrived, Khalifa hid him until on January 1, 1928, the Baluchi slave along with Khalifa and Muhammad's supporters from among the Manasir tribe murdered Saqr. At first the Bani Yas were furious that the Manasir who were not Bani Yas had killed their chief, until Khalifa explained he had ordered the killing (Lienhardt 2001: 181). Khalifa turned over Abu Dhabi fort to Sultan's sons, Shakhbut and Hazza, and ordered Saqr's sons to leave Abu Dhabi (Rush 1991: 96, Zahlan 1978: 44). Some sought refuge with their mother's relatives in Dubai (Rush 1991: 152) while others went to Saudi Arabia.

The Difficulties of an Outcast Lineage

A year later, on July 28, 1929, the Political Resident based at Bushire sent a letter to the Shaikhs of Dubai, Abu Dhabi, Sharja, Ajman, and RAK complaining about the practice of brothers killing ruling shaikhs and declaring themselves rulers. The Resident noted that this was against God and advised the rulers not to recognize perpetrators of such deeds. He said he would gladly assist in any effort to end such activities (Rush 1991: 161). Saqr was the last of the Nahyans to be removed by assassination, and although his descendents were not subjected to physical retaliation for his role, they suffered what may have been worse, a form of family shunning. For the rest of the century the rulers of Abu Dhabi did not forget who killed their father.

Up until this time, assassination was a common instrument of succession in Abu Dhabi, with the murderers almost always becoming ruler. Most attempts were mounted in rough birth order to enhance the legitimacy of the contenders' claims. Once the murderers became rulers, they kept a close watch on the next-in-line kin, and tried to address the resentments of victims' kin so they would not try to restore their lineages to power. One public sign of reconciliation was the marriage of children. This was not the case with Saqr's descendents who were deliberately excluded from power. Most of them eventually married outside the Nahyan family, a sure sign of stigmatization, especially in the case of women. The Saqr name was no longer given to children of the Nahyan ruling branch, and certain rules about visiting Abu Dhabi were applied exclusively to Saqr's family. Khalifa Zaid, Saqr's grandson, for example, was allowed to visit Abu Dhabi but had to leave the city before sunset.

Saqr, as noted, was the first of Zaid's children to marry a daughter of an "outsider" merchant family, a fact some thought made his murder of Sultan more understandable. The Utaibas were neither tribal in the purest sense nor connected to tribal sections associated closely with the Nahyan. The fact that he was the fourth son and not likely to become ruler may have made it easier to arrange an outsider marriage. The marriage to Muza Ahmad Khalaf Utaiba was probably arranged through his mother who was from Dubai and would have known the family. When no sons resulted, his mother may also have encouraged marriage to Saliha Ahmed Dalmach, from a pearling merchant family. She was related to the Bu Falasa family into which the daughter of Saqr's earlier victim Hamdan married (Lienhardt 2001: 175).

Saliha bore Saqr's five sons (Diab, Rashid, Zaid, Tahnun and Hilal) and two daughters (Hissa and Shamsa). His third daughter Khadija was born to the Utaiba wife. After Saqr was killed, his sons fled to their Bu Falasa grandmother in Dubai (Rush 1991: 152). Later they inquired in Bahrain whether the Wahhabi agent there would support them in regaining the rule in Abu Dhabi. He sent them to Ibn Jiluwi, the Wahhabi Governor of Hasa, who discouraged them from attempting a comeback (Zahlan 1978: 44).

Much later in 1954, Diab and Zaid,[15] conspired with the Saudis to assassinate Abu Dhabi's ruler, Shakhbut. The Saudis saw in them a chance to undermine border negotiations with Abu Dhabi over Buraimi. Diab and Zaid were given a large sum of money by Ibn Jiluwi, but when they tried to recruit members of the Bani Yas, Awamir, and others through the Manasir, the Manasir warned Shakhbut and the plot failed (Kelly 1964: 180). These two sons also told a 1954 investigating committee on Buraimi, that agents of the Saud family traditionally collected taxes there, in support of Saudi claims. The brothers' desperation shows, when in January 1955, Diab admits in a letter to taking Saudi money.[16] He and his brothers were exiled to Sharja and then "travelled all over the world to get a handful of rice." They asked Shakhbut for money but he only gave them Rs. 2,000 per year and so they turned to the Saudis. For several years the Saudis gave them little "and our names were recorded among those of undistinguished persons." Eventually in 1954, the King gave them a more generous amount of Rs 70,000 (Rush 1991: 211). Later Diab settled in Sharja where he built a house and imported dates from Qatif (Rush 1991: 211).

A major problem for the Bani Saqr was their children's marriages. Before Saqr's assassination and the "unnatural" situation it created, he contracted marriages to daughters of the Utaiba and Darmaki, probably reflecting Zaid's political ambitions more than his own. Certainly his mother from the Bu Falasa also influenced the choice. Reports state that his sisters also married Darmakis. This would make the children, their mother, and their spouses a close group of Darmaki relatives, creating a strong block of outsiders within the Nahyan family.

Saqr's eldest son Diab probably also married before the assassination since he was born in 1900 and would have been about 26 at the time. His wife bore him two sons, Saqr, named after his grandfather and Sultan, possibly named for the uncle Saqr had murdered. No information is available on Saqr's other sons, Rashid and Tahnun.[17]

The rest of the family marriages probably occurred after the assassination and therefore reflect sanctions imposed on the family. Hilal Saqr married a Shamsi member of the Naim tribe, traditional enemies of Nahyan allies, the Dhawahir. Zaid Saqr who, with Diab, became involved in the mischief with the Saudis, married twice outside the Nahyan family to Fatima Muhammad Dalmuk and later to Hamda Ahmad Majid, a Ghurair whose mother was a Darmaki, putting him again within the circle of Darmaki-related kin. His wife's sisters were married to the rulers of RAK and UAQ. Zaid Saqr's son Saqr, married a Qassimi, Nawal Salem Salim, granddaughter of the Ruler of Sharja (1924–1951).

Zaid Saqr's son Abdalla was the only descendent given a position of any consequence in the government of the UAE. In 1989 he was appointed Ambassador to the United States and later to Spain in 1992 before he returned to private business in Dubai.

The daughters and granddaughters of Saqr had an even more difficult time finding appropriate marriage partners. Compared to Saqr's sons, however, they had the advantage that their children would carry their fathers' names and would later marry based on his status. Thus the women could be absorbed into lineages and lose their "affliction" while the men continued to bear the tarnished name of their forefather. The convention of marrying women within the family was not an option since none from the Nahyan branches wanted them as spouses. And it was not easy to find nonrelated families with a status high enough to marry Nahyan women. Perhaps more than others, the family needed spouses who could increase the family's economic and political base. But few families wanted to risk the displeasure of the Abu Dhabi ruling family.

Saqr's eldest daughter Hussa may have married just before the assassination in about 1926 if estimates of her daughter's age are correct. She married Muhammad Khalifa Nahyan who later opposed Sultan's murder by her father. She married at the age of 13 and died within the year giving birth to her daughter, also named Hussa. This daughter became the wife of Sultan's son, Zaid, suggesting that more stock was given to her father's than her mother's origins.

Saqr's second daughter, Khadija, from the Utaiba wife did not marry. His third daughter from the Darmaki wife, was probably born in the early 1920s and therefore not old enough to marry until well after the assassination. She was married "properly" to a Nahyan cousin, Hamdan Hamdan Zaid. He is the only Nahyan who had good reason to marry into Saqr's family. His ruler-father, also Hamdan, was assassinated by Sultan with the help of Saqr. When Saqr killed Sultan, Hamdan's family would have seen the act as revenge for Sultan's key role in the elder Hamdan's death. Hamdan's Mugrin wife and Sultan's Qubaisi wife were quarelling. Since the Qubaisi wife was the mother of the next two reigning Abu Dhabi rulers she may have snubbed Hamdan's children by his Mugrin wife as well as Saqr's children because their father murdered her husband. Thus a marriage between Hamdan's and Saqr's children was essentially a marriage between two Nahyan branches that were ostracized by the then Nahyan rulers and their mother. The explanation gains force when we see that two of Saqr's grandchildren also married grandchildren of Hamdan in a sister-brother to brother-sister exchange (Saqr Zaid to Fawziyya Hamdan and Salha Zaid to Muhammad Hamdan). Conventional wisdom expects such marriages to bring families closer, in addition to the advantage of exchange dowries.

Marriage difficulties continued into the generation of Saqr's grandchildren where the women (with the exceptions above) were still unable to marry Nahyans. One, Fatima Zaid Saqr, married the Ruler of Ajman, Rashid Naimi. Her uncle, Hilal Saqr, married a Shamsi member of the Naim tribe closely connected to the Ajman rulers and he may have been helpful in arranging her marriage. The Naim were not particularly close to the ruling Nahyans after the latter reduced their influence in Buraimi. Consequently this marriage had advantages to both sides, Saqr's family because it gave them respectability to marry into a ruling family, and the Naim because it aligned them with a renegade branch of the Nahyans. Saqr's family married Darmakis (a section of the Nahyan allied to the

Dhawahir) before becoming outcasts. Now his granddaughter was marrying a Dhawahir rival.

Hilal's daughter, Muza Hilal Saqr, also had some difficulty marrying. She was raised in Saudi Arabia, but eventually returned to marry Faisal Sultan Salim Qassimi, son of the Ruler of RAK deposed in 1948. In the early 1970s Faisal was the Chief of Staff of the Abu Dhabi Defense Force She bore seven children. Her eldest son Khalid was married in about 1994, to a Darmaki, again an accommodation arranged by maternal relatives. While Nahyan men previously married Qawasim women, Muza was the first Nahyan woman married to a Qassimi.

The marriages of Saqr's descendents stand out as anomalies to previous patterns of Nahyan marriages. Yet, although the marriages of Saqr's daughters and granddaughters violated Zaid I's norm of only marrying Nahyan girls to paternal cousins, the renegade family retained their "dignity" by marrying into ruling families of other emirates, to maternal relatives, and to tribes with status. Their only Nahyan marriages were to descendents of Hamdan who suffered a similar estrangement from the Abu Dhabi rulers. The fact that none of Saqr's descendants have married into the ruling lineage or, after Hussa, into the Bani Muhammad suggests a reconciliation has not occurred. Thus the long rule of Sultan's sons and their memory of their father's death has been a disadvantage for Saqr's descendents.

Discussion

Zaid I was without doubt the consummate political leader in the region up until his death in the first decade of the twentieth century. This chapter looked at how he managed his relations with the British, other rulers, allies, traditionally loyal tribes, the Bani Yas, and his own kin members. Zaid took pains not to confront the British, a force he recognized as too powerful to challenge. He sought their permission before taking actions they might not approve, as for example, when he brought the Qubaisat back to Abu Dhabi. He passively resisted when he wanted to avoid their directives.

Zaid had several advantages in his long, productive reign. The first was long-term support from the Bani Yas tribes, and the independent but loyal Manasir and Dhawahir. His situation contrasted with the Qawasim who had few long-term relationships with other tribes and certainly none that compared with the steadfast loyalties of the Bani Yas. Zaid used these trusted allies to expand his interests up the northeast coast and into Buraimi. While he could be ruthless in military matters, he also understood when to use incentives to encourage compliance. He developed a reputation for generosity to his enemies, and avoided long-term animosities through reconciliation after a conflict was over.

A personal advantage for Zaid was the fact that he had only one brother who remained loyal throughout his reign. Zaid made Diab his deputy and married his daughters to Diab's sons, signifying his high level of trust in him. A second personal advantage was ruling long enough to see his many sons reach adulthood and support his interests.[18] In old age Zaid continued to command their respect and they neither challenged his rule nor challenged one another during his lifetime. He took pains to ensure that his sons agreed on a successor before he died, anticipating the conflict that might ensue.

During Zaid's rule, more personal information is available and consequently we see for the first time the importance of marriage links to the political process. Each type of marriage had characteristic implications, but whether or not it accomplished its mission, the act of the marriage alone communicated the ruler's intentions to pursue a certain course. What may not be recognized as much as it should, is the impact of maternal influences on the lives of rulers' children. Zaid's Mansuri wife changed the course of the succession by keeping her son and grandson from accepting the position of ruler. Several maternal relatives provided refuge for the children of murdered rulers, and socialized them to their roles as leaders, arranged marriage partners for them, and advocated support of their political ambitions. However, the role they played, was restrained by the knowledge that children's futures depended on paternal more than maternal connections.

The importance of marriage is clear too in the negative example of the Bani Saqr who were cut off from their Abu Dhabi relatives. The Nahyans, with one exception, were unwilling to marry Bani Saqr children. This sanction forced them into highly unusual marriages including ones where they gave their daughters to outsider men arranged through sympathetic maternal relatives. The marriage sanction proved tantamount to ostracizing them from the family, a serious penalty in a society where social benefits flow from family membership.

Zaid refused, as a point of honor to use his daughters as political pawns. Although he was disproportionately a "wife-taker" for himself and his children, he married his daughters conventionally to paternal cousins (their FaBrSo), and when there were no more paternal cousins available, the rest remained unmarried. He may have feared he would become vulnerable through them in his dealings with other chiefs. Maybe he felt no other families were of comparable status. By recognizing others as equal, he would have been compelled to cede some of his power.

Considerable time has been spent on Zaid's marriages, largely because his is such a good example of the implications of marriage in the political process. Many scholars have noted the importance of marriages in the Arab World,[19] but what is new here is the refinement on conventional practice that they show. Where the original intent may have been to create harmony between groups, the marriages did not invariably lead to that outcome. Several Nahyan rulers confronted their wives' families in ways that must have left the women emotionally torn. Yet most remained loyal to their husbands' families and the long-term interests of their children. Royal marriages make sense at particular times and places, but the original rationales often disappear as political realities change. In many cases marriages were hardly better than alliances in producing their intended outcomes.

One hoped-for advantage of multiple marriages was the production of many sons. As Lienhardt points out, having many sons strengthens the position of a shaikh in relation to other family members (2001: 19). Falah, Shakhbut, and Zaid all had numerous sons, six, eight, and seven respectively. Sons are an advantage while a father is alive and able to use them to extend his outreach. After his death, the reverse is true. The multiple sons compete for the rulership thus weakening their father's gains. This is especially true when sons as half brothers grow up in separate households with mothers from different backgrounds. Inevitably these mother-blocks of sons compete for power. Their conflicts constitute an important weakness in a system that provides no clear order of succession. On the other hand, if succession were rigidly prescribed, there would be no mechanism for talented leaders to bypass ineffective leaders and rise to the top. The rulership is essentially synonymous with the person occupying it, and when his interpersonal skills and acumen are weak he invites challenges from his kin.

During Zaid's rule, the role of traditional leader changed from "first among equals" held accountable by his followers, to an authority figure who had to account to the British for the transgressions of his subjects. It was a two-edged sword, in that, he had to maintain the loyalty of followers while still meeting British demands. Zaid lived at a time when the British were becoming more involved in internal politics, but before the discovery of oil caused them to take even stronger actions affecting local governance. In many respects Zaid was the right man to take advantage of the new conditions—he consolidated the tribes and territories of Abu Dhabi before the British fixed the boundaries and assigned tribal locations. As a result, his descendents became heirs to the largest territory along the Trucial Coast. Although the sons fought continually after his death there was never any question of fragmenting Zaid's empire. They weakened the ruler position but continued to preside over the state he created. It was not until the generation of Zaid's grandsons, the Bani Sultan, that Abu Dhabi again enjoyed the kind of stability Zaid Khalifa provided.

CHAPTER 5

THE BANI SULTAN AND THE TRANSFORMATION OF ABU DHABI

Our experience in federation . . . arose from the ties that bind us, as well as the conviction of all that they were part of one family, and that they must gather together under one leadership . . .

—Shaikh Zaid

Abu Dhabi Rulers in the Twentieth Century

- Shakhbut Sultan   1928–1966; nephew (FaBrSo) of predecessor, deposed
- Zaid Sultan   1966–2004; brother of predecessor; died natural death
- Khalifa Zaid   2004–present; son of predecessor

This chapter continues the Nahyan story by spotlighting three of Zaid I's grandsons. Two, Shakhbut and Zaid, were sons of Sultan and a third was their cousin, Muhammad Khalifa, who stepped aside to support Shakhbut as ruler. Shakhbut and Zaid, are inexorably linked. As brothers they shared the same fate of losing their father and as rulers they provide contrasting examples of leadership qualities. Intelligent but weak, Shakhbut found it difficult to respond to modern changes, while Zaid, like his namesake Zaid I, saw changes as opportunities. Zaid oversaw the transformation of Abu Dhabi from a little known traditional society to one of the most modern states in the world. His son Khalifa succeeded him in 2004.

The story starts in 1905 when Sultan, then about 24 years old, married Salama Butti Khadim Qubaisi, then about 13. She was from Muzaira in the

72

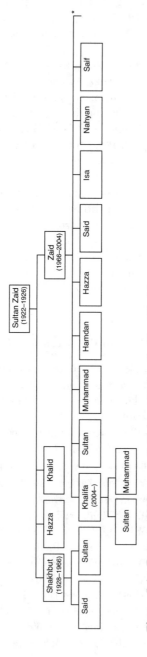

Figure 5.1 Recent (1928–present) Nahyan Rulers in Abu Dhabi

*Zaid's sons also include: Tahnun, Falah, Mansur, Hamid, Ahmad, Nasir, Diab, Abdalla, Umar, and Khalid

Liwa and sister of Hamid Butti who was a major pearling merchant of Abu Dhabi (Butti 1992: 134) and a prominent member of the Qubaisat tribe. This was the tribe that left Abu Dhabi three times in the nineteenth century in 1835, 1849, and 1869 until prevailed upon to return. Her father had been chief in the third exodus. Initially he was held hostage in Abu Dhabi by Zaid I to convince the Qubaisat to return but was later rescued and taken to Udaid. They eventually returned to Abu Dhabi in 1880. Relations between the Qubaisat and the Nahyan later improved, and an event considered important in strengthening the relationship was the marriage between Sultan and Salama (Boot n.d.: 4). Salama's mother, Muza Hamid, came from the Sultan tribe mentioned by Lorimer as a major section of the Bani Yas in Liwa. Salama remained Sultan's only wife, bearing his four sons, Shakhbut born in 1906, Hazza in 1907, Khalid in 1909, and Zaid in 1916 or 1918,[1] and one daughter, Miriam.

As described earlier, Sultan Zaid I became ruler by killing his brother Hamdan in 1922. He was about 41 at the time. Four years later in July 1926[2] he sent Salama with several of their children to Buraimi where the weather was better in the summer. Shakhbut was 20 at the time and Hazza 19. Ten days later at a dinner on August 4th, Sultan was killed by a half brother, Saqr. His son, Khalid, was wounded but managed to flee to his Qubaisat uncles (Rush 1991: 137). Saqr tried to entice the older sons, Shakhbut and Hazza, back to Abu Dhabi to kill them but they took refuge with Ahmad Hilal Dhahiri, the Nahyan representative in Buraimi (Rush 1991: 96; Kelly 1964: 119). Hamid Butti[3] sent a message to Salama in Buraimi warning her that Saqr planned to kill the children with her. So she sought protection from the Naim Shaikh of Hamasa in Buraimi (Rush 1991: 96) until at the urging of her husband's brother, Khalifa, she left for Sharja.

A year and a half later Saqr was killed by agents of Khalifa and Khalifa's son, Muhammad. Tribal elders convened to consider who would be the next ruler. Several candidates were suggested including Khalifa, who had previously declined the offer. With British approval, they eventually decided on Sultan's eldest son Shakhbut, who was about 22 at the time. Some felt he was not the best choice, including, Ahmad Khalifa Suwaidi, who argued for Sultan's second son, Hazza, who was more popular (Heard–Bey 1996: 33).

That year, Salama, concerned by the fratricide that had plagued the rulership since Zaid I's death extracted an oath from her sons that they would not kill one another. They complied and there were no further Nahyan fratricides. Salama's influence on her sons was said to be considerable, even to the point where they consulted her daily (Heard–Bey 1996: 150).

When Shakhbut began his rule in 1928, he was expected to perform the role of traditional leader, but his personality was such that he was uncomfortable in that role. People who knew him describe him as high strung, intelligent, and keenly interested in world events. He listened to BBC broadcasts daily and enjoyed discussing current events with foreign visitors, sometimes correcting their knowledge of facts. What he learned about the outside world concerned him about the future of his own country where changes were occurring more quickly than he thought good for the people. He disliked ceremonial duties and the largely pro forma visits to the tribes. Most of his travels, outside of summer sojourns in Buraimi, were last minute affairs to solve crises or deal with tribes claiming allegiance to the Saudis in Buraimi. Fortunately for him, rulers were no longer as vulnerable to overthrow. Lienhardt says that during the nineteenth and into the twentieth centuries, the two main checks on a shaikh's authority were his fear that part of his population might desert him or that he might be overthrown by his competitors (Lienhardt 1975: 62). Previously, a ruler's success in internal politics depended on his "engagements, actual or potential" with other shaikhdoms (Lienhardt 1975: 75). That was no longer true in Shakhbut's reign.

Consequently Shakhbut played a quiescent role, doing little to maintain relations with tribes normally loyal to Abu Dhabi, the rulers of other emirates, or even members of his own family. As his wealth increased, his disgruntled followers complained of his miserliness. He neither shared his resources in the traditional way nor invested in the basic services that were becoming commonplace in other states.

Shakhbut's inward focus was carried over to his marriages that were conventional and risk-averse. He married four women, including, traditionally, as first wife, his paternal cousin (FaBrDa), Fakhra Hazza Zaid I, who bore all six of his children. He probably married her around 1924 or earlier when he was roughly 20 years of age and before he became ruler. Their first son Said was born in 1926 and their second, Sultan, in 1934. Four girls, Rawda, Muza, Aisha, and Quth were born in the years separating the two boys. After Fakhra died giving birth to Sultan, Shakhbut married three wives from the wealthy Utaiba merchant family: Hamda Ahmad Khalaf, Muza Abdulla Ahmad, and Miriam Rashid Khalaf who was his last wife and the one to whom he was married longest. By the time he contracted the Utaiba marriages, the pearling industry had collapsed and the economy was in desperate straits. The marriages to the wealthy Utaiba daughters would have been economically advantageous to him in a period before oil brought him independent sources of revenue.

Three of Shakhbut's daughters married sons (FaFaBrSoSo or classificatory paternal cousins) of Muhammad Khalifa and his Utaiba wife. Muhammad had restored the rule to the Bani Sultan, giving up his own claims,[4] and Shakhbut appears to have reciprocated by marrying his daughters to Muhammad's sons. The fourth daughter also married a paternal cousin (FaBrSo), son of her uncle Khalid Sultan.[5] Shakhbut's eldest son, Said, married several times including to Maitha, a daughter of Muhammad Khalifa by the Utaiba wife, to Mahra a daughter of his paternal uncle Khalid Sultan, and to Salama, the eldest daughter of his paternal uncle, Zaid Sultan. Shakhbut's second son, Sultan, who was eight years younger, married a Suwaidi and then a Mazrui.[6] Shakhbut's sons were carousers and not liked in the family or by the citizens.

In the 1950s, during Shakhbut's reign, Lienhardt commented that among the important Nahyan sheikhs, only three of them had daughters old enough to marry—Shakhbut, his brother Khalid, and his cousin Muhammad Khalifa—and that all possible marriages had been arranged among the men and women of these families outside the prohibited degrees of kinship[7](2001: 183). Thus Shakhbut's aim in some of the cousin marriages may have been to conserve property within the paternal lineage. And in the marriages to wealthy Utaibas he may have hoped to expand his resources. This theory is supported by the exchange marriages he contracted for his children with the children of his brother Khalid Sultan. He also took his cousin Muhammad Khalifa's daughter while giving him three of his own daughters, in this case, coming out ahead by two dowries. There is no obvious political vision in these marriages, nor did they prevent the Bani Muhammad from eventually supporting his overthrow (Van Der Meulen 1997: 130).

Shakhbut was criticized for not investing in the shaikhdom's development. His supporters counter that his projects had not come to fruition when he was deposed. Certainly there were modest projects underway most of them financed by private initiative. The British deserve much of the blame for the lack of social services since, as they acknowledged, they made no funds available for development until 1953 (Tuson, Vol. 9: 25). By the 1950s, with the prospect of oil, roads were being built and private benefactors were establishing health clinics and schools. In 1952 the contractor to Petroleum Development Limited, Khan Sahib Hussain Amad, built a bridge across the creek at Muqata (Rush 1991: 175) that made it much easier to travel between Abu Dhabi island and the mainland. Guards stationed there protected the town (Heard-Bey 1996: 120).

Still the grumblings about Shakhbut continued. In 1952, a Political Agent reported that, according to Zaid and Hazza, Shakhbut had become more miserly over the previous five years and this along with his generally discourteous behavior toward visitors was seriously damaging Nahyan prestige. He would refuse to see visiting tribesmen for days, deny them rooms in his guesthouse, and then dismiss them with paltry sums barely covering their expenses in Abu Dhabi. The Agent added that these reports may have been back-biting but that hostility toward Shakhbut was indeed widespread among the tribes, particularly the Manasir, and warned that Shakhbut's personality and attitude were causing a drift of tribal loyalties toward the Saudis. The Manasir complained that Shakhbut should have paid them a share of the oil concession money, had refused to protect them in the war with Dubai in 1946–1947, and then prevented them from taking revenge on their enemies. What perhaps rankled Abu Dhabians the most, given the economic privations of the times, was the profligacy of Shakhbut's sons. One report criticized them "for their carnal and alcoholic indulgences," and said it was clear that ". . . whoever succeeded Shakhbut would not be Said" (Rush 1991: 169). Said died of complications from alcoholism in 1968 at age 42, and Sultan a year later of the same cause at 35.

A British report of 1952 assessed the various potential successors for Shakhbut. It said Khalid was not well liked, Hazza was liked for his understanding of tribal matters, but that Zaid was universally popular. The glowing report said Zaid was ". . . respected, almost revered as a man, the only real man among the four brothers, a man of physical and mental strength used to taking big and bold decisions, a fine organizer and a clean liver" (Rush 1991: 169–170).

Throughout 1952 relations worsened between Hazza and Zaid on one side and Shakhbut on the other. Shakhbut's neglect of Buraimi caused especial dissatisfaction among the tribes. A Saudi Emir passed through Tarif to discuss with the Manasir the possibility of allying with the Saudis (Rush 1991: 174). Eventually Shakhbut sent chiefs of the Hawamil and the Bu Khail sections of the Bani Yas to Liwa and Bainuna to mollify his critics (Rush 1991: 175).

Meanwhile two sons of Shakhbut's maternal uncle, Hamid Butti broke relations with Shakhbut and decided to leave for Saudi Arabia. When Shakhbut heard of their plans, he told their father he would expel the entire family from Abu Dhabi. This crisis resulted from Shakhbut's failure to provide them allowances (Rush 1991: 199), even though Hamad Butti had generously protected the family after Sultan's assassination. Another report similarly criticized Shakhbut for not providing payments to the Bani Muhammad who put him in power. Shakhbut went further and reduced the allowances of his three brothers, Hazza, Zaid, and Khalid, in March 1954. Hazza with their mother Salama's support protested to Shakhbut (Rush 1991: 201). He threatened to resign but changed his mind (Rush 1991: 202–203). In September 1954, to gain sympathy, he told his family he was dying (Rush 1991: 197).

After their mother's intervention, Shakhbut provided more generous allowances to his brothers but the amounts didn't cover the costs they incurred on behalf of the emirate. Zaid was unable to support the costs of administrating Al Ain where he had been governor since 1946, and when he had to deal with a siege at Hamasa, he supplemented his meager income with gifts from his mother and uncle. During the 1950s, discontent reached such heights that an exodus began from Abu Dhabi to the more lucrative environment of Qatar led by members of the Sudan and followed by the Rumaithat, Qubaisat and other Bani Yas families (Heard-Bey 1996: 33; Rush 1991: 213).

Meanwhile Hamid Butti decided to go to Saudi Arabia via Bahrain. The British worried that the Saudis might use him to claim Udaid where his grandfather Khadim Butti had established a settlement in 1869. They urged Shakhbut to recall him (Rush 1991: 204) but he refused. The problem might have escalated if other Qubaisat followed,' strengthening Saudi claims to Udaid and Liwa and the offshore islands (Rush 1991: 204–205, 214). In the end the Saudis lost interest in Hamid, as Shakhbut predicted, and he returned to Qatar. All these uncertainties created anxiety for the British who were anticipating the discovery of commercial quantities of oil[8] in Abu Dhabi and wanted to establish a political agency there. They knew Shakhbut might oppose the idea and decided to appoint an agent after oil royalties came in to gain his trust (Rush 1991: 205–206).

In 1954, Salama fell dangerously ill with pneumonia and Shakhbut traveled to Buraimi to see her. The Saudis feared Shakhbut was using his mother's illness to strengthen Abu Dhabi's claims on the oasis, and persuaded him to leave after two weeks. Upon his return to Abu Dhabi, his son Sultan told him that Diab (of the Saqr lineage that killed his father) had received large sums from the Saudis to foment a coup. In panic, Shakhbut sent out patrols, imposed a curfew, and purchased rifles—the expenditures delighting everyone. But by the end of the year Diab, "a worthless character," showed no suspicious behavior and Sultan tired of his duties as militia commander (Rush 1991: 215).

Shakhbut still refused to pay for the country's development, including a proposed 25 million pound development project, saying he did not have the money. People were now having more contact with the outside world and saw the amenities other states enjoyed. News reports noted that Shakhbut's mother and his daughters traveled to India for medical procedures, Hazza, with his brothers Khalid and Zaid went to the United States and Britain for medical consultation, and Muhammad Khalifa visited India (Rush 1991: 217). Also, increasing numbers of foreigners were coming to Abu Dhabi. One report mentions the arrival of five school teachers in Abu Dhabi: three Jordanians, one Iraqi, and one Omani arranged by Thani

Abdulla in Dubai (Rush 1991: 219). Others reported that Zaid went to Lebanon to put Khalifa in school; Saqr Sultan, Ruler of Sharja, went to Cairo for holiday; and Shakhbut's son, Sultan, spent his holidays in southern Iran (Rush 1991: 221). These experiences made the lack of basic services in Abu Dhabi all the more obvious.

The oil revenues pouring in after 1962 aggravated the complaints that the wealth was not benefiting the residents. It rankled that Shakhbut spent lavishly on his younger son Sultan's wedding in the 1960s, and planned to build two palaces for himself and one for each for his sons (Herb 1997: 267). By 1966, conditions became so intolerable that, as Zaid said later, Abu Dhabi was becoming depopulated from the residents fleeing to states with better economies.

The events that followed have several versions. The British version stressed the British role in announcing to Shakhbut that he must abdicate in favor of his younger brother Zaid (Rush 1991: 231). Some non-British foreigners said that after consultations with the family, Zaid went to England to ask permission to take over from his brother. At first Zaid told Shakhbut he could remain ruler but that he (Zaid) would take over the finances. Shakhbut refused and Zaid replied that the only alternatuve was for him to step down. Zaid said the palace was surrounded by Trucial Scouts, and Shakhbut answered, "So be it." An airplane took him into exile.

The official version (Tammam 1983) says the Nahyan family convened and decided unanimously to replace Shakhbut with Zaid. In deference to his brother, Zaid did not go to the palace but rather delegated the Deputy British Political Representative to relay the family's decision to Shakhbut. Shakhbut received the news in August 1966 while Zaid and the family waited at Police Headquarters. Shakhbut argued with his brother by phone for an hour, until he was told that the best course was to abdicate with honor. He was driven to the airport through an honor guard of troops that Zaid insisted on as a means of honoring his elder brother (Tamman 1983: 74). The British flew Shakhbut to Bahrain and then Beirut. Four years later Zaid allowed him to return to Al Ain as long as he didn't interfere in politics. Zaid did not meet Shakhbut until 1978 when they both attended their mother's funeral. After that, they saw each other occasionally until Shakhbut died in 1989 at age 83.

Why was Zaid chosen to succeed Shakhbut? According to those present, Hazza who had been the popular choice in 1966 died of cancer in 1958.[9] The third brother Khalid, whom people called "cold coffee," was disliked and never considered.[10] One report said he had never recovered from the shock of being present at the murder of his father and remained high strung and nervous the rest of his life. He married a maternal cousin (MoBrDa)

Muza Butti Qubaisi, a gentle woman who was a good wife to him. Their children, Muhammad and Mahra, married Shakhbut's children in an "exchange" marriage.

Zaid was the popular choice among the groups with an interest in the next ruler: the Nahyan, Bani Yas leaders, and the British. His leadership qualities, his selfless generosity, and his abilities in negotiating and pacifying the tribes during the difficult reign of his brother were legendary and contributed to the high esteem in which he was held. He cultivated personal friendships among other Nahyan branches and with tribes traditionally loyal to the Nahyan. His links through marriage reinforced commitment to the Nahyans despite the failings of Shakhbut.

Zaid credited his experiences growing up with the shaikhs of the Qubaisat, the Bu Shamis, and his maternal grandmothers' tribe, the Sultan, with preparing him for his future role as leader. From age 30 until he became ruler, he had been Abu Dhabi's representative in the eastern region, including the period when the dispute between Saudi Arabia and Abu Dhabi over Buraimi came to a head between 1952 and 1955. The Saudis based their claim on Wahhabi occupation at the start of the nineteenth century and until 1869 when Oman assisted the Naim in expelling them. Since then, Oman and Abu Dhabi occupied Buraimi even though some tribes continued to pay taxes to the Saudis. In 1952, in anticipation of oil discoveries, the Saudis occupied the village of Hamasa. The British protested and a tribunal in Switzerland convened in 1954 to resolve the issue. When negotiations broke down in 1955, Omani forces with British officers retook parts of Buraimi occupied by the Saudis. Luckily for Abu Dhabi, British policy after World War II was aimed at preventing the Saudis from taking control of the entire Arabian Peninsula. The Saudis, however, continued to claim Buraimi as well as a third of Abu Dhabi (Litwak 1981: 53; Rush 1991: 231).

The Buraimi crisis could well have lost Abu Dhabi considerable portions of its territory. Zaid knew this, but also knew that the way the crisis was handled could later impact his relations with the tribes. The Saudis were spending large sums of money to bribe tribal leaders into claiming they were clients. Abu Dhabi had little to counter the Saudi pressure, and it looked as if the Saudis might win even though historical evidence supported Omani and Abu Dhabi claims. Zaid kept channels open to the shaikhs who defected, promising them safe passage if fighting turned against them. When the British decided to oust the Saudis, Zaid directed the battle from a distance. He feared that if his men were involved and there were deaths it might start a cycle of revenge that would make it hard to control Buraimi once the conflict subsided. The British won the crucial battles against the Saudis. When disloyal sheikhs from two Abu Dhabi families realized the Saudis had lost, they returned to Zaid's camp to ask his forgiveness. A moving moment is described when they approach his camp with their head scarves draped on their shoulders and their head ropes around their necks, and try to kiss his feet. He raises them up and tells them to return home in peace (Henderson 1999: 219–242).

The dispute with the Saudis came to a head again in 1967 during Zaid's rule and intensified in 1970 when Aramco discovered oil deposits in Saudi Arabia near Abu Dhabi's border. Eventually the Saudis exploited the field, even though part of it extended under Abu Dhabi territory (Abdullah 1978: 16). The terms of the 1974 agreement that negotiated this border were not published because of the strong opposition they might raise in Abu Dhabi. Shaikh Zaid agreed not to exploit the Zarrara oil in return for the Saudis renouncing their claims to Buraimi and recognizing the newly formed UAE. In addition Zaid gave Saudi Arabia a corridor across Abu Dhabi to the coast ending at Udaid. Some say Zaid later felt he had been mislead by his advisors and the agreement was a mistake, but others believe he needed Saudi recognition of the newly formed UAE for it to survive. The Ruler of Qatar was incensed because he believed Udaid was his territory. Oman also was not consulted although Zaid believed an aide had obtained their agreement. Oman was so angry that it massed troops at its border with Abu Dhabi. In the agreement several villages were retained by Oman while the rest came under the jurisdiction of Abu Dhabi. The potential for friction continued but did not erupt during Zaid's lifetime, and later he supported the Omanis during the Dhofar rebellion (Litwak 1981: 55). Oman settled its argument over Buraimi with the Saudis in 1990.[11]

Shaikh Zaid acted throughout these border negotiations in the manner of an old-time tribal leader, offering a generous (some say too generous) concession both to obtain a settlement and to reestablish cordial relations with his neighbors, both crucial to him. The future of these ambiguities according to one writer will depend on the strength of the UAE federation. Should there be a weakening, both Oman and Saudi Arabia might intervene to readjust their boundaries (Litwak 1981: 55). In 1971, when the UAE was still fragile, Iranian forces moved onto the islands of Abu Musa and Tunbs, claimed by Sharja and RAK, causing Arab residents to protest. With the British withdrawal from the Gulf, Zaid was unable to confront the Iranians directly. Yet he needed to defuse the anger of the non-UAE Arab residents, so he allowed Arab residents to demonstrate and even damage Iranian property, but told the police not to let the protests get out of control. Afterward he quietly compensated Iranians for their damaged property.

The UAE Federation

The most significant event of Zaid's tenure was the formation of the UAE in 1971. Up until 1951, there was little coordination of activities among the Trucial State rulers other than on an ad hoc personal basis. In 1952, the British established a Trucial States Council that included the seven rulers presided over by a British political officer. In the 1960s, a Development Fund under the jurisdiction of the Council received grants from Britain as well as Bahrain, Qatar, and Abu Dhabi. By the 1970s, Abu Dhabi was providing 80 percent of the funds. When Britain announced in 1968 that they would withdraw from bases east of Suez by 1971, the Trucial rulers, and Bahrain and Qatar began thinking about the governments they would establish. Zaid argued strongly, despite opposition in his own family, for a federation of states that would be more powerful and economically viable than states acting individually. Several states hesitated to become involved in a federation that would be dominated by Abu Dhabi with its vast oil wealth. One was Dubai. People present at the time credit the strong relationship between Zaid's advisor, Ahmadi Suwaidi, and the Maktum's advisor, a Bahraini Mahdi Tajir for bringing the leaders of the two most important emirates together (Peterson 2001: 581). Zaid eventually convinced other rulers that they would benefit from a relationship with the oil states. They all believed oil would eventually be discovered in their emirates and so agreed.

After three years of negotiations, six rulers signed the Provisional Constitution of the UAE in July 1971. Bahrain and Qatar refused to sign and RAK joined two months after the UAE became a state on December 2, 1971. The Provisional Constitution provided strong legislative and executive functions, accepted mainly because a supreme council composed of the seven rulers would make all the significant decisions by simple majority, including Abu Dhabi and Dubai. The chairman of this group, also president of the UAE, would run federal affairs in the absence of an operational authority. Zaid was re-elected president by the Supreme Council Members every five years until 2004 when he died and his son became president. The president appointed the prime minister, deputy prime minister, cabinet ministers and other officials. Day to day management was carried out by a council of ministers. This body started with 12 ministers in 1971, expanded to 19 in 1972, and then to 29 in 1973 when Abu Dhabi abolished its separate cabinet in exchange for more seats on the federal cabinet (Rugh, W. 1997: 19). The Cabinet announced in 2004 on the day of Zaid's death reduced the number to 19 by restructuring and merging ministries. A Federal National Council composed of 40 members was also appointed on the basis of each emirate's proportion of the population: eight each for Abu Dhabi and Dubai, six each for Sharja and RAK, and four each for Fujaira, UAQ, and Ajman. In late 2006, the UAE Government announced that half of these seats would be put forth for election.

The Provisional Constitution was to be replaced by a permanent constitution in five years, but a new draft prepared by the ministers and Federal National Council members was defeated in 1976 by the Supreme Council. A constitutional crisis in 1979 pitted those who supported centralized, presidential power against those who wanted to continue power in the hands of the individual ruling families. Of particular importance to the former group was unification of the armed forces, dropping internal borders and distributing oil wealth more equitably. Abu Dhabi led those wanting more centralization and Dubai those wanting to maintain the status quo. The status quo eventually won, and every five years thereafter the Provisional Constitution was extended until it became permanent in 1996 (Heard-Bey: lecture 2004).

From its start, Zaid was the most active backer of the Federation. In 1971, he pledged to finance 85 percent of the federal budget but because other emirates contributed little he often paid as much as 95 percent. He transferred resources and personnel from Abu Dhabi government institutions to the Federal Government and in 1976 incorporated the Abu Dhabi Defense Forces into the Union Defense Force, while other emirates retained their individual forces. To encourage participation, Zaid subsidized the rulers of the poorer states so they could function in their roles as tribal sheikhs. Much of the development money also supported the poorer northern emirates whose citizens disproportionately sought jobs in the civil service of the Federal Government. Despite the important positions it was assigned, Dubai played a largely passive role in the Federation. Zaid worked to strengthen the Federation until he died, but with the exception of general services, most of the day-to-day governing of the separate emirates still remains in the hands of their individual rulers. He was careful not to push centralization faster or further than the other rulers could accept.

Zaid's Marriages

When compared with those of his brothers, Zaid's marriages show a sense of political acumen unsurpassed from the time of his grandfather, Zaid I, and probably modeled partially on his example. Not all the details are known but over his lifetime Zaid married at least nine wives although most people believe there were others. He had at least 30 children, 19 of them boys. His first son was born about 1946 when he was around 30 (if born in 1916) and his last child in 1978 when he was in his 60s. He reportedly married two women before his "senior" wife Hussa but little is known about them. One may have been Alia, a daughter of Muhammad Salimin Rahma of the Sunaina, the Chief of the Bedouin section of the Bu Shamis. This Chief's pledge of loyalty to the Sultan of Muscat (rather than the Saudis) was an important turning point in the Buraimi negotiations of 1955 (Kelly 1964: 196–197), causing other shaikhs to align themselves in favor of Muscat and Abu Dhabi.[12] A relative was a chief of Hafit a village in Buraimi (Zahlan 1978: 181). Alia died soon after marriage leaving no surviving children, probably the reason she is not usually listed with his wives.

The wife who became his senior wife was a Nahyan, daughter of his benefactor, Muhammad Khalifa and Hussa Saqr Nahyan, daughter of Saqr who murdered Zaid's father. Hussa died at the birth of a daughter, also Hussa, whom Zaid married. The fact that she was a granddaughter of Zaid's father's murderer suggests the greater importance of her paternal bloodlines. Hussa bore Zaid one child, in 1946. Khalifa conveniently connected the two main Nahyan branches, the Bani Sultan and the Bani Muhammad, a fact that should give him strong support as ruler. Zaid and Hussa were reportedly married ten years during which time she suffered numerous miscarriages before she bore Khalifa. This means they could have been married as early as 1936 when Zaid was 20. What is unusual is the length of time it took him to marry again. Were he politically ambitious, he might be expected to want more children. At the time however his brother Hazza was the obvious next in line to succeed Shakhbut. Hussa continued to live in al Ain, remaining Zaid's senior wife until his death. In his later years Zaid lived mainly in Abu Dhabi with another wife, Fatima Qitbi, who played a prominent role in women's affairs there.

The third known wife was Fatima (family name unknown to me). Some say she was the mother of Zaid's first daughter, Salama, who later married Shakhbut's son, Said, but had no children. Fatima was probably divorced after a short period, and quickly faded into obscurity.

Zaid's subsequent wives were mostly from prominent tribal sections. The nonroyal Shaikha Ma'azid al Mashghuni was Zaid's fourth wife and the mother of his second son Sultan, who was born in 1955. The Mishaghin are one of 14 major sections of the Bani Yas Federation. Although relatively small in number,[13] their importance lay in the fact that they resided in areas of Buraimi disputed by the Saudis (Kelly 1964: 36). Zaid probably married her in the mid-fifties when Saudis were bribing tribes to claim loyalty to them. Zaid divorced her soon after the birth of her son who was then raised by Zaid's brother Hazza and his mother Salama.

The next five marriages (one to Muza from the Bu Samra was short and produced no children) took place within a short space of five or six years—between 1959 and 1965—in the period just before Zaid became ruler. The rapidity with which he contracted these marriages is noteworthy since he was in his 40s by then and already had two sons and a daughter born over two decades of marriage to four wives.[14] Suddenly his wives and children increased dramatically.

Two events may provide an explanation. The first, of a personal nature, was the death on January 21, 1958 of his favorite brother, Hazza. The second was the discovery of oil off the coast of Abu Dhabi in 1959 and, two years later, deposits on the mainland that would lead to enormous increases in revenues when exports started in 1962. Hazza's death left Zaid alone to deal with Shakhbut while at the same time increasing his chances of becoming ruler if the crisis could not be resolved. Zaid must have realized the increasing revenues made it all the more important to have a farsighted leader who could bring prosperity to the region. He made his move in a characteristically tribal way by mobilizing supporters and preparing his own dynasty.

Four of the five wives he married at this time, Fatima Mubarak Qitbi, Muza Suhail Awaidi Khaili, Aisha Ali Darmaki and Amna Salah Badawi, bore children throughout the 1960s and up until the end of the 1970s, altogether producing 27 of his estimated 30 or more children. Between 1966 and 1971 Zaid's wives were producing children at a rate of two or three a year.[15] His last child, a son, was born in 1977 to Muza Suhail.

Each of the wives brought political advantage to Zaid. The first, Fatima Mubarak, is the wife most often referred to in the press. People say she is Zaid's favorite wife. A romantic story claims he saw her drawing water from a well and immediately fell in love with her. This presumably made theirs a love marriage but given Zaid's tendency to marry wives from strategically important tribes, this could not have been a bad marriage in the late 1950s when he was still Wali of Buraimi (1946–1966). The Qitab, though small in numbers, roam a strategic area of the hinterland and the coast. They were the main Bedouin tribe in Sharja, and also in large tracts south of Buraimi. Up until 1891 they constituted the land-based allies of the Qawasim but turned their allegiance to Zaid I as Qawasim power declined (Van Der Meulen 1997: 370). Animosity developed between them and the Qawasim Shaikh Saqr Khalid, and escalated in 1927 when his son Sultan allowed Dhaid, where some Bani Qitab lived, to be taken over by RAK. At various times Abu Dhabi, Dubai, Ajman, and UAQ all made alliances with the Qitab to tilt the balance of power in their favor. By the 1930s the Bani Qitab controlled the interior of the Trucial States (Zahlan 1978: 145) and British exploration parties in 1936 and 1938 were turned back by the Bani Qitab even though they had agreements with the Ruler of Sharja. Had not World War II caused an interruption in oil exploration, the Bani Qitab almost certainly would have seriously delayed the discovery of oil. The Qitab were also enemies of the Naim and therefore helpful to Abu Dhabi and the Dhawahir in keeping the Naim under control in Buraimi (Van Der Meulen 1997: 370). Because at various times they paid *zakat* to the Wahhabis, they were key players in the dispute over Buraimi where the British used *zakat* payments to determine rightful control. Zaid's marriage to Fatima in the late 1950s may have been meant to encourage the long-term loyalty of her tribe.

Fatima bore Zaid six sons (Muhammad in 1960, Hamdan in 1963, Hazza in 1965, Tahnun in 1969, Mansur in 1971, and Abdulla in 1973) and two daughters (Shamma in 1967 and Alyazia in 1968) over a thirteen-year period. They all occupy important positions in the government with support from their mother. Her eldest son Muhammad is now Crown Prince of Abu Dhabi.

The next wife, Muza Suhail Awaida Khaili,[16] was from a section of the Manasir located in the area between Abu Dhabi and Dubai. They acted as transporters for the Nahyan during their annual migrations to Buraimi oasis and owned date palms in Liwa, Khatem and Buraimi. Their center was Tharwaniya in Liwa with their main grazing areas west of Buraimi. They were listed among the Bani Yas in the Saudi Memorials and remained loyal to the Nahyan during the Buraimi crisis (Kelly 1964: 236). Although independent, the Manasir could usually be counted on for support, and from as early as Zaid I's reign, their children intermarried with the Nahyan.

Zaid probably married Muza not long after the Buraimi settlement while the memory of her tribe, the Bu Khail's, help in that crisis was still fresh in his mind. She bore Zaid five boys Saif in 1968, Ahmad in 1969 (some sources say 1971), Hamid in 1970, Umar in 1973, and Khalid in 1977) and two girls (Shamsa in 1960 and Afra in 1966). Muza lived in Al Ain (Zakhir) where her daughter, Shamsa, and her husband Tahnun Muhammad Khalifa built a house. Her other daughter married a son of Muhammad Khalifa from his Dahihri wife. Muza's eldest son Saif married his maternal cousin (daughter of Awaida Suhail Khaili), thus perpetuating her family connections into the next generation.

The next wife was Aisha Ali Saif Darmaki who Zaid probably married in the early 60s. The Darmakis as noted earlier, are a main section of the Dhawahir tribe. They are prominent in Abu Dhabi and Al Ain, and some live in Qatar where they are related to the Qatari ruling family. Through them the Nahyan strengthened their influence in Dhawahir villages where they acquired landholdings. In 1960, some Dhawahir had a dispute with Shakhbut and 120 of them left for Saudi Arabia where they stayed until asked by Zaid to return. Since the timing of this dispute coincided with Zaid's marriage to the Darmaki wife, there may have been a connection. Marriages with Dhawahir women were common in the Nahyan family. Zaid I, two of his sons (Tahnun and Hamdan), Muhammad Khalifa and two of his sons (Tahnun and Said), and one of Shakhbut's grandsons (Khalifa Sultan) married Dhawahir wives, as did the outcast Saqr Zaid I.

Aisha's first child, a daughter, Latifa, was born in 1963, and later four sons (Said born in 1965, Nahyan in 1968, Falah in 1970, and Diab in 1971) and four more daughters (Muza in 1964, Wadima in 1969, Shaikha in 1974 and Maitha in 1976). The eldest of her sons married a granddaughter of Muhammad Khalifa (daughter of Hamdan) and the second eldest son, a daughter of Muhammad Butti Hamid Qubaisi. Three daughters married classificatory cousins: a grandson of Shakhbut, a great grandson of Zaid I (through Hamdan Zaid I), and a grandson of Muhammad Khalifa, spouses that distributed their influence across three main Nahyan lineages. The Qubaisi marriage, echoed[17] several times in the marriages of Zaid's children, was to a granddaughter of the brother of Shaikh Zaid's mother, Salama. Her father, Muhammad Butti, became governor of Taraf in 1968, and later chairman of the Abu Dhabi Municipality. One of his jobs was land distribution in Abu Dhabi.[18] The special prominence of this family came from Zaid's residence with his maternal kin as a child and Nahyan efforts to maintain close relations with a Bani Yas tribe that fled Abu Dhabi several times in the past.

Aisha Darmaki was divorced from Zaid and lives in the Hili area of al Ain, one of five areas that used to be almost exclusively Dhawahir but where the Nahyan bought property in the last decades of the nineteenth century: Al Ain, Hili, Jimi, Al Qattara, and Mutirid (Heard-Bey 1996: 38). Several Darmakis have held positions of prominence in the Abu Dhabi government.

Amna Salah Badawi was the fourth of the wives Zaid married in the 1960s. She was also from the Darmaki tribe, and came from Hatta, north of Al Ain. Zaid probably married her in about 1965, the last of his known marriages that produced children. She bore two sons (Isa born in 1966, and Nasir in 1968) and a daughter (Rowda in 1970). She was divorced and lived in the Al Ain village of Masudi.

Zaid's wives exerted different degrees of behind-the-scene influence on the politics of Abu Dhabi, either because of their especially close relationship to Zaid or because their multiple sons have formed a political block. In the first category are his senior wife Hussa Muhammad Khalifa who resides in Al Ain and his Qitbi wife Fatima who lived with him in Abu Dhabi. Zaid talked frequently on the telephone with Hussa and is said to have respected her judgment. There is no doubt Hussa and Fatima used their closeness with Zaid to promote their sons. Other wives who were divorced from Zaid and returned to their own communities probably had less influence. Those who bore several sons seem to have had a special influence with Zaid. Three such "mother-blocks" include the Bani Fatima (six sons), the Bani Muza (five sons), and the Bani Aisha (four sons). The other mothers of sons bore only one or two, not enough to form an important pressure group.

Altogether, aside from his one Nahyan wife, Zaid chose eight tribal wives who came from the Bu Shamis, the Mishaghin, the Bu Khail, the Darmaki/Dhawahir, and the Qitab. These tribes were mostly from areas near Al Ain/Buraimi and Liwa. Several were helpful in the dispute with Saudi Arabia over possession of Buraimi. The wives also came from and several returned to live in the four main villages of Al Ain/Buraimi where the Nahyan bought property from the Dhawahir in the nineteenth century. These tribal marriages proved useful well into the second half of the twentieth century until land disputes were resolved and borders rather than tribal leaders' skills defined the scope of a ruler's supporters. By the end of the twentieth century the political value of such marriages was waning, and Zaid changed course and began consolidating power within his own lineage, first broadly and then narrowly. The marriages of his children reflected this new strategy.

The Bani Muhammad

Figure 5.2   The Bani Muhammad of Abu Dhabi

In examining the links between Zaid and other Nahyan lineages, those between the Bani Sultan (Zaid and his brothers) and the Bani Muhammad (his cousins) are the most interesting. Khalifa Zaid I and his only son Muhammad removed Sultan's murderer, Saqr, and restored the rule to the Bani Sultan. Based on age, birth order, and influence, the Bani Muhammad could have ruled if they wanted. Their refusal was attributed to several factors, including the influence of their Manasir wife/mother, their dismay at earlier bloody succession conflicts, and their fear of leaving their own families without heads if they should meet the same fate.[19] Khalifa and Muhammad appeared content to remain "king-makers." As long as Muhammad lived (he died in 1979) he remained loyal to the Bani Sultan and none of his sons dared attempt a takeover. However Zaid and his family were not sure his sons and grandsons might not make a move after the death of their patriarch. The Bani Sultan thus watched as the Bani Muhammad became more numerous and powerful.

Mindful of his indebtedness to the Bani Muhammad, Zaid immediately appointed several of them to positions of importance in September 1966 a month after he came to power. At that point his sons were still young—the eldest, Khalifa was 20—and his own brothers dead, exiled or "cold coffee" so he had little support from immediate kin should the Bani Muhammad move against him. The Executive Council consisted of six shaikhs and a commoner to advise him. They included Zaid's own son Khalifa as Deputy Ruler or Crown Prince, five Bani Muhammad, including their three most prominent members from the Utaiba wife, and two younger members from the Dhahiri wife, and Ahmad Hamid, Zaid's maternal cousin (MoBrSo). Zaid signaled through this arrangement that he intended, unlike Shakhbut, to extend political influence to the Bani Muhammad while keeping control of the council through his eldest son. Zaid followed up by marrying ten of his children as they came of age to the Bani Muhammad. In two cases he gave daughters to the Bani Muhammad with whom he had the closest relations—Tahnun from the Utaiba wife and Surur from the Dhahiri wife.

Khuri (1980) notes that it is now usual for rulers in the Gulf to appoint relatives to positions of authority, but it was a departure at the time for Zaid to formalize relations with relatives in this way. The appointments accomplished several aims: (1) They publicly recognized his special indebtedness to the Bani Muhammad; (2) They showed his intention to share power, and (3) They eased the transition from a largely self-appointed group of community elders advising rulers, to a defined group of people he could interact with on a personal basis. Later Zaid expanded the group to others in the society.

Unfortunately for the Bani Muhammad, subsequent events removed the likelihood they would come to power. Their senior member, Hamdan, (showing the most leadership potential) moved from Chairman of Public Works to Deputy Prime Minister in the 1970s, but became ill and finally died in 1989. The second son Mubarak who had risen to Minister of the Interior and in charge of internal security, had a car accident in 1979 in England that seriously crippled him and forced him to resign. The third son Tahnun continued to serve in several important positions: on the Abu Dhabi Fund for Arab Economic Development (ADFAED), as Vice Chairman of the powerful Abu Dhabi Executive Council, and on the Abu Dhabi Investment Authority (ADIA). He also served as Chairman of the

Abu Dhabi National Oil Company (ADNOC) Board, and in several other organizations. He was eventually replaced in all of those positions, and since August 1974, has been representative in the eastern region, an important position well away from the capital. Surur was Director of ADNOC, Vice Chairman of ADFAED, and a Director of ADIA until he also was replaced in all these positions. Later he was Chairman of the Electricity and Water Board until removed from that job in 1998. He was also on the Supreme Petroleum Council, the Abu Dhabi Executive Council and was Chamberlain of the Court, but was not active in these roles and now focuses entirely on his business interests. As Zaid's sons grew older they were appointed to the powerful Abu Dhabi Executive Council and later, after 1971, to the Federal Council of Ministers. By Zaid's death in 2004 only two Bani Muhammad were left on the Federal Council and one on the Abu Dhabi Executive Council.

Bani Zaid and the Succession

As the influence of the Bani Muhammad waned, Zaid's sons, the "Bani Zaid" were taking on responsibilities commensurate with their ages and birth order. The eldest son, Khalifa, became his father's representative in the eastern region between 1966 and 1969, until he became the chief of the new Abu Dhabi Defense Department, and Brigadier in the Abu Dhabi Defense Force. Between 1971 and 1973 he was Prime Minister, Minister of Defense and Minister of Finance, and then Deputy Prime Minister in the federal government. From 1971 he was Crown Prince and administrative head of Abu Dhabi.[20] In March of 1980 he assumed daily control of Abu Dhabi government operations, retaining the important position of Chairman of the Abu Dhabi Fund for Economic Development (ADFED) that he had held since 1972. In November 2004 when Zaid died he became ruler.

What does Khalifa Zaid bring to the rulership besides long administrative experience and membership in the paramount family? First he is Zaid's only son with a Nahyan mother. As a daughter of Muhammad Khalifa, Hussa brings Khalifa the support of the Bani Muhammad, and as granddaughter of a Darmaki chief some Dhahairi support. Hussa is a strong presence in Al Ain, highly respected as Zaid's senior wife, and uncompromising in support of her only son.

Khalifa's wife is a Mazari, one of the tribes traditionally loyal to Abu Dhabi (Heard-Bey 1996: 29). They were the principal Bedouin section of the Bani Yas, and also owned pearling boats. In the 1950s, the Mazaris that had been guards and retainers of the Abu Dhabi rulers were employed to protect the oil industry (Heard-Bey 1996: 206). Khalifa married Shamsa Suhail Mazrui in about 1964. She was his only wife and bore all eight of his children, two boys[21] and six girls.[22]

When it came to marrying his own children, Khalifa, as Zaid's eldest son by 9 years had difficulty finding traditional paternal cousins for his oldest children, especially the girls, since the cousins were not yet of appropriate age to marry. Consequently he married them to Muhammad Khalifa's grandchildren, who were the next best thing, classifactory paternal cousins.[23] The girls married: Hamad Tahnun, Khalifa Saif, Sultan Hamdan, and Mansur Tahnun. Another daughter married the son of the patriarch of the Bani Muhammad, Hamdan, around the time of his death. Khalifa's oldest son, Sultan, married a granddaughter of Muhammad Khalifa, Shaikha Saif, whose father's sister, Hussa, was at the same time Sultan's paternal grandmother. In 1999, Khalifa's second son Muhammad, married a daughter of Khalifa's half brother, Sultan (FaBrDa), who like Khalifa is the only son of his mother. All the marriages but one were to the Bani Muhammad, diplomatically divided among the children of Tahnun, Saif, and Hamdan. This could have been a coincidence but historically there are enough cases of "balancing" to believe it was intentional. Note too that Hamdan and Tahnun are sons of the Utaiba mother and Saif of the Dahiri mother so the "mother blocks" are also represented.

The political ramifications of these marriages are too important to be a matter of chance. In theory, such marriages have the effect of strengthening the mutual interests of collateral branches at the expense of other branches of the family. In this case Khalifa, who already had ties to the Bani Muhammad through his mother, simply strengthened these relations further. This act basically guaranteed Bani Muhammad support for Khalifa's rule after Zaid's death by offsetting the growing prominence of the Bani Fatima half brothers with their nonroyal mother. The marriage of Khalifa's second son to the daughter of his half brother, Sultan Zaid, showed a similar effort to put together a coalition of the two oldest sons to balance the Bani Fatima.

Why were these marriages so important to Khalifa since most people felt after years of running the day-to-day operations of Abu Dhabi Khalifa would automatically step into the rulership position when his father died. At issue was not so much whether Khalifa would succeed Zaid, but who would be named the next Crown Prince. All else being equal, the main candidates should have been the two Sultans, Zaid's son Sultan because he was the next oldest son, and Sultan Khalifa because he was Khalifa's oldest son. Realizing the tension, Zaid made his choice known before his death, by naming his third son Muhammad Zaid, Deputy Crown Prince. This was a blow to Khalifa's desire to see his own son in the position.

Why had Zaid's second son, Sultan, been eliminated? Sultan was born in about 1956 to Zaid's wife, Madhad Mishghuni (from a section of the Bani Yas) and was raised in the household of Zaid's favorite brother, Hazza, and Zaid's mother, Salama. In 1975, he married Shamsa Muhammad Khalifa, a highly respected woman of the Bani Muhammad. Her mother was a Dhahiri. Their marriage made Sultan brother-in-law to Muhammad Khalifa's sons from his Dhahiru wife: Hamdan, Mubarak, and Surur, and it tied him closely to his older brother, Khalifa, whose mother was a half sister of his wife. Sultan was educated at Sandhurst and upon his return in 1978, at 23, his father made him Chief of Staff of the UAE Armed Forces, a largely symbolic role since most of the emirates had their own military forces. In February 1982, Sultan became Deputy Prime Minister in the Federal Government, a post suggesting a possible future high position in the Abu Dhabi Government.

Sultan Zaid however fell out of favor for several reasons. First, he had a tumultuous youth that left questions about his ability to hold important leadership positions. The final crisis occurred in February 1982 in an incident involving a Dubai girl and a shooting. Zaid was furious and ordered Sultan brought to him—one report said "dead or alive"—dismissed him from his position, and sent him to the United States for drug treatment. When he later returned to the UAE, Zaid made him Deputy Prime Minister, but he never fully regained his father's favor. The incident is cited as an example of Zaid's uncompromising standards, especially in comparison to his predecessor's handling of his sons. Although unlikely to regain a place in the line of succession, Sultan still has four advantages that make his support helpful to Khalifa: his age and birth order among Zaid's sons, his popularity with the tribes, his links to the Bani Muhammad, and his independence from other mother-blocks of Zaid's sons.

The other "natural" candidate was Khalifa's son, Sultan. Sultan Khalifa graduated from the Emirates University, and later from Zaid Military Academy. After he failed graduate courses at a U.S. institution, Sultan entered the UAE military where he became a commissioned officer. In 1984, he married a granddaughter of Muhammad Khalifa, Shaikha Saif. Her father Saif, is the most powerful of the younger group of Muhammad Khalifa's children through his Dhahiri wife. Shaikha also has connections through her Utaiba mother to the business community. With this combination of connections she makes a perfect wife for an aspirant to the throne.

Sultan Khalifa was preparing himself for the position until Muhammad's appointment. In the 1990s, he completed a doctorate in England and took on responsible positions in the Abu Dhabi administration. He was director of his father's office, and member of the Abu Dhabi Executive Council.

Sultan has three boys and five girls. The girls are closely protected to prevent any hint of impropriety. Their mother established a private school where they could be safely educated, ensured that they had special tutoring in languages, and the older girls studied at the all-girls Zaid University. During the late 90s the family built a tastefully decorated palace suitable for entertaining.

Crown Prince Muhammad is Zaid's third son and the eldest of Shaikha Fatima's sons. Zaid seems to have selected him based on his special leadership skills, as well as quite probably on Shaikha Fatima's urgings that her son be given the position. Several local observers noted that the "one who shares the bed has access to the ear." Muhammad Zaid was in any case the next in birth order after the discredited second brother Sultan and therefore the choice was not as likely to elicit criticism, as it would if he were a younger, less well-established son. Muhammad is the eldest of six full brothers and two full sisters in the Fatima "mother block." The brothers are close and are usually thought of as a single power group. They will use whatever influence they have to bring their eldest brother to power.

The influence of the Bani Fatima block needs to be considered in its totality. All eight children married. Muhammad married Salama Hamdan Muhammad Khalifa in about 1981 when her father was still patriarch of the Bani Muhammad. Her mother was a Bu Falasa from Dubai. The second brother, Hamdan, married his cousin (MoBrDa), Aisha Suhail Mubarak Qitbi in about 1981 but later divorced her and married Shamsa Hamdan Muhammad Khalifa in 1988, reportedly after seeing her abroad and falling in love with her. Shamsa is a half sister of Muhammad's wife, with a Dhahiri mother. Fatima's two daughters, Alyazia and Shamma, in 1982, married Hamad Hamdan and Surur Muhammad respectively, again both members of the Bani Muhammad. The third brother, Hazza, married Muza Muhammad Butti, a great granddaughter of Zaid's maternal uncle (his FaMoBrSoSoDa) in about 1988. Her father was one of the most powerful nonroyals in the government. The fourth brother, Mansur, also married a daughter of Muhammad Butti, Aliya, in 1994. Tahnun married in 1997 to Khawla Ahmad Khalifa Suwaidi, the daughter of the one-time close confident and advisor of Zaid. The youngest son Abdulla, sometimes said to be his mother's favorite, married Ilyazi Saif, granddaughter of Muhammad Khalifa in 2002.

Shaikha Fatima's eight children thus married in ways that reinforced their interconnectedness. The five Bani Muhammad Khalifa marriages included three to progeny of Hamdan Muhammad, the late patriarch, one to his brother and one to a granddaughter. These marriages, focused on Hamdan's lineage, offset some, although not all, of the new ruler, Khalifa's, strong Bani

Muhammad support. Three Bani Fatima sons also married women related to Zaid's mother, Salama Butti Khadim Qubaisi, certainly welcomed by Zaid who was fond of his maternal relatives. The final marriage to the Suwaidi woman carried little political advantage other than to recognize an old colleague of Zaid's who for some years was estranged from him.

It was highly unusual for Zaid to choose a Deputy Crown Prince before his death. This act can only be explained in terms of the growing tensions among his sons. By appointing Muhammad Zaid to the position he hoped to calm the fears of his other sons, especially the Bani Fatima that Khalifa might cut them out of the line of succession. Some argue that in the modern era, power is so concentrated in the sitting ruler that, after some time passes, Khalifa could still appoint his own son Crown Prince. But he could probably only do this if he wins the support of a substantial part of the Nahyan family which is unlikely.

Discussion

After the Bani Muhammad turned over the rule to Shakhbut and he was deposed in a bloodless coup, Zaid dominated the politics of Abu Dhabi for the rest of the twentieth century. He was not a man who ruthlessly pursued political advantage but rather intuitively knew how to deal with people so that in the end they would see things his way. He gave his adversaries space to recant voluntarily, and when their disagreements with him were over he offered generous concessions so they would not lose face. Zaid was the most visionary, generous, and sympathetic of all the rulers yet described, a man who tried at all times to serve the needs of his people. He was genuinely loved by the people of the Emirates until the day he died. Heard-Bey at a lecture in 2004, describes him as possessing a "referred" kind of power—characteristic of effective tribal shaikhs—where a ruler seeks power in the satisfaction of his subjects. Zaid used his power to please his subjects, not to suppress them, and valued himself to the extent that he succeeded.

Where does such idealism come from? Certainly much of it comes from tribal values and the inherent sense of responsibility that is a basis of morality and civility. It also comes from the upbringing of children in the best of the paramount families where they observe the mannered behavior of their elders. There they learn the ritualistic art of hospitality—sensitivity to the reactions of others, the conventions of the *majlis*, and the responsibilities of the powerful—saturating their young minds until the art of leadership becomes an automatic part of their personalities.

Unlike some rulers before him, Zaid knew how to make kin feel they were being fairly treated. In retrospect, one sees the progression of steps he took to gain the support of his Bani Muhammad cousins until he could promote his own sons to positions of dominance. The first step was the placation of the Bani Muhammmad cousins by appointing them to the Executive Council. The second was to marry his children to Bani Muhammad spouses in order to sustain the generally friendly relations with them. This was a departure from the tribal marriages Zaid contracted to expand his own influence. Third was the appointment of Khalifa as Crown Prince. Khalifa was not only the eldest son but the son most closely linked to the Bani Muhammad through his mother. This was the first time a crown prince was formally named by a Nahyan ruler before he died. The fourth was Zaid's gradual consolidation of the most powerful governmental positions in the hands of his own sons. Fifth was the contracting of later marriages to spouses within his family or to members of lineages with emotional ties but no claim to the throne. Finally he skipped over other candidates to appoint his third son Muhammad as Deputy Crown Prince, another first, to reduce family tensions over who would be Crown Prince under Khalifa. With threats from outside his lineage no longer absorbing his attention, Zaid's final challenge was the growing competition within his immediate family. In the meantime he had been absorbing his sons into positions of responsibility and influence, and trying to create cordial relations among the half brothers through frequent contacts, even sending some of them abroad to study together. Yet despite these efforts, the brothers coalesced into political blocks around their separate mothers—the Bani Fatima, the Bani Muza, and to lesser extent, the Bani Aisha. Even though their competitiveness is not likely to end in Khalifa's overthrow, they will demand a share of power in exchange for their support.

Even while he drew his kin into government, Zaid saw the need for educated outsiders to advise him. Early on he brought in Mana Otaiba (Petroleum), Ahmad Suaidi (Foreign Affairs) and Muhammad Habroush (Finance) to advise him on matters that required expertise. At the same time he was never comfortable with fully delegating decisions and administration to others as the complexity of a modern state requires. In this he remained a tribal chief who feared the delegation of authority might be seen as a sign of weakness, detracting from the support base he had created. It was common to see him driving around the city, checking on projects he initiated and personally ensuring they were carried out well.

The death of a long-term ruler is a momentous time in the political history of tribal societies, even modern ones, since as Khuri (1990) notes, the deceased ruler's networks collapse and have to be reconstituted in the new networks of his successor. Zaid ruled largely by tribal tradition, adapting practices pragmatically to address modern exigencies. His relationships with his sons, family, extended relatives, and nonkin members were all dictated by the tribal values he placed great stock in. If history is any guide, Khalifa will increasingly develop a relationship with his half brothers like that his father developed with the Bani Muhammad. He may start by supporting them in positions of importance until his own sons and maybe some of his Bani Muhammad supporters are secured in major positions. Or he may favor blocks of his younger half siblings like the Bani Muza or the Bani Aisha to counteract the influential Bani Fatima. He faces the challenge of having many ambitious half siblings without the support of many sons of his own to counteract them. In this he differs from his father. Khalifa's presumed goal to situate his two sons favorably will take considerable strategy in the future, and since he is already nearing 60 he will be pressed to move quickly before the Bani Fatima take over under Muhammad Zaid. In chapter 12 we will look at Khalifa's initial moves after the death of Zaid.

CHAPTER 6

THE MAKTUMS (AL BU FALASA) AND THE DEVELOPMENT OF DUBAI

The Bu Falasa Rulers to the Present

- Maktum Butti — 1833–1852; ruled with Ubaid Said for first three years
- Hashar Maktum — 1852–1886; son of his predecessor
- Rashid Maktum — 1886–1894; brother of his predecessor
- Maktum Hashar Maktum — 1894–1906; nephew (BrSo) of his predecessor
- Butti Suhail Maktum — 1906–1912; cousin (FaBrSo)of his predecessor
- Said Maktum Hashar — 1912–1958; cousin once removed (FaBrSoSo)of his predecessor
- Rashid Said — 1958–1990; son of his predecessor
- Maktum Rashid — 1990–2005; son of his predecessor
- Muhammad Rashid — 2006–present; brother of predecessor

Dubai is different in several respects from the other emirates. Although small in land size—about 4 percent of the UAE with 3,885 square kilometers—it has roughly one third of the population. The capital, Dubai city, is located on a deepwater creek that divides the old city, Bur Dubai, from the northern, more modern section of Dera. Dubai's inland town of Hatta is a tourist haven roughly 100 km southeast of Dubai city on the road to Fujaira and Oman.

Next to Abu Dhabi, Dubai is the wealthiest emirate, and the only one that was wealthy before oil. Oil was discovered in Dubai in 1966 and production

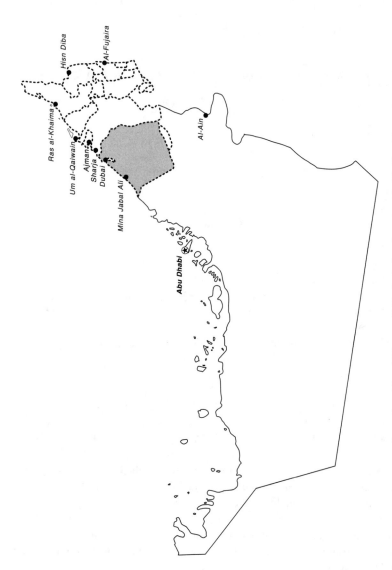

Hisn Diba
Al-Fujaira
Ras al-Khaima
Um al-Qaiwain
Ajman
Sharja
Dubai
Al-Ain
Mina Jabal Ali
Abu Dhabi

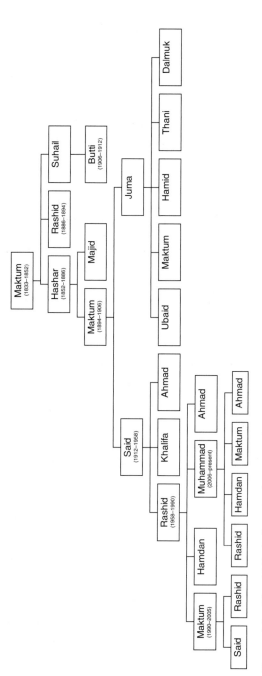

Figure 6.1 The Al Bu Falasa (Maktum) Rulers in Dubai

began in 1969. It peaked in 1991 at 420,000 barrels a day and its reserves will only last a few years. Dubai successfully invested in infrastructure to diversify its economy, keeping its main focus on commerce and trade. Although early Dubai families participated in plundering ships, they preferred stable conditions suitable for trade. The rulers also focused on maritime activities and de–emphasized almost to the point of ignoring the inland tribes. But they welcomed prominent trading families from Iran, India and other countries wanting to do business in the emirate (Van Der Meulen 1997: 173).

Little is known of Dubai before 1833 but Lorimer says the Omani Ruler in 1799, coveted the area where the town now stands (1986: 772). Although most coastal settlements possessed sufficiently deep harbors for safe anchorage, Dubai's harbor and creek were particularly favorable for shipping. From the time of the British protectorate, the creek marked the line between Qawasim and Abu Dhabi territory until the Bu Falasa settled on the Abu Dhabi side in 1833 (Heard-Bey 1996: 242). Dubai's boundaries with Abu Dhabi and Sharja remained in contention for a long time, and fighting broke out as recently as the 1940s over the border. In 1968, a neutral zone was also created in disputed areas between Sharja and Dubai (Litwak 1981: 63) which remained until a settlement in the 1990s.

The Bu Falasa's history was largely synonymous with that of the Bani Yas in Abu Dhabi until the 1830s. The first sign of Dubai's separate existence was the signature on the 1820 General Treaty of Peace by a minor chief Hazza Zaal on behalf of Dubai. On his death in 1825, Hazza was succeeded by his son Muhammad whose sister the Qassimi Shaikh, Sultan Saqr, married to gain influence in Dubai (Rush 2 1991: 22).

In 1833, about 800 members of the Bu Falasa section of the Bani Yas left Abu Dhabi permanently to set up residence in Dubai. They were angered by the choice of Khalifa Shakhbut as ruler[1] and refused to comply with British demands that they pay compensation for attacks on British shipping. With the help of Abu Dhabi's enemy, the Qassimi shaikh, the Bu Falasa managed to create an independent state (Rush 1991: xix.), although at the time Dubai was governed on behalf of Abu Dhabi (Lorimer 1986: 772).

The leaders of the exodus ruled jointly, with the eldest Ubaid Said taking the prominent position and Maktum Butti the junior one (Rush 1991: 237),[2] until Ubaid died in June 1836 and Maktum Butti (1836–52), although "haughty and inexperienced" became ruler. Although the relationship between the two chiefs was not clear—possibly uncle and nephew—Maktum was the eldest of Butti Suhail's three sons (Lorimer 1986: 772).

Freed from the control of Abu Dhabi the Bu Falasa plundered a number of Gulf vessels and even a village on the Batina coast of Oman before the British brought them under control (Rush 1991: 237). Dubai quickly realized the advantages of being located where it could side with the Nahyan of Abu Dhabi or the Qawasim of Sharja.[3] Soon after their arrival in Dubai, they joined the Qawasim in attacking Abu Dhabi, and although they were defeated, they continued as a nuisance factor by offering refuge to Abu Dhabi's enemies and plundering its ships. Their incursions became so frequent the British sent a squadron to resolve outstanding property issues (Rush 1991: 238–239).

In 1841, a fever ravaged Dubai and people fled across the creek to Dera where Dubai's chief, Maktum, had constructed a fort with the permission of Shaikh Sultan of Sharja. Maktum signed a document saying that the land belonged to Sultan and would be vacated when he requested it. About this time, 500 of the Muhair tribe who had accompanied Maktum to Dubai deserted him and settled in Sharja. Shaikh Sultan was delighted because, shortly before, Maktum had encouraged Sultan's son Saqr to rebel against his father. Meanwhile Shaikh Khalifa of Abu Dhabi with 150 men took over the lightly guarded fort of Dubai while the townsmen were away. The invaders destroyed stores, houses, and boats, and then withdrew to protect themselves from counterattacks by Maktum and Sultan and the 200 men they had assembled. The Abu Dhabi Chief continued to attack surrounding towns until turned back by Sultan when he approached the Qawasim stronghold of RAK (Rush 1991: 240–241).

For a time in 1843, Dubai's Maktum refrained from becoming involved in the conflicts between the Qassimi and Abu Dhabi Chiefs, but in a turn-about, suddenly allied with Abu Dhabi and offered his services as mediator between the two powers. After concluding a peace, however, he encour-aged the Abu Dhabi Chief to break it by attacking Qawasim territories (Rush 1991: 241). Eventually this treachery was discovered and the two enemies joined forces against Dubai in 1845, but Maktum and "his staunch ally," the Chief of UAQ, defended themselves against their attacks. When the two instigators were about to attack the fort of Dubai in 1846, they quarreled and made peace overtures to Dubai instead. Maktum made offensive and defensive alliances with the Sharja Chief while rebuffing Khalifa's successor Said Tahnun in Abu Dhabi. The Qawasim-Maktum agreement held and in early 1848 they concluded a closer alignment to oppose Abu Dhabi's moves against their territories. This time they were joined by the Shaikh of Ajman. When later the Wahhabis from the south were defeated, leaving the Bani Yas of Abu Dhabi at the pinnacle of their power, the three chiefs sided with Said Mutlak of Buraimi to challenge Abu Dhabi's influence in the oasis. By February 1848, with the help of a mediator the hostilities ceased (Rush 1991: 242–243).

Maktum continued friendly relations with the Qawasim Chief, and together they urged the Emir of Qatar to rebuild Udaid and encourage the Qubaisat to leave Abu Dhabi in 1849 and relocate there. This alienation of a major Bani Yas tribe so angered the Abu Dhabi Shaikh that he took extreme measures against them—"measures untempered with mercy or honesty that eventually reduced . . . the tribes to a state bordering on nothingness" (Rush 1991: 243). In 1851, Maktum agreed to reverse his position on Udaid. But in March 1851, his men intercepted a letter from the Shaikh of Sharja to the Shaikh of Abu Dhabi agreeing to an alliance. Maktum threatened the Qassimi Shaikh but, although appearing to back down, he concluded the agreement anyway by sending a messenger to Abu Dhabi through his Al Hula allies. With his neighbors to the east and west allied against him, Maktum turned to the Wahhabis in the south, and sent his brother to offer support to the Imam of Muscat in a fight for Sohar against Qawasim aggressors (Rush 1991: 244). He used the same tactic in 1847 to refocus Abu Dhabi and Qawasim attention toward the far side of their territories and away from himself. It was a tactic frequently used by chiefs of smaller emirates when pressures became too intense.

Shaikh Maktum contracted smallpox and died in 1852 while on board a ship returning from a visit to the Sultan of Muscat (Rush 1991: 245). Maktum spent much of his rule fending off attacks by Abu Dhabi and Qawasim shaikhs. The constant threat helped consolidate his authority internally (Lorimer 1986: 773). He also had good relations with the British. Captain Kemball wrote that Maktum had distinguished himself among the chiefs for generally fulfilling his commitments and understanding that British policy was "conducive to the advancement and prosperity of the Arab States . . ." (Rush 1991: 245). As chief of a small tribe located on territory claimed by Abu Dhabi, Maktum was forced to play off his neighbors against one another. The extreme measures Abu Dhabi had taken in the past to bring defectors home increased the Bu Falasa's sense of vulnerability.

Said Butti (1852–1859), Maktum's younger brother, succeeded to the rulership. His rule was soon contested by two of Maktum sons, Hashar and Suhail. When Said was visiting Muscat in October 1852, Maktum's sons took over the fort of Dubai and ousted Said's maternal uncle who had been left in charge. The uncle was imprisoned and then released, and soon regained the fort. Maktum's sons fled to Sharja. When Said saw there might be further difficulties with the Shaikh of Sharja, he concluded defensive agreements with Abu Dhabi and UAQ thus ending Qawasim intrigues against Dubai (Rush 1991: 246).

Shaikh Said obliged the British when they sought signatures to the Perpetual Treaty of Peace in 1853. He was the only ruler who was not visiting the son of the Wahhabi Emir in Buraimi (Lorimer 1986: 773), although he sent his maternal uncle to pay his respects. He supported British policy opposing the presence of a Wahhabi force in Oman, suppressed the maritime "irregularities" committed by his people, and showed himself "anxious to cultivate the good will and friendship of the British Government" (Rush 1991: 246). He died in December 1859 of smallpox along with his brother Butti and a nephew, Suhail.

Maktum's son, Hashar (1852–1886), who earlier challenged his uncle Said's rule, was the next to succeed. He ruled uneventfully until his death in November 1886. A third brother, Rashid Maktum (1886–1894), succeeded after a dispute with Hashar's son, Maktum, was settled peacefully by the elders. Rashid's letter to the Political Resident on December 6, 1886 made the following points: (1) His brother was dead; (2) The relevant people had given him authority "of their free will and consent"; and (3) He recognized all agreements existing with the British (Rush 1991: 261). The Political Resident wrote back that he recognized Rashid, saying that the people's free choice was the preferred way to settle issues. He added that the Residency Agent was ready to advise him and hoped he would attend to any advice he was given (Rush 1991: 261). By this time the British were giving final approval for successions, ostensibly to ensure agreement for existing treaties.

During his brother's reign, Rashid had not been groomed for the rulership, probably because Hashar wanted his own son to succeed. Hashar sent Rashid on commissions, and gave him 28 boats for his own maintenance, but otherwise did not involve him in the affairs of government. During Hashar's reign, Rashid was prohibited by the British from building a stone house in Dera that might be defended if there were troubles with the incumbent (Rush 1991: 257).

After he became ruler of Dubai, Rashid, like his predecessors, kept up his connections with Muscat. On one trip to Muscat in 1892, he married a woman from the breakaway Bu Shamis division of the Naim in Buraimi, thus linking himself to a group that normally opposed Abu Dhabi's long-term allies, the Dhawahir. The Bu Shamis had originally ruled Ajman but were replaced by another Naim branch. In December of the same year, he had a paralytic stroke and died a year and a half later on April 7, 1894 (Rush 1991: 250). [4]

Rashid was succeeded by his cousin and earlier challenger, Maktum Hashar (1894–1906). Rashid's six sons were still young with the oldest only 23, but in what was becoming a pattern in Dubai, they decided to unseat Maktum. He learned of their activities and imprisoned them for five months before exiling them to Sharja where they received small allowances from the Qassimi Shaikh (Rush 1991: 250). As usual the "enemy shaikh" saw the benefit in welcoming well-connected family members who might later come to power.

It was during the enlightened reign of Maktum, assisted by the decline of the port of Linga that Dubai began to flourish as a locus of commercial shipping (Rush 1991: 250). Earlier the Qawasim governed Linga but in 1887, the Persian government appointed Persian officials in their place. Linga now became subject to Persian customs. Consequently much of its trade moved to Dubai with the encouragement of Shaikh Maktum. Dubai quickly became the entry point to the interior of Arabia and the city filled with a variety of merchants and traders from many nations.[5]

In 1887, at the height of the Persian crisis, Maktum married the sister of Ahmad Ubaid, the Shaikh of Hanjam, a strategically located island off Qishim, near Linga. This marriage conveniently connected him to an influential family in this contested area. His son appears to have maintained an active connection with these maternal relatives from reports of his hunting expeditions there until the early 1930s (Rush 1991: 309–310).

At the time, Dubai employed the largest numbers of men in the pearling industry even though it had fewer boats than Abu Dhabi. Although it imposed taxes on the community, there were so many exemptions that eventually a number of pearlers moved to Dubai from other settlements along the coast (Heard-Bey 1996: 243). The decline of the pearling industry in the 1930s and World War II brought hard times to Dubai. Many turned to smuggling the rations provided by the British to the Persians. One positive outcome of the hard times was a decline in slavery (Heard-Bey 1996: 251).

Maktum maintained exceedingly good relations with the British, so much so that they expressed great regret when he died suddenly of a heart attack in February 1906 after a short illness (Rush 1991: 251). The British felt Maktum's oldest son Said was too young[6] when his father died to assume the rulership (Rush 1991: 276). So the rule was given without opposition to an elderly 55 year-old cousin (FaBrSo) of Maktum, Butti Suhail (1906–1912). He was the son of the Suhail who died in 1859 of smallpox. Butti turned out to be "somewhat uncouth and less civilized than his predecessor" (Lorimer 1986: 774), and was of generally unsatisfactory character (Rush 1991: 251, 288). The British felt he did not show the same "friendly cooperation" as Shaikh Maktum (Rush 1991: 296).

When Butti died six years later in 1912, also of paralytic stroke, his sons, Said, Rashid, Muhammad, and Suhail, ranging in age from 8 to 13 years, were too young to claim the rulership. The British Political Agent reported two competing factions emerging, the sons of the previous ruler, Maktum

(1894–1906) and the sons of an earlier ruler, Rashid (1886–1894) both saying they represented Butti Suhail's young sons. The Political Agent brought them to an agreement whereby Said, Maktum's eldest son, would succeed (Rush 1991: 291). This resolution follows earlier patterns where the more recent the ruler, the more entitled the sons, all else being equal. After Butti's sons were rejected because of age, Maktum's sons were considered before the sons of an earlier ruler. Although ostensibly ruling on behalf of Butti's sons, Said Maktum remained ruler once installed.

Said (1912–1958) was 24 or 30 by various reports when he became ruler. He married Hussa Murr Huraiz of the same Bu Falasa branch as the rulers. Her mother's father was Chief of a Shihuh village in the Musandam. She was reportedly much loved by Said and was his only wife during her lifetime. She had enormous power and influence. The extraordinary Hussa,[7] according to Lienhardt, first made herself available to hear women's problems, then received the Shaikh's retainers to solve their problems while he was away, and eventually she held a public majlis[8] that was often convened at the same time as her husband's. She became well known for her business acumen and for her generosity. She owned and rented out boats that ferried people across the Dubai creek, and also owned a number of shops in the market. During World War II she made a fortune smuggling scarce commodities into Dubai. She died in 1948 and her husband survived another ten years. Said's youngest son Ahmad was born to a woman of RAK whom he married after Hussa's death. Shaikha Hussa became famous as a businesswoman and played a pivotal role in the political affairs of Dubai. Her daughters, Muza and Shaikha, inherited much of the Dera bazaar and some gardens in RAK given to them by their father (Lienhardt 2001: 171–172).

One of the stories told about Hussa was that in 1940, a member of the Mahairi tribe who conspired against Dubai fled to Sharja. Hussa demanded he be handed over to her, but the Shaikh of Sharja refused. Since it was one of many disagreements with Sharja, a war broke out. Hussa was so infuriated by her husband's and sons' opposition to the war that she ripped off her veil put on trousers and took charge of the fort and army. Eventually the British concluded a peace between the parties (O'Shea 1947: 64).

While Said's succession was still being contested, the British considered making it a condition of their approval that the new ruler agree to the establishment of a telegraph station and other facilities the British wanted (Rush 1991: 288). They put the facilities issue to Said with an argument calculated to appeal to his vanity. Dubai, they said, needed "measures of progress" comparable to those of other principalities, and informed him "of the benevolent and public motives of the British authorities" in seeing such measures implemented. Shaikh Said referred the matter to his relatives who responded that they had enough trouble protecting themselves against Bedouin marauders without having to protect foreign staff of the facilities (Rush 1991: 296–297). The British found the answer unsatisfactory and worried that the new shaikh would continue "like his predecessor in the hands of a camorra of his ignorant and reactionary relatives . . ." (Rush 1991: 291). The British Political Resident also complained that the Arab in the Residency was not helpful in promoting British interests (Rush 1991: 291). He laid out two options: coercive action against Dubai or British occupation of Zura Island, north of Ajman (Rush 1991: 292). The Resident saw Zura[9] as the best option if the British Government would invest money in a settlement there. He reasoned that this option would be best "in the interests of our commerce and political predominance on the Coast" (Rush 1991: 293). Nothing came of either option but the report indicates that the British were increasingly abandoning their rhetoric about noninterference in internal affairs.

Fifteen years later in 1927, the senior naval officer in the Gulf expressed a better opinion of Said when he recommended raising his salute from three to five guns as a reward for his help in negotiations with UAQ, Hamriya, and Sharja. The officer felt he had much greater influence than the Shaikh of Abu Dhabi, and also supported the British government in preserving law and order (Rush 1991: 302).

Eventually Said's authority was challenged by the sons of predecessors, Butti and Rashid. The first major challenge came in 1929 when the citizens became angered by several aspects of Said's rule: his submission to the British (Rush 1991: 313), his strict enforcement of the payment of debts, his inability to protect the outskirts of Dubai from marauding Bedouin, and the seizure of a Dubai ship that the British had not been able to restore to its owners.[10] The challengers were Mana Rashid and his brothers, Hashar, Said, and Maktum and the sons of Butti Suhail, Said, Rashid, and Suhail. If they succeeded in removing Said, Mana was to take over as his successor (Rush 1991: 316).

No longer able to command the support of the *majlis* of elders, Said wrote the British to say that if they did not back him, he would resign. The British sent a boat in April 1929 to Dubai and found Said and Mana Rashid both claiming the rulership (Rush 1991: 317). The *majlis* met under Muhammad Ahmad Dalmuk, the father-in-law of Mana Rashid. Not surprisingly the members of the *majlis* declared Mana ruler. Mana immediately informed the British Resident Agent that Said had resigned and that he was now ruler. The British insisted on evidence that the change was what the people wanted. A larger *majlis* of about 400 men was convened and the

British sent a message saying they would accept the majority opinion. The British insistence on evidence bolstered Said's position and he returned to power.

Another major challenge occurred five years later in September 1934 when the same sons of Rashid and Butti made an attempt on Said's life. When that failed they met to depose him. The British insisted once again that their differences with Said were an internal matter. However they sent an airplane to fly overhead and a sloop to lay off Dubai to ensure the security of British lives and property. When the Agent visited Said to report that there were 30 members of the Bu Shaar section of the Manasir ready to attack his enemies (Rush 1991: 324), Said sought a meeting with the Bu Falasa (Rush 1991: 329). He sent his cousins[11] an ultimatum to meet him by November 1 or he would turn them out of Dubai with the help of the Manasir.[12] At first the cousins feared he might kill them or put out their eyes, a means of ensuring they would not become future challengers[13] (Rush 1991: 325). Finally, on November 2, Hashar went to Said and swore allegiance on behalf of Rashid's sons. Later, Said Butti also came and swore allegiance on behalf of his siblings. The British were confident their presence had contributed to the positive resolution of the problem (Rush 1991: 326).

On a visit to a British ship in September the same year (1934), Said was given a five-gun salute, and his brother a one-gun salute (Rush 1991: 333) in recognition of their status. In discussions with the British, Said tried to prepare for the eventual succession of his own son by expressing his fear that Mana Rashid might still try to succeed him (Rush 1991: 334).

Meanwhile, during the 1930s and 1940s, the global decline in pearling was affecting many Dubai families who had become wealthy in the trade. The families of Persian origin engaged in other types of trade—food-stuffs and textiles—and therefore were not as affected by the decline as many local traders. The ruler himself gained much of his income from taxes, so he and the Persians thrived while others felt the economic pinch. Later, oil exploration fees were paid directly to the ruler for his private or public purposes. Therefore, by the end of the 1930s, he was considerably wealthier than the rest of his extended family and this eventually led to their opposition. Local discontent was further fueled by the news that in 1938, the Kuwaitis had forced their ruler to establish an elected council of reformers (Heard-Bey 1996: 252–254).

In June 1938, the feud between Shaikh Said and his cousins erupted again and to strengthen their argument, the cousins occupied the defensive towers of the town. Their list of grievances included demands for a "Budget and Civil List," proper arrangements for health and sanitation, a "Watch and Ward Service," reorganization of the Customs Department, fixed allowances for members of the ruling family, and abolition of monopolies held by the Shaikh, his wife, or his son with respect to landing cargo from ships, ferries, motor services, and so on. The Political Resident felt the demands indicated that ideas of progress were infiltrating the Trucial Coast (Rush 1991: 340). A conciliation committee was formed under the Residency Agent and a truce was arranged. The ruler of Sharja offered to send 200 men to help Said against the opposition in Dubai, and the Ruler of RAK suggested on a visit that the truce be abandoned because it had been arranged by outsiders. Both Shaikhs were told by the Political Agent and the Resident to mind their own business, and the Shaikh of RAK was told to go home. Again the presence of the British agents and aircraft were felt to have hastened reconciliation (Rush 1991: 340–341).

In late September 1938, Said's brother visited the Political Resident in the Gulf and the Agent in Bahrain and reported that Said was again having problems with the family. The Resident wrote saying he would not interfere, but advised Said that popular demands might be met with fewer concessions if addressed early rather than waiting until they escalated. He noted that if the Bu Falasa[14] have a strong group of backers then it shows that the demands are popular, and if they were not popular, Said had nothing to fear and need not come to the British for support (Rush 1991: 368). With this rebuff, fighting between the factions began in early October. Rashid's sons were on the Dera side and Shaikh Said's men on the Dubai side of the Creek. Said tried to borrow arms and ammunition from the Shaikhs of Qatar and Abu Dhabi but they refused. He told the Political Resident he could no longer be responsible for the approximately 70 British subjects in the area, so the British sent a sloop (Rush 1991: 361–363). The Resident reiterated that the British were not required to get involved in this internal dispute, and worried that they might get "the odium of supporting the Shaikh against popular feeling" (Rush 1991: 342). By October 9, a five-day truce was arranged by the Shaikhs of Abu Dhabi, the Bani Qitab, and the Bakha.

Meanwhile the Rashid group demanded a representative council modeled on the one in Kuwait (Rush 1991: 345). The British noted that the ruler had gone back on promises he made the previous June (Rush 1991: 347), and opposition demands were escalating. This time they wanted a permanent council to replace the advisory *majlis* of notables (Rush 1991: 348). The Rashid faction also wanted the Shaikh removed from an active role in decision-making, but the Political Agent said the British could only deal with Shaikh Said himself (Rush 1991: 361).

By this time, Said recognized his weakened position and was ready to accept almost any terms (Rush 1991: 364). By October 20, Said agreed to the terms of the Bu Falasa that largely involved the disposition of state income. They argued that this income should be expended in the name of the state under the control of a council (Heard-Bey 1996: 256). Specifically they wanted a council of 15 leaders, presided over by the ruler to decide all matters by majority vote. The ruler would be required to carry out the council decisions and he would receive one-eighth of the state income for his own use—a small amount considering his private properties. The ruler would have to attend meetings and if he were absent the members of the council would make and implement decisions themselves (Rush 1991: 351, 370–371). The Political Agent again warned the Bu Falasa that the British relationship was with the ruler and that he was responsible for carrying out treaty agreements. They agreed that matters affecting treaties would be conducted in the presence of the ruler (Rush 1991: 351).

The Political Resident responded to the Political Agent by suggesting that a letter be written with the following points: the British government considers the Shaikh as head of state with whom they would conduct official relations; there would be no change in existing treaties or in long practice where the British government would be responsible for Dubai's relations with external powers and regulate matters affecting foreigners in Dubai. The Resident assumed the Bu Falasa accepted these terms and directed the Political Agent against guaranteeing any internal agreements between Shaikh Said and the opposition (Rush 1991: 354–355).

Later the Resident wrote confidentially saying that the Dubai Shaikh has not formally agreed to British jurisdiction over foreigners but that since the British had a responsibility in these matters he had thought it wise to bring up the subject. The Agent in Bahrain wrote the Resident in Kuwait that more local movements toward the Kuwaiti model were likely and noted that there had been evidence of this in Bahrain (Rush 1991: 357–358). Another report in 1938 also noted that agitation in Dubai was livelier than in Kuwait because of local objections over the Shaikh enforcing British demands. It added that British control over the Trucial Coast was looser, implying that the agitation may have been due to this fact (Rush 1991: 360).

The Dubai council promptly took steps to achieve reforms. They organized the customs, appointed a watchman, opened three small schools, and started a sanitation system. The Rashid family dominated the meetings, ignoring the Shaikh who came only infrequently. Instead of a committee to run the municipality, they appointed an individual and ". . . gradually a feeling spread that for one despot there had merely been substituted a board of despotism" (Rush 1991: 375).

The attempts of the Shaikh and the Bu Falasa to widen participation in government changed abruptly in March 1939. Although Said attended some council meetings at first, he soon stopped going. Several council members also lost the support of followers who expected to gain employment from the new arrangement, and public opinion turned again in favor of Said. The Bedouin especially were attracted to Said because of his generosity, while Mana on the other side of the Creek was too occupied setting up new offices to become involved.

Said eventually extended his control to both sides of the Creek. One account relates how in 1940, his son Rashid contracted a marriage on Mana's side of the Creek and visited his bride's family daily. When he lulled the suspicions of Mana, he launched an attack that defeated Mana and killed one of his brothers (Lienhardt 2001: 219). A later British version says that under the cover of the festivities surrounding Rashid's marriage to Latifa Hamdan Zaid I, Said brought in large numbers of armed Bedouin loyal to the family,[15] and soon took control of Dera. There was little fighting but Hashar Rashid and his son (or brother) Butti were killed. Half of the Council surrendered and on March 30, Mana and his followers fled to Sharja (Rush 1991: 373–375). This was one of the few times there was bloodshed in conflicts over the rulership in Dubai.

The British as usual sent a sloop "to steady the town." After the Political Agent suggested its advisability, Shaikh Said appointed an advisory council to form a transition between the Shaikh's autocratic rule that had become so unpopular, and the Executive Council that had not been effective. He also formed a committee of merchants to settle commercial disputes. A number of innovations started by the council were adopted and five of the old members were reinstated. The British believed Said finally realized the importance of staying in touch with popular opinion. The report claimed that the Shaikh of Dubai's problem (like that of the Shaikh of Kuwait) was in not taking British advice earlier to form an advisory council (Rush 1991: 377–379). Heard-Bey feels Said might not have been so opposed to reform if he had trusted his relatives more, but by that time they had tried too many times to unseat him (1996: 255). Said never regained his previous control over Dubai and before long had delegated its administration to his son Rashid (Heard-Bey 1996: 258). The British remarked that Said was now under the control of his wife and his son (Rush 1991: 400).

The British intervened on behalf of the Bu Falasa who fled to Sharja, and Said agreed that if Mana and the other leaders went to a distant shaikhdom their properties would be restored and their followers could return (Rush 1991: 378). But before this happened, Said's brother Juma took over Mana's forts and property. When Rashid wanted to reconcile with the exiles, Juma opposed the move so that he would not have to give up the seized property.

After the 1939 civil war ended, Said married his younger son Khalifa to Mana's daughter Sana, in an effort at reconciliation (Lienhardt 2001: 221).[16] Sana's brother Suhail, was allowed to stay in Dubai until it was learned in the 1950s, that he visited Dubai dressed as a woman to assassinate Rashid. He was expelled to Buraimi but kept in contact with his sister. For some time cars were inspected on Dubai's border to prevent such incidents (Rush 1991: 383; Lienhardt 2001: 174).

Meanwhile, after 1936, negotiations were underway to settle boundary issues between Dubai and Abu Dhabi. In November, Said and Juma visited Shakhbut in Abu Dhabi and agreed to arbitration. After long negotiations they agreed verbally to a line demarking Abu Dhabi and Dubai territory. In 1938, the Political Resident commissioned political officers to finalize the boundaries for all the Trucial States by determining tribal loyalties to the rulers (Abdullah 1978: 294).

By 1955, Rashid was increasingly being obstructed by his uncle (FaBro) Juma and his six sons who were setting their own taxes, reversing Rashid's orders, and issuing title deeds that were illegal. Worse still, from the perspective of the British they vetoed a scheme for court reform that the British convinced Rashid to adopt. They consistently took an anti-British and pro-Saudi stance, and ordered that Shaikhs of other Emirates be fired upon or robbed when they approached Dubai. Rashid was left trying to resolve these issues with neighboring Shaikhs. In an effort to mollify Juma and his sons, Rashid paid them large allowances, but then his brother Khalifa, became so jealous that the wives of their two families would not visit one another. Lienhardt observes that rulers often try to hold the ruling family together by stressing more distant, less reliable ties, but the result is often that they increase the enmity between close and distant kin (2001: 221).

Matters came to a head when Juma demanded his faction take control of the government. The Political Agent advised Rashid to exile Juma and his family (Rush 1991: 389–391). With the approval of his father, Rashid summoned Juma and his three eldest sons, Ubaid, Maktum, and Hamid, and told them in front of elders and merchants that they would have to leave. Juma was told he had no alternative, given that two and a half squadrons of Levies were waiting outside. He asked to go to Saudi Arabia instead of Bahrain and with the consent of the Political Agent, this change was made (Rush 1991: 393). The exiles were provided a comfortable living by the Saudi ruling family (Rush 1991: 395). British ships were sent during these tense events but Rashid persuaded them to stay at a distance so he would get credit for solving the problem himself.

Juma left on May 14 (Rush 1991: 395), but less than a month later, Shaikh Said embarrassed Rashid by changing his mind about exile and complaining to the Political Agency. He decided it was shameful to exile a brother and wanted to take a more neutral position in case the situation changed (Rush 1991: 396). A few months later, under pressure from Juma's supporters, Said wanted to renounce Rashid as his successor "in favor of his other son, Khalifa, who is a nonentity" said British reports (Rush 1991: 402). Said considered traveling to Saudi Arabia to see his brother, but Rashid feared his father might sign compromising papers there (Rush 1991: 403). The Resident suggested that if Rashid could not get his father to abdicate, he should tell him unequivocally that he should step down and turn over the rule to Rashid (Rush 1991: 402, 405). The Foreign Office in London rebuffed their Resident saying it was too early for such action, which would then have to be enforced, and suggested that Said be told privately that the British would not recognize Khalifa as the successor (Rush 1991: 407). The Political Agency made it clear that although Shaikh Said could go to Bahrain for medical treatment, they would not approve travel to Saudi Arabia (Rush 1991: 409).

Said made several attempts to resolve his differences with Juma, including marrying a daughter Shaikha, to Juma's son (FaBrSo) Maktum who had been active in the opposition. When Juma was exiled, Shaikha's husband was the only son allowed to remain in Dubai (Lienhardt 2001: 174). She maintained a close relationship with the women of Rashid's household and later arranged marriages between her son Ahmad Maktum and Rashid's daughter Hussa, and her daughter Hind and Muhammad Rashid in brother-sister exchange marriages.

British reports point out parallels between Juma's rebellion in 1955 and Mana and his brothers' rebellion in 1937. Both wanted the rulership, had a "defiant attitude towards HMG and (were) always attempting to put an obstacle against the Political Officer . . ." (Rush 1991: 399). While this was the British view, time was clearly running out for these relatives to obtain the rulership. The 1930s rebellion involved cousins, while the one in 1950s involved an uncle worried about his nephew becoming too entrenched in a position he felt should be his. Eventually he realized the futility of his efforts against strong British support for Rashid.

Rashid now had to demonstrate that the stability from his uncle's exile made reforms possible (Rush 1991: 397).[17] The three critical concerns for the community were the courts, the Dubai school, and town sanitation. As regards the courts, the British Resident felt there would not be much improvement since Shaikh Rashid found it difficult to delegate authority. As for schools, Rashid himself was not educated, nor did he send his children to school but he was willing to consider the Kuwait ruler's offer to help with education. The issue that energized Rashid most was sanitation and soon he arranged contracts to remove garbage (Rush 1991: 398), an arrangement that enhanced his own business interests.

Said Maktum died of natural causes on September 10, 1958, (Rush 1991: 417) at the age of 76 (Rush 1991: 416) or 78 (Rush 1991: 426), finally leaving his son Rashid, to rule without interference. Eyewitnesses described the wailing of his daughter Muza and other women marching in his funeral procession. A Saudi Qadi repeated "*Haram*" (forbidden) and tried to silence the women but an Adeni Qadi said they should be allowed to wail "as their religion permitted" (Rush 1991: 417–418).

The economy of Dubai changed dramatically during the rule of Said and later his son. The change started in 1902 when duties imposed on goods passing through Persian ports caused traders to divert them to Dubai where they were sold locally or redistributed to places like Buraimi, or reshipped to Persia. The migration of Arab traders from Persia began slowly in the last decade of the nineteenth century and throughout the first decades of the twentieth century. But when more restrictions stifled trade in Persia in the 1920s, large number of traders accepted Said Maktum's invitation and moved permanently to Dubai. Writers reporting on problems in the pearling trade noted that merchants who had previously assisted the shaikhs of Dubai and Sharja were no longer willing to do so since Sharja had become comparatively wealthy and the Shaikh of Dubai was "no longer poorer than his merchants" (Rush 1991: 333). In November 1938, one of the first actions of the Dubai council was to level a duty of 2 percent on imports, but require no charge on exports, while a committee fixed the annual price of customs due to the ruler (Rush 1991: 372).

In 1952, attempts were made to drill for a reliable source of water for Dubai and start a company for electricity. Both projects failed but an ice factory succeeded (Rush 1991: 381–382). In 1953, Persia's falling market precipitated a depression in Dubai with few able to buy the goods piling up on the docks. Dubai merchants reacted by expanding trade with Saudi Arabia through Buraimi (Rush 1991: 383–384).

After Said's death, his natural successor was Rashid who had been de facto ruler since 1938. The British were at first unsure how to accord him recognition. The precedent set with the Rulers of Sharja and Fujairah in 1951 and 1952, required them to accept conditions that ". . . by present standards might be thought humiliating . . ." At the same time, the agreements with Abu Dhabi and UAQ in 1928 and 1929 were more general. The Foreign Office decided the more general precedent should be applied and on October 4, 1958, in a formal ceremony, Rashid became Ruler of Dubai (Rush 1991: 426–427) after agreeing to abide by all the treaties and agreements that had been accepted by his predecessors (Rush 1991: 435).

The following year in June of 1959, Rashid and his two eldest sons visited England as guests of the British government. The British believed him to be one of the most important rulers of the Trucial States, particularly noting his cooperation during the Buraimi, Suez, and Oman crises (Rush 1991: 447). In Britain, Rashid raised questions about his contract with the Petroleum Development Trucial Coast Company that had not discovered oil on his territory. He felt bound by the contract and worried that with the discovery of oil in Abu Dhabi, they might improve their port facilities and impoverish him (Rush 1991: 457). While in England, Rashid appointed his cousin (FaBrSo) Muhammad Hasher as acting ruler. Muhammad belonged to a branch of the family that had remained loyal to Said and his son. By August, Rashid and his sons were back in Dubai (Rush 1991: 460).

Rashid continued developing Dubai. In 1961, an airstrip was completed and a year later air service was established. In 1963, a bridge opened to connect Dubai with Dera, paid for by Rashid's son-in-law, the Shaikh of Qatar (Heard-Bey 1996: 260). Heard-Bey notes that in Dubai the construction of infrastructure was never simply a response to people's immediate needs but rather showed the ruler's ambitious plans for future development that were mostly realized (Heard-Bey 1996: 261) despite pessimistic British predictions. Finally, in 1966, oil was discovered in Dubai and exported in 1969. The revenue, considered the personal income of the ruler, was far less than that of Abu Dhabi and consequently Dubai continued to develop its commercial activities. The Shaikh also owned most of the undeveloped land in Dubai and the land dredged from the Creek.

In 1957, a municipal council was created, allowing Rashid to run Dubai like a large corporation with the help of advisors. Eventually there was a Chamber of Commerce, an international airport, a modern banking system, and the largest dry dock in the world that opened in 1972. In 1985, Dubai possessed its own airline, Emirates Air, competing with Gulf Air that was owned jointly by the UAE, Bahrain, Qatar, and Oman. Medical services were established with an Indian doctor in 1940, and expanded in 1950 when the British government employed a British doctor to run the first hospital. Soon modern medical practices such as immunization were being put into effect. Education, which started in the 1930s and was suspended during the war, was reinstated in the 1950s. Dubai became so prosperous that when the British announced they were leaving the Gulf, Rashid was reluctant to join the new UAE federation. But eventually he decided Dubai was too small to survive on its own and agreed to join, becoming the first Vice President of the UAE. However, in 1976, he refused to sign a permanent constitution, and demonstrations in 1979 supporting Abu Dhabi's desire to see a stronger union seemed to assign blame to Rashid for his reticence. With Kuwaiti mediation, Rashid agreed to become Prime Minister (Zahlan 1989: 96–97) but the constitution remained transitional until much later. Tensions continued between Abu Dhabi and Dubai over matters including choosing a site for the permanent federal capital; a commercial policy Dubai felt should be more liberal to attract business; military issues—both emirates maintained their own defense forces; and allocation of positions in the federal bureaucracy. The tensions that existed over much of their history were due mainly to differences between a tribally oriented oil-rich society (Abu Dhabi) and an ethnically diverse urban commercial center (Dubai). The problems also derive from long-term tensions between the two ruling families (Rush 1991: xix) starting with the defection in 1833 of the Bu Falasa to Dubai and the fact that Dubai territory once belonged to Abu Dhabi (Zahlan 1989: 96). At times they cooperated as in 1972, when they opposed the succession of a usurper in an attempted coup in Sharja.

By the 1980s, Rashid's sons Maktum, Hamdan, and Muhammad had taken over many responsibilities for governing and expanding the economy. Maktum was appointed Crown Prince in 1964 and between 1971–1979 was first Prime Minister of the UAE. His father assumed the position of Prime Minister in 1979 and held it until his death in 1990 when Maktum was reappointed. The same year Maktum became Ruler of Dubai. Hamdan was considered next in line because he was the second eldest son but with the agreement of the family, the younger brother Muhammad, was chosen instead to became Crown Prince. On the death of Maktum in 2005, Muhammad became Ruler. He has a close relationship with Zaid's son, Muhmmad and is extremely active in the development of Dubai.

The ruling family of Dubai does not now conduct itself in the traditional manner of open *majlises* as is the case in some other emirates. Shaikh Muhammad Rashid appears on behalf of the family at openings of buildings and other events. And members of the family appear at international sporting events, tennis, horse racing, golf, etc., even participating in some events themselves. Muhammad's children, both girls and boys, are accomplished equestrians. Dubai promotes tourism and the amenities that encourage foreign businessmen to relocate to the emirate. They build world-class hotels, serve alcohol, construct golf courses, develop their beaches, and organize activities such as "dune bashing" and visits to "Bedouin encampments" that appeal to foreigners. In this they contrast with the more socially conservative emirates of Abu Dhabi and Sharja.

The matter of foreign wives has been an issue in Dubai. Perhaps because of the city's more international and cosmopolitan flavor, more marriages of this kind have taken place there among ruling family members and in some cases have been publicly acknowledged. Over the years, the King of Morocco encouraged UAE ruling family members to take Moroccan wives in an effort to forge closer links between the two countries. Foreign marriages cause tensions within the families, especially among female members who strongly prefer that men marry Emirati wives. In the early 1990s, the Ruler Maktum Rashid took a second wife, a young Moroccan woman who bore him several children. Family members had trouble accepting her for several reasons including that she was not from the ruling family or even from a local family. One irritation was that royal women were finding it increasingly difficult to marry because royal men were marrying so many unrelated or foreign women.

The three sisters of Maktum were examples of what happens when appropriate local men are not available. The eldest, Hussa, married a fairly distant relative, Ahmad Maktum Juma (FaFaBrSoSo). The second, Miriam. married an al Thani from the ruling family of Qatar and the third, Shaikha, at age 35 married Sultan Abdul Aziz Saud from the ruling family of Saudi Arabia. While these were good marriages, the fact that two were foreigners meant the brides had to move to distant families, which most do not like to do.

Another reason for hostility toward the Moroccan wife was sympathy for Maktum's first wife, Aliya Khalifa Said. She was his paternal cousin in the approved pattern. Aliya was highly respected and people felt her husband should not have taken a second wife. After his marriage to the Moroccan, Aliya left on pilgrimage to Saudi Arabia, and after the *Iid* holidays, went to the United States. She planned to spend four months in countries away from her husband and, according to some sources, said she would not return home until the marriage to the Moroccan was dissolved. When asked to mediate, Muhammad Rashid refused, suggesting he too disapproved of the Moroccan. The final embarrassment was the Moroccan's frequent appearances in public and in newspapers in "immodest" dress with her face and hair showing, unlike most well-covered royal women. The end came—the story goes—when she appeared in skin-tight clothing in a British magazine and the King of Morocco urged Maktum to divorce her. Maktum told her not to return from London.

Muhammad Rashid also married several women but, until he divorced her, his main wife was Hind Maktum Juma, (FaFaBrSoDa).. She and her brother Ahmad, were married in the brother-sister exchange that linked the Rashid Said and Maktum Juma children. Although from the line that opposed Muhammad's father's rule, their father was not forced into exile because of his marriage to Rashid's sister. Muhammad Rashid also had an Iranian wife (who bore a daughter) and an Algerian wife. In 2004, he married the daughter of King Hussain of Jordan by his Jordanian wife Aliya. His new wife gives Muhammad an international connection useful for Dubai as well as strengthening his influence in the UAE federation. However, people say that it is the couple's common interest in horses that is more important than political strategy in this case.

Dubai's position as an economic center, a political refuge for exiled members of ruling families from other emirates, and as strategic middle ground between the northern and southern emirates made rulers of other emirates eager to marry into its ruling family. The common Bani Yas origins of the Bu Falah and the Bu Falasa, made finding equivalent status families for their royal women easier. Zaid I of Abu Dubai married a Bu Falasa woman. Her son Saqr married a daughter of Ahmad Dalmuch, a prominent pearl merchant from the same Bu Falasa section as the ruling family. Mana Rashid, the one-time contender to replace Said Maktum, also married a Dalmuch. Both married the women before the pearling industry failed, when such marriages were financially useful.

Hamdan Zaid I of Abu Dhabi married Shamsa Sultan Mujrin,[18] from a nonruling branch of the Bu Falasa. After Hamdan's murder,[19] his Bu Falasa wife fled to Dubai where she bore Hamdan's son. This son[20] married a daughter of Sultan Mujrin from his mother's branch of the Bu Falasa. Her sister was married to Juma Maktum from the opposition branch of the Bu Falasa, while Juma's son Thani, married a daughter of Mujrin Sultan Mujrin, suggesting a multigenerational closeness in these two families, probably resulting from their estrangement from ruling branches. Thani's daughter Fatima, went on to marry the Ruler of Fujaira, thus providing options for her family to remain active in politics.

The fate of two of the estranged Juma's sons show the difference marriages can make. Maktum, married to Shaikh Rashid's sister, was not exiled while his brother Thani married to a distant Bu Falasa was, and had to marry his daughter to a faraway ruler. The marriages of the Juma group are comparable in some respects to the outcast Saqr group of Abu Dhabi. The latter could not marry into the main Nahyan branches because of Saqr's murder of Zaid's father. Juma's descendents mostly married Bu Falasa lineages outside the ruling family, or other Dubai families, and so, although similarly restricted they were not as severely penalized. After his marriage to Rashid's sister, Juma's son Maktum took as second wife, a woman from Awir, in the hinterland of Dubai. A grandson Hashar Hamad Juma married the daughter of a prominent business family (Tayer) while another grandson, Butti Maktum Juma, married a daughter of the UAQ Ruler, Rashid Ahmad Mualla.

Caught between the Qawasim and the Nahyan, the Dubai rulers sought marriages that fortified their position. Intermarriage between Nahyans and the Bu Falasa were suitable, while marriages with the Qawasim were rare.[21] Numerous Nahyan families sought refuge in Dubai with Bu Falasa relatives, growing up and marrying there, and depending on maternal networks for the kind of support usually provided by paternal networks. The Maktums also sought marriages outside the Trucial States. Rashid married two daughters to ruling families of neighboring states: Miriam to the ruler of Qatar and Shaikha to a cousin of King Fahad of Saudi Arabia. In 1972, when his son-in-law was deposed in Qatar, Rashid invited him to Dubai despite close ties to other Al Thani family members.

The ruler also used political appointments to consolidate his political control. The most important positions in Dubai were held by Rashid's sons. Maktum was Ruler of Dubai and Vice President and Prime Minister of the UAE until his death in December 2005. Hamdan was Deputy Ruler for a time and Minister of Finance and Industry in the UAE Council of Ministers. Muhammad was appointed Crown Prince in 1995 and is now ruler. He is also UAE Defense Minister, as well as Prime Minister and Vice President of the UAE. This powerful third son for years was head of the Dubai Central Military Command (CMC). The final son Ahmad, born later than his brothers in 1952, became Commander of the CMC.

Several secondary positions were held by members of the Juma lineage. The jobs, involving the Dubai military, require a trust that is only accorded to one branch of Juma's sons, that of Maktum, the son married to Shaikh Rashid's sister. Butti Maktum is Deputy Commander of the CMC, while two other brothers Marwan and Ahmad, also have high positions in the CMC. Another brother Hashar is head of the Information Department and editor in chief of Al Bayan, a semi-official daily newspaper. His son Muhammad, is head of the courts department. Through their mother's connections, Maktum's sons grew up in proximity to the ruler's sons. Their sister was married to Shaikh Muhammad who is now Ruler. In effect, Muhammad surrounded himself in his military capacity with his brothers-in-law. Another grandson of Juma from a different branch, Muhammad Ubaid Juma, is Under Secretary for UAE Defense and therefore deputy to Muhammad Rashid. This federal position although ostensibly higher, is less important because of the largely passive role Dubai has played in national affairs.

Shaikh Maktum also appointed his paternal uncles Khalifa and Ahmad, to important positions. They remained loyal throughout the time the Juma branch was opposing his father. They are closer in blood terms than the Juma branch and therefore, conforming to theory, should be more loyal. Ahmad was Chairman of Dubai Civil Aviation Department, Chairman of Emirates Airlines, and has an important influence over Dubai's oil and gas industry, its commerce and tourism board, its Aviation College, and at one time the CMC. The other uncle Khalifa, was represented by his sons Muhammad, as head of Dubai's Land Department, Mana as head of the Ruler's Diwan, and Rashid as head of the Traffic Department. These appointments are meant to recognize families even though individuals occupy the positions. Dubai's dilemma is in managing an effective balance between the technocratic needs of a modern state and satisfying those groups that expect recognition for their political importance.

The absence of groups from Dubai's patronage appointments is as instructive as the presence of others. After the Bani Yas, the numerically largest group living in Dubai is the Bu Shamis from the Naim tribe. Because they also live in significant numbers in other emirates, it lessens the obligation to give them "due representation" in Dubai (Van Der Meulen 1997: 182–183). They have a few positions but not commensurate with their numbers. The Manasir and Mazari tribal sections also have substantial populations in Dubai but their traditional ties with Abu Dhabi means they too are not key to Dubai. Large numbers of Iranians are naturalized citizens in contrast to other emirates where citizenship for foreigners is only granted in unusual cases. These mostly Iranian-Arabs have considerable economic influence (Van Der Meulen 1997: 183) but are not represented in government other than individually as technocrats. Political power in Dubai thus concentrates in the hands of the Bu Falasa, but is offset by committees that decide administrative matters. Ruling family members and residents alike have a common interest in keeping an environment congenial to business.

Discussion

Dubai's commercial interests encouraged a particular adaptation of personalized rule. The state has little oil, a small land area, and not much in its hinterland except a tourist center. Even its undefined border with Sharja was not of great concern until rising land prices stimulated interest in its development. Dubai's main advantage was its good harbor and penetrating creek that provided ideal conditions for commercial vessels. Much later, the Jebal Ali Free Zone added up-to-date technology for offloading and warehousing goods. The rulers and residents were single-mindedly focused on building an environment where business would flourish. In this they differed from Abu Dhabi's tribal disdain for commerce, and their focus on property holdings and oil wealth. One Dubai ruler commenting on the few trees in Dubai compared with Abu Dhabi reportedly said, "There is no profit in trees."

Observers note the lack of tribal atmosphere in Dubai. The segmental nature of tribal society where units converge and diverge depending on threat level is not important to rulers of Dubai—partly because of their mainly commercial interests and partly because the Bu Falasa have little tribal depth in their relationships. They spent comparatively little time cultivating the tribes of their interior, and they essentially cut themselves off from the Bani Yas when they left Abu Dhabi. Although Shaikh Said was generous with the Bedouin and called on them to back him against kin challengers, his interest in the tribes was more to maintain stability than to mobilize aggressions against other states. The polyglot people of Dubai were more interested in public services, wider participation in governance and state expenditures, jobs, and limiting the powers of the ruler. These were goals that were appropriate in a free trade atmosphere but not in a tribal society where people expected rulers to organize services and distribute the largesse equitably. The Maktums still control enough of the wealth to position close family members favorably and exert their considerable influence over infrastructure projects that increase their revenues and those of the citizens of Dubai.

Three discernible policy directions emerged from Dubai's history. The first was the rulers' interest in maintaining independence from other regional powers. Dubai rulers realized their early vulnerability when defecting from Abu Dhabi. Dubai's location was also problematic—on land claimed by Abu Dhabi (Heard-Bey 1996: 239) and coveted by Sharja, at a place where Nahyan land abutted Qawasim land. Both these powerful neighbors could have destroyed the Bu Falasa, were it not in their interest to see them survive as a buffer. Fresh in Dubai rulers' memories was the forcible return of another Bani Yas tribe that defected from Abu Dhabi. The Bu Falasa answered these challenges by making short-lived alliances with whichever regional power could best defend them in a crisis, and then often worked behind the scene to weaken their allies. Their strategy worked so successfully that except for a few aborted attempts by Abu Dhabi and the Qawasim, there were no long-term threats to Dubai's independence. Dubai's desire for independence translates until now into minimal participation in the UAE government where Dubai fears restrictive rules might jeopardize trade or require significant financial contributions to public services. With Shaikh Muhammad now in the Prime Minister role, that passivity is likely to change.

The second and perhaps most important policy direction in terms of economic viability was Dubai's skillful exploitation of international opportunities during its history. The first period came when Dubai took advantage of Persian controls on trade and welcomed merchants to their more open environment. Later, Dubai merchants became middlemen in the lucrative gold trade between Europe and India, and much later in the 1970s, Dubai replaced Beirut as entrepot and tourist haven for the citizens of oil-rich countries during Lebanon's civil war.

A third and final preoccupation of Dubai's rulers was the constant challenges from kin. Here their approach was two pronged. On one side they encouraged the support of nonthreatening kin lineages and "bought-off" threatening ones with marriages, financial support, and positions of influence. On the other they maintained good relations with the British who several times made a show of force in support of their preferred Maktum candidates (Heard-Bey 1996: 239). Interestingly all the Maktum rulers died natural deaths and few were deposed before their deaths, even though most dealt at one time or another with strong challenges from kin. The usual pattern was for sons of a past ruler to challenge an uncle or cousin incumbent. Most challengers were caught and imprisoned or deported before they could act. Natural longevity explains the length of Maktum reigns rather than preemptive assassinations as in Abu Dhabi.

Dubai's successions were unusually characterized by uncle-nephew tensions. Possible explanations for the constant challenges include: (1) The small risk of challenging candidates, given that successions occurred with little bloodshed; (2) The more recent establishment of the Maktums as a paramount family compared with the Nahyans or the Qawasim; and finally (3) The rulers' longevity meant sons and nephews were mature enough at the time of the succession to seek their rights. The basic presumption of succession based on age-ordering was, as in Abu Dhabi, interrupted in this generation when the Maktum brothers agreed that the youngest Muhammad, would become Crown Prince. Muhammad has proved the most active in developing Dubai's infrastructure and demonstrating a temperament and personality for the job.

Marriages connections proved no less important in Dubai than in Abu Dhabi, but with a different purpose. Several marriages united the vulnerable Dubai ruling family with ruling families of other emirates and outside states. Others simply served as a barometer of tensions among branches of the ruling family. Some consolidated ties among loyal family members while others co-opted disgruntled lineages. As Lienhardt says, ruling families often try to repair rifts by giving their daughters to principal rivals (2001: 173–174). Marriage to a rival family is recognized as an act of generosity, especially when a daughter is concerned. It implies willingness to share resources or, when women are taken, openness to the risk of maternal influences on children. The point highlighted once again by the Dubai example is that marriages form a unique configuration for each individual.

The father's plan in contracting marriages for himself and his children shows his own ambitions that may differ from the implications to his children. The relationships however continue to have implications for the ensuing generations.

The wives of two Dubai rulers, Said and Rashid, stand out as occupying unusually strong public positions. Their husbands declined in health after they died. These women were consulted, kept up with politics, even contrived to save their husbands during crises, and one was reportedly more successful in business than her husband. There are other examples of women's influences on politics, in one case through maintaining links between an out-of-favor husband and the ruler, and in others solidifying important political relationships through her children's marriages. In some cases, the tensions men could not acknowledge in public were acted upon openly by their wives.

CHAPTER 7

SHARJA AND RAS AL KHAIMA (RAK) DURING EARLY QAWASIM RULE

The Qawasim Chiefs and Rulers of Sharja and RAK up to 1866

- Qasim
- Kaid
- Qadhib Kaid
- Matar Kaid [1]
- Rahma Matar
- Rashid Matar   1747–1777; Rashid resigned in favor of his son Saqr.
- Saqr Rashid   (Sharja and RAK) 1777–1803; son of predecessor
- Sultan Saqr   (Sharja) 1803–1866; son of predecessor

The experience of the Qawasim family of Sharja and RAK was quite different from the Nahyans or Maktums. They started as a major maritime power in the Gulf in the eighteenth century with interests on both Persian and Arabian shores. The Qawasim were gradually contained and diminished in the nineteenth century and by the twentieth century their territories were ruled separately by various branches of the family or lost altogether to non-Qawasim chiefs. These events reduced their once proud empire to political and economic insignificance in comparison with Abu Dhabi. These consequences resulted from a number of factors including their maritime activities that inevitably put them in conflict with powerful foreign powers; the uncompromising stance some Qawasim leaders took regarding the British; competitive family lineages unable to consolidate their

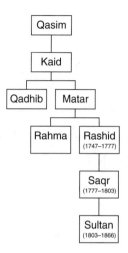

Figure 7.1   The Early Qawasim Chiefs and Rulers of Sharja and RAK up to 1866

interests behind single strong leaders; and the accident of location with no windfall of oil to provide an alternative means of livelihood and power.

In the eighteenth century the Qawasim ruled most of the northern portions of the Trucial States not controlled by Oman. Their capital was the port of RAK, conveniently located near the mouth of the Persian Gulf and only a short distance by sea to the Persian coast. Their other main port of Sharja was located on an inlet near the then edge of Abu Dhabi territory. Virtually all the territory between RAK and Sharja was controlled by the Qawasim. By the nineteenth century, when their locus of relations turned to other Trucial States, Sharja became a more convenient center for their activities. Today Sharja and RAK are ruled independently by separate branches of the Qawasim family. Both are now small emirates with limited political and economic power. In land mass, Sharja and RAK occupy roughly 1,000 (3 percent) and 660 (2 percent) square miles of the UAE. RAK has two major land units, one on the Persian Gulf coast that extends into the Hajar mountains, and the other adjacent to Fujaira and Oman with no outlet to the Gulf of Oman. Sharja has six land units including several on the coast of Oman and one it administers with Fujaira. In population, Sharja is the third largest with 636,000 (16 percent) and RAK the fifth largest with 195,000 (5 percent) compared with Abu Dhabi's 1.6 (40 percent) and Dubai's 1.4 million (35 percent).[2] Without significant oil resources, RAK now depends for its income on cement and gravel industries, shipbuilding, fishing, and subsidies from Abu Dhabi. It has recently established a major porcelain factory. Sharja depends on commerce, tourism, a small amount of oil and gas, and benefits from its location close to Dubai.

The Qawasim were the first—in 1648—of the Trucial families to be mentioned in historic documents. They descend from inhabitants of the Najd, the Bani Gafree or Bani Nasir (those on the left side of the Kaaba in Mecca) (Rush 2 1991: 5). Their ancestors, the Quraish of Yemen, emigrated eastward five or six centuries ago. Most tribes under Qawasim rule sided with the Ghafiri faction in the Omani conflicts (see chapter 2). They follow the Hanbali tradition of Islam and cooperate at times with the Wahhabis of the Arabian interior. Some who immigrated from Persia were Maliki Sunnis (Heard-Bey 1996: 133). This is in contrast to the generally Hinawi and Maliki Sunni persuasion of the Bani Yas. Another difference is the nature of the authority they wield over the tribes. The Nahyan emerged as a paramount family from a dominant tribe of the Bani Yas, the Bu Falah, while the Qawasim either imposed their authority or persuaded unrelated nearby tribes to support them (Heard-Bey 1996: 68). The character of their territories also differed. By 1850, besides the seacoast, the Qawasim controlled much of the mountainous areas of the interior with their water-supplying valleys while the Bani Yas mostly occupied the deserts between the two coasts (Heard-Bey 1996: 69).

In this and the next chapter Qawasim rule is divided into three parts: the first describes the early Qawasim leaders up to and including the indomitable Sultan Saqr (1803–1866) during whose rule the British severely restricted the Qawasim, even though he managed to hold on to many areas north of Dubai. The next chapter details the period of Qawasim decline from 1866 to roughly 1950 as the children and grandchildren of Sultan Saqr struggled among themselves for control of various Qawasim territories. Finally, the third period (1950 until the present), in the same chapter, describes the recent Qawasim rulers in the emirates of Sharja and RAK.

The Early Years

Four powers dominated the southern shore of the Gulf in the eighteenth and early nineteenth century: the Persians, the Qawasim, the British, and the Bu Said of Oman. Qawasim influence extended over numerous seacoast towns including two that are now independent states within the UAE Federation, Ajman and UAQ. At that early period the Qawasim were recognized rulers of five towns and their dependencies: Sharja, RAK, and Kalba on the Arabian Peninsula, and Linga on the Persian Coast. In the early eighteenth century they also took over the town of Basidu on Kishim

Island in the Gulf, thus competing in trade with the British East India Company that was headquartered with the permission of the Persians at nearby Bandar Abbas. From their convenient bases the Qawasim attacked long distance commercial traffic and local fishing and pearling boats. When challenged, they often called on their Wahhabi allies of central Arabia to fight their common enemy, the Bu Said rulers of Oman. Since the British were the main supporters of the Bu Said, the Qawasim felt no qualms about attacking their ships as well.

At their peak in the eighteenth century the Qawasim were the most important maritime power in the Persian Gulf (Rush 1991: xvii). They might have maintained their influence were it not for Britain's concern that trade was being disturbed by "piratical" attacks committed by inhabitants of Coastal Oman, then including the emirates. The main offenders in the British view were the Qawasim. A less self-interested view might have excused Qawasim activities as not unlike those of desert nomads exploiting trade routes across their desert environments. Qawasim "oases" were the settlements dotting the Omani and Persian shores of the Gulf, and the waters in-between were areas where they felt they could legitimately challenge their competitors. But the British did not take these challenges lightly and with their massive naval power set about ensuring that the Qawasim could no longer interfere with shipping. Another view of these events sees the British exaggerating Qawasim piracies to draw their Foreign Office into committing the necessary force to suppress their competition (al Qassimi 1986).[3]

The first Qawasim leader about whom more details are known was Saqr Rashid, Shaikh of Sharja from 1777 until his death in 1803. He married a daughter of the Shaikh of Kishim and Hormuz, Abdalla of the Bani Main, who earlier had expelled the Qawasim from Persia. At the time Hormuz was a strategically located Qawasim stronghold on the Gulf shipping lanes. The marriage conveniently linked Saqr to the local chief and signaled their rapprochement. Saqr had four sons, Saqr, Muhammad, Sultan, and Salah, the last being the son of a slave. Sultan and Salah later played major roles in Qawasim history.

The fact that no power in the Gulf in the latter part of the eighteenth and early nineteenth century could completely control the Gulf dampened trade (Heard-Bey 1996: 229). The groups who depended upon trade soon turned to attacking shipping as a lucrative alternative. The incident that is the precursor for later British actions occurred in May of 1797 when Saqr and his men captured their first British vessel, the Bassein Snow, which they released two days later. This was followed in October by Saqr's nephew, Salah, attacking the British ship Viper at anchor in Bushire.

The Qawasim at the time were at war with the Imam of Muscat who was supported by the British. They claimed they thought the boat was Omani. Salah called on the British Resident at Bushire and promised to keep any British cargo intact if the British would refrain from protecting Omani dhows and cargo. Thereafter, Salah asked for balls and powder and then attacked the cruiser before he was repelled.

When the Resident complained to Saqr about Salah's behavior, Saqr tried to disassociate himself from his nephew, saying Salah had gone to live on the Persian Coast where he "married a woman of the Bani Khalid tribe which was one of a villainous nature and character." From the moment the Qawasim started fighting with Oman, Saqr claimed, Salah acted independently. He stressed that RAK had no fight with the British, and only considered Oman its enemy (Rush 2 1991: 7).

The British felt these problems stemmed mainly from the unstable situation in Oman, where after the death of Imam Said Ahmad, and the usurpation of his rule by Said Sultan, the acts of aggression against British ships had come mainly from Arabs supporting the cause of the deposed Imam (Rush 2 1991: 7). The rivalry between the Omani pretenders meant both sides tried to coopt the support of the Qawasim. Finally in May 1802, the Wahhabis subdued both coasts from Udaid to Dibba including settlements in Qawasim territory.

Shaikh Saqr died in 1803 and was succeeded by his son Sultan (Sharja and RAK from 1803 to 1866). Sultan was born around 1780, thus making him about 23 when he became chief. He was Saqr's third son by the daughter of Shaikh Abdalla of the Bani Ma'in.

By the end of 1804, the Wahhabis had killed the Omani Imam, Said Sultan, and taken over control of Muscat, leaving the Gulf leaders in a state of confusion. About this time, the Qawasim again took up their "piratical depredations" against British vessels, capturing the Shannon and the Trimmer and firing at the Mornington. Badr who succeeded as Imam, started planning to destroy the Qawasim (Rush 2 1991: 8) and soon was able to retake Bandar Abbas, Minao, and Hurmuz from them with the help of the British. Things became so bad for Qawasim on Kishm Island that they finally negotiated a cessation of hostilities. The British were afraid of offending the Persians and the Wahhabis who were Qawasim allies, and so did not pursue them. The Qawasim sent an agent to conclude a peace and convey the message that the Qawasim only wanted to return to trading. Peace was concluded on February 6, 1806 without the knowledge of the Wahhabi Shaikh. The Qawasim stuck to their agreement as far as the British were concerned, but supported attacks by their former rival, Imam Said Badr, on Said Ghes of Sohar who refused to sign the agreement until he avenged the death of the former Imam by the Utaibas and Wahhabis.

In the early period of Sultan's rule, the far ranging nature of Qawasim interests becomes apparent. Through alliances with Omani factions, the Wahhabis, and the Persians at different times, the Qawasim maintained a strong presence in the area, even when the opposition seemed overwhelmingly against them. However, the British eventually proved the most formidable of their opponents. The nonaggression pact signed by Sultan in 1806 was the beginning of a series of agreements meant to limit Qawasim influence (Rush 1991: xvii).

By 1808, Shaikh Sultan's authority was reduced to the area around RAK although he managed to recover Khaur Fakkan from the Omani Sayyids. The Wahhabis began encouraging independent groups of Qawasim to plunder ships off the coast of India without the permission of Sultan (Rush 2 1991: 9). One of these minor chiefs, although against piracy himself sent his subjects off to work on other ships when they could no longer make a living by trade. They proved extremely successful at capturing boats and in October of 1809 in the first breach of the treaty, captured and then lost a British cruiser. In the following year attacks continued against Qawasim, Utaiba, and Persian boats.

In further attempts to claim control over Qawasim territories, the Wahhabi Chief appointed Hussain Ali, then Qassimi Shaikh of Ramse, to govern RAK and assigned Wahhabi officers to oversee affairs throughout Qawasim territory. This was a low point for Sultan who was invited to go to Dera to discuss matters with the Wahhabis. But upon his arrival they imprisoned him. Eventually he escaped by way of Yemen and Mokha to Muscat where he sought the protection of his former enemy, the Imam. The Imam immediately put him in charge of Sharja to counter the growing influence of the Wahhabis.

The British determined to stop the attacks at sea and so set out in September 1809 to suppress the Wahhabis and their sometime Qawasim agents. They sent an armada to bombard RAK in November and after a stiff fight in which the town and over 50 boats including the British Minerva were burnt, drove the inhabitants inland (Rush 2 1991: 10). After the Shaikh of RAK had the temerity to demand tribute to let British ships pass safely, the armada continued to Linga where they destroyed 20 dhows, and finding no ships in Bandar Mullim and Humram, proceeded to Luft on the north side of Kishm where they took the town and burned the boats but could not take the fort. The Chief, Mulla Hussain, surrendered and delivered the Imam's property worth 2 lakh rupees to the head of the Naim to hold in trust for him. The British armada continued to Muscat, where the commanders expressed their willingness to recover other ports belonging to the Imam. The Imam accompanied them to the town of Shinas north of Muscat, but upon arrival there on December 10, 1810 the fort was so well defended that by the time they forced its surrender, the building was demolished and no longer of use. The Imam decided against attacking the next village, Khaur Fakkan, where the same thing might happen and the British concurred since they had no interest in ports that had no pirate ships (Rush 2 1991:11).

The British commandeer could not contract a treaty with RAK because Shaikh Sultan had been seized by the Wahhabis and his government overthrown, and he was unwilling to deal with the Wahhabi-appointed governor. The British were satisfied that they had destroyed all the major boats of the petty chieftains from Ramse to Abu Kail on the Arabian shore and Mugu on the Persian side and decided their mission was complete. They felt it was unnecessary to destroy small boats that belonged to the poorer residents for fear of creating "an odium against the British name" and since in any case many had been forced to take part in the piratical activities. The British also did not attack Khaur Hassan whose Utaibi inhabitants had not interfered with British trade. The British felt that as a consequence of their expedition, "the Qawasim had been rendered quite incapable of committing any further depredations by sea" (Rush 2 1991: 12). The British however still did not trust the Qawasim or the Wahhabis, under whose jurisdiction they now came, and proposed a prohibition against the importation of timber to prevent them from rebuilding their boats. But the Qawasim proved they were not entirely subdued and in 1812 destroyed boats in Bussura and Cungun, including some under British flag (Rush 2 1991: 12).

It was not long before Shaikh Sultan had ingratiated himself with the Imam[4] who along with the British was concerned about Wahhabi advances into Qawasim territory. In 1813, the Imam decided to attack RAK and reinstate Sultan as chief. Sultan promised he would refrain from piracies and consider himself a "vassal" of the Imam if he regained his possessions. The British agreed feeling by this time he must surely know they would not leave the slightest infraction unpunished. The Imam's first expedition failed but a second one in 1814 succeeded, and a peace treaty was concluded. Sultan agreed to the Imam possessing RAK, and to himself taking over Sharja (Rush 2 1991: 13). But he continued to live in Linga (Rush 2 1991: 15) and left the administration of RAK in the hands of the Wahhabi-appointed Qawasim deputy there.

This Qassimi Shaikh, Hussain Rahma, remained de facto chief of RAK for some time after these events. British reports said there were continuous complaints made to him and the Wahhabis about attacks against British ships. The Qawasim assured them they would do their best to restrain their members from committing such acts. But they hoped the British would not prevent them from attacking their enemies, since according to the law of Arab nations, blood had to be repaid by blood and if they did not comply "they would lose their rank amongst the Arab States, and that their enemies would come to their very homes to attack them . . ." The Qawasim claimed they had been forced by the Wahhabis to bring the Muslims of the Gulf under the political control and religion of the Wahhabis, but said they would halt their continual warfare if the British guaranteed that none of the Arab States would bother them or their vessels and would protect them from the vengeance of the Wahhabi Chief. Otherwise they would have to confront the other Gulf States (Rush 2 1991: 14).

These statements show the importance chiefs felt in maintaining an appearance of strength or alternatively, the need for protection against those who interpreted their restraint as weakness. Confrontations were a demonstration of strength as much as responses to aggressions. This explains the Qawasim's occasional "irrational" attacks in the face of treaty agreements. The Qawasim attacks, outrageous demands, and temporary alliances often constituted a performance for local audiences that applauded courage and fearlessness. The Imam and others viewed the Qawasim as fearless adversaries better mobilized in support of their own causes than against them. The British however saw their attacks and broken agreements as duplicitous, and had little intention of playing protector for "trouble-makers." The Qawasim meanwhile used the British to highlight their audaciousness and intervene when they needed to regroup. At times the British seem bewildered by such "inexplicable" acts.

In August 1814, when the Qawasim seized boats with a British pass, the British representative sent a boat to RAK with complaints to Hussain Rahma and also to Sultan in Linga. The boat's cargo of dates was confiscated in RAK and the boat itself in Linga, proving to the British that they could not trust "such lawless banditti." The act was at variance, they said, with the conduct that characterizes Arabs, where they offer hospitality even toward an enemy seeking their protection. The Qawasim followed up this insulting comment by capturing an Omani boat and six more off Karachi and Sind (Rush 2 1991: 15).

The Qawasim so increased their prestige through these actions that others decided to mount their own attacks. The Qawasim meanwhile defeated the Imam's fleet, and attacked both British and American cruisers, and people so feared them that the British representative could no longer find a ship willing to take his complaints to RAK. When some messengers got through, they were told that the Qawasim only respected Christians and not unbelievers from India whom in any case they did not recognize as British (Rush 2 1991: 16). Some believed the Qawasim's tendencies toward Wahhabi fundamentalist beliefs meant they could deal more aggressively with those they considered infidels (Heard-Bey 1996: 281).

Attacks by the Qawasim continued throughout 1817 and 1818. In 1819, expecting an attack by Turkish troops, the Qassimi Chief sent men from RAK to build a fort at Bassadore (Basidu) on Kishim Island. They intended to retreat to the fort if unable to drive out the Turks. It was a place where only boats of shallow draft could enter and had been used for defense by the Portuguese who built water reservoirs, a fortified town, and a pier. The British noted this activity with anxiety believing the Qawasim would use the fortified port to disrupt trade. When the RAK Chief heard that a British expedition was being mounted out of Bombay, he sent a message to the British saying he wanted to be on good terms but the British rejected his overtures (Rush 2 1991: 17).

By this time the British were fed up with Qawasim violations of the maritime agreements and decided to destroy their capacity to attack by sea. In October 1819, they assembled an expedition of 3,000 men including half Europeans and half local people for the purpose of completely crushing the Qawasim (Rush 2 1991: 18) in RAK. The Imam of Muscat agreed to send 4,000 men by land and three ships by sea. The British also sent letters asking for support from the Prince of Shiraz against the Persian towns, Linga, Mugu, Tawuni, and Charrak, allied with the Qawasim. The naval forces assembled at Kishim and proceeded to RAK where they blocked the harbor and destroyed 80 Qawasim ships. On land European and Muscati troops attacked Sultan's army and after strong resistance for six days the town fell on December 9 and the local chiefs surrendered. Other chiefs on the coast, seeing this massive destruction, sent offers of submission to the British. A month later, finally recognizing the overwhelming power against him, Sultan signed a General Treaty of Peace (Rush 1991: xviii).

The Treaty was concluded in RAK on January 8, 1820 with the aim of completely suppressing piracy. Major General Keir represented the British and all the Chiefs of the Arab Maritime States in the Persian Gulf signed. A separate treaty was signed with Hussain Rahma of RAK, agreeing to the surrender of all his remaining boats (except those for fishing), the release of Indian prisoners, and British occupation of RAK and Maharra. A similar treaty was concluded with Shaikh Sultan for the surrender of the towers, guns, and vessels of Sharja, Ajman, UAQ and their dependencies in return for which the British would not enter their towns (Rush 2 1991: 19). The British General returned to Bombay leaving a garrison in RAK, but a week later he ordered the garrison to Kishim, leaving the town to Sultan of Sharja. Sultan refused to accept responsibility if RAK's defenses were destroyed as ordered by the British. The order was carried out and the town abandoned on January 18, 1820.

From this low point Shaikh Sultan began rebuilding his power base. In 1823 he began construction of a defensive fort in Sharja but was told he would have to await permission from the British. A similar case was pending in RAK where inhabitants who returned to the town wanted to build a protective sea wall across their harbor. The British government decided there was nothing in the treaty to prevent these constructions. About this time, Sultan deposed the Shaikh of Ramse and appointed Muhammad Abdul Rahman, son of a former Qassami shaikh to govern the town. All the formerly Qawasim ports except Ajman pledged their loyalty to Sultan (Rush 2 1991: 20).

A British Captain visiting the Qawasim in 1823 described the commercial activities he saw. The people procured building materials and war stores from Muscat, Bahrain, and Persian ports in the lower Gulf. They sold pearls on the spot, since the foodstuffs they raised were not sufficient for export. They fished, dove for pearls, and imported dates, grains, and other necessities with income from the pearls. They bought dates from Bahrain and Bussura, and grain and cloth from Muscat and Persia. They were still poor and could only carry goods for others in commercial trade, "although it is said they at one time pursued a very extensive trade" (Rush 2 1991: 21).

Meanwhile the Wahhabis were winning against the Turks, and fearing for their safety, Shaikh Sultan of Sharja and Shaikh Rashid Humaid of Ajman who was under Sharja's control, negotiated with the Wahhabis to preserve their positions. Other problems arose in 1824 with external groups. In one case two Sharja boats seized a boat of the Mehra Tribe, committing the first serious breach of the Maritime Treaty. Still cautious, Shaikh Sultan reported the incident to the British, and with no place to go, the perpetrators abandoned their booty and the British dropped the case (Rush 2 1991: 21–22).

A more important issue was a dispute between the Imam and Sultan over the latter's occupation of the towers of Buraimi that had been declared neutral. In this case Tahnun of Abu Dhabi supported the Imam. Meanwhile in a related incident, members of the Sudan under Salmin Nassir attacked some Sharja boats. The Sudan had previously deserted the Qawasim and taken refuge in Dubai where they were constructing a fort at Dera to the consternation of Sultan.[5] The British Resident arranged a reconciliation where the parties agreed that the two incidents should be resolved at the same time so that the Buraimi towers would be destroyed in return for the destruction of the Dera fort.

Shaikh Sultan however did not carry out his side of the bargain, saying the Imam had convinced his agent not to destroy the Buraimi tower. Sultan said he would send an agent with one appointed by the Resident to prove his good intentions. The Resident sent his agent with the Imam's troops in May 1825, but before the mission was complete, Sultan attacked the fort at Dera. Tahnun of Abu Dhabi sent troops to support the Sudan who had been repulsed by Sultan and 150 of Tahnun's men were killed, a large number for the times. It was clear that the problems in Buraimi had been instigated by Sultan (Rush 2 1991: 23) wanting to create a diversion so the Sudan would leave the area near Qawasim territory By this time, exhausted by warfare and loss of income from pearling, Sultan and Tahnun in October 1825 accepted the Imam's mediation. The problem with the Sudan continued however until the Imam demolished Dera tower in March 1827 (Rush 2 1991: 25).

Meanwhile Sultan was involved in other intrigues. The 1820 General Treaty of Peace showed a separate signature for Dubai by a chief named Hazza Zaal, before the Bu Falasa migrated to Dubai. He died in 1825, and was succeeded by his son Muhammad whose sister Sultan married in hopes of eventually gaining possession of Dubai. The same year Sharja attacked a Bahraini boat, and the British demanded satisfaction for the loss of life and property. Sultan was told if he refused their terms, the British would remove the British Agent from Sharja and confiscate all the boats of the area. Sultan immediately agreed. But later he backed down and when a notorious resident of Bidda belonging to Bahrain, captured a UAQ boat, Sultan felt the account was even (Rush 2 1991: 22–24).

The Imam of Muscat, either attempting to compensate Tahnun of Abu Dhabi for the Dera towers or simply to cause problems between Tahnun and Sultan, gave arms to Tahnun and encouraged the people of Dubai to pledge their loyalty to him. The Imam may also have heard of Sultan's marriage and suspected he had designs on Dubai. Encouraged by his support Tahnun captured the Dubai Chief and took over the town. By the pearling season the two rulers called a truce but this only lasted until November 1827 when Sultan threatened war on Tahnun, but failed to carry out his threat (Rush 2 1991: 26).

Another incident increased the tensions between the two Chiefs. A boat carrying supplies to Abu Dhabi was boarded by some Qawasim, and although the agent had sold the goods to Sultan, the captain had not been informed and Sultan disavowed any connection with the case (Rush 2 1991: 28). The Imam, wanting to visit his properties on the African Coast, decided to ensure quiet in his Arabian territories by providing allowances to each of the Qawasim Shaikhs. Sultan was allotted 2,000 German Crowns a year. But despite this payment, he sent 400 men to help the sister of the Governor of Suwaik wage war against the Imam for his imprisonment of her brother, but the elders of his tribe convinced him it would be disgraceful to help her while receiving payment from the Imam, and the British supported this view (Rush 2 1991: 29).

A general peace settled over the Gulf during 1828, with the exception of a single piratical act committed by a RAK inhabitant on an Omani boat, the act swiftly and summarily dealt with by Sultan (Rush 2 1991: 27) who seems not to have wanted any more confrontations with the British or the Omanis. The escalating tensions between Sharja and Abu Dhabi seemed largely a consequence of the Qawasim's position with regard to the other powers of the region. Sultan's vulnerability after the destruction of his fleet in 1819 invited others to expand their influence at his expense. The Qawasim reacted violently to being squeezed by the British on one side and Abu Dhabi on the other. It was only fear of Wahhabi encroachment that made the Imam and the British willing to preserve a suitably weakened Qawasim in the area. Sultan however was fighting to restore Qawasim glory and was not content to take a passive role. He still had a few surprises left for his enemies.

By 1830, Turki Saud, the Wahhabi Chief, successfully suppressed the northern Bani Khalid tribes and began moving south. Sultan saw the Wahhabi advances as opening the possibility for renewed piratical attacks that the Wahhabis previously supported. The Shaikhs of Ajman and UAQ saw the advance differently, as an opportunity to remove themselves from dependence on Sultan. Sultan saw that Wahhabi successes might diminish his own influence, and cause revenues that normally flowed to him to revert to the Wahhabis. Publicly he supported their advances but privately sent messages to the British saying he would cooperate with moves to stop them. The British responded as usual by replying that they were only interested in suppressing piracy and not in interfering in the internal affairs of the regional states (Rush 2 1991: 29). Sultan's fears were somewhat allayed when he learned that the Wahhabi Chief had refused the Ajmani Chief's request for troops to take over Qawasim territories. The Ajmani was told that the Wahhabis considered Shaikh Sultan and the Imam of Muscat the chiefs of the Arabian Tribes in larger Oman (Rush 2 1991: 30). The Wahhabi threat soon passed and Sultan managed to retain what influence he possessed along the coast.

Over the next few years Sultan consolidated his authority within Qawasim territories, preferring to address internal concerns rather than upset the British with maritime incursions. By this time his sons and nephews had reached adulthood and were helping administer his widely scattered holdings. In the early years, he appointed his brothers as governors and in later years replaced them with his sons or grandsons. In RAK, for example, Sultan appointed his brother Muhammad Saqr in 1823 to replace the Wahhabi-appointed governor. He probably remained there until he died in 1845. Sometime before 1860, Sultan appointed his son Ibrahim to administer RAK. Ibrahim was still governor when Sultan died in 1866. Ibrahim's son, Mashari, became subgovernor of Dibba, a dependency of RAK, in 1855 until he was murdered by Shihuh tribesmen from the interior.

In Sharja, Sultan appointed his half-brother, Salah to administer the town. Even though he was considered one of the most intelligent and enlightened members of the family he was deposed in 1838 in favor of Sultan's son, Saqr. In 1840, with the encouragement of Shaikh Maktum of Dubai, the new Chief Saqr, tried unsuccessfully to cast off his father's authority and rule Sharja as an independent principality. He was deposed for a time but his father soon relented and returned him to the post, where he remained until he was killed in an 1846 battle with UAQ. He was succeeded by a half-brother, Abdulla Sultan who tried unsuccessfully to retake Ajman. He continued in office in Sharja until he was killed in fighting at Hamriya in 1855 (Rush 2 1991: 68–69). Sultan then appointed a grandson, Muhammad Saqr, but he was challenged by his uncle, Khalid Sultan, who took over part of the town.

By then Sultan was too infirm to exert much control over the disputes developing among his family members. In 1859 Khalid and Muhammad were still presiding over their separate sections of Sharja town. But in 1860 or 1861, Khalid managed to decoy Muhammad a distance out of town on horseback, and shot him, throwing his body into a well. Khalid's subsequent efforts to see the British Resident and state his claims as Governor of Sharja were rebuffed because he had "so recently and so fearfully polluted" himself (Rush 2 1991: 70). British reports said Khalid defended his actions by claiming he feared his nephew was plotting his death, and was only taking preemptive action against him. In the end, Khalid governed Sharja from 1861 to 1868 (Rush 2 1991: 93–94) while Sultan continued to maintain nominal control over his governors until his death in 1866.

One of Sultan's last major crises occurred in 1854, when the residents of Hamriya rebelled against his authority. The reason was a blood feud between the Huwaiah of Sharja town and a body of Shuwaihiyin[6] (about 500 fighting men) that Sultan had moved into Hamriya on the advice of the Wahhabi representative in Trucial Oman. No sooner were they settled than at the direction of their chief, they began agitating for independence from Sharja. At the time Sultan was having problems with his relative,

Khalifa Said, in Linga, and was away trying to resolve problems there, leaving the Wahhabi's representative, Ahmad Sudairi, to handle Hamriya. Ahmad tried to establish a Wahhabi garrison but failed, and when Sultan returned, encouraged him to blockade Hamriya, an action expressly forbidden by the British (Rush 2 1991: 69). Although the Hamriya rebels numbered only 800 men, they had the support of the Shaikhs of Dubai and UAQ. Most of the killed consequently were on the side of the beseigers, including Sultan's own son, Abdulla. By the time the Political Resident appeared, both sides were anxious for a settlement. The terms were that Hamriya would pay 500 dollars in submission to Sultan and after the pearling season the Shuwaihiyin would leave and settle where they pleased.

Sultan Saqr continued to influence the course of Qawasim affairs during the remainder of his life, even though his relatives increasingly assumed the burden of administration. When he died the British noted that Sultan, born around 1780 and ruling over the course of two generations, had witnessed, "the whole process of change from barbarism to civilization in the Persian Gulf" (Rush 2 1991: 67). Much of the time he was considered chief of both Sharja and RAK but it remains unclear whether he lived mainly in one town or the other. Certainly he spent considerable time at Linga. By 1850, he extended his rule to all the Shamaliya tract on the Gulf of Oman by taking Kalba, Dibba, and Fujaira as well as Khaur Fakkan from the Sultan of Muscat. According to the British, he was considered so duplicitous by Arab and outsider alike, that everyone distrusted him and in his later life was unable to mobilize actions of any consequence (Rush 2 1991: 68).

Like the most successful Nahyan leaders in the previous chapters, Sultan married numerous times, using his marriage connections to his advantage. His wives and concubines produced numerous sons who helped him consolidate Qawasim power as they grew older. The wives included a Qassimi, an Abyssinian, a Bani Yas, a Marzuqi. an al Ali from Tavunch, and one or more slaves. He was said to have married his last wife, a 15-year-old Bedouin girl, at the ripe age of 115 (other more reliable reports say he died at the age of 86). Shortly after marrying her he contracted "a paralysis of the loins" for which he was in search of a cure when he died (Rush 2 1991: 89). From his multiple marriages, he had at least 11 and probably more sons.[7] These sons are the subjects of the next chapter.

Discussion

A number of comparisons can be made between the reigns of Sultan Saqr Qassimi (1803–1866) and Zaid I Nahyan of Abu Dhabi (1855–1909), even though their tenures only overlapped for a decade—Sultan Saqr dominated the first half and Zaid I the second half of the nineteenth century. The first noteworthy similarity is that each ruled more than a half-century, unusually long tenures compared with the generally shorter-lived reigns of their predecessors and many of their successors. It was not until the mid-twentieth century in a period when it became more difficult to overthrow rulers that we find a Qassimi, Saqr Muhammad (1948 on), and a Nahyan, Zaid Sultan (1966 to 2004) who challenged their longevity records. Both the early rulers skillfully used multiple marriages to encourage the loyalty of tribal leaders and resolve their differences with opponents. Both produced numerous sons and grandsons who with other family members helped consolidate control over areas of importance. After their deaths these family members actively contested the rule and through their conflicts essentially reduced the power their predecessors had so laboriously built.

The two leaders employed other similar political strategies. Both were strong active leaders constantly looking for opportunities to extend their influence and strengthen their control over existing territories. They maintained law and order, punished or sought retribution for offenses, aggressively dealt with enemies, and fluidly created short-lived coalitions to achieve their aims. They were not adverse to breaking agreements when it was in their interest to do so, or seeking truces when they needed breathing room from their opponents.

There were also noteworthy differences. The first was in the nature of their authority, which in the case of the Qawasim came largely from their imposition of force on the disparate, unrelated local tribes of their regions. The Nahyan family by contrast was widely accepted in their leadership role by the Bani Yas tribes from whom they emerged. A second difference was the character of their relationship with the British. The Qawasim frequently opposed the British frontally with their attacks on shipping or neighboring states, while Zaid I worked cautiously around them, operating mainly in the interior and mostly staying away from British maritime interests to the extent he could. Consequently Qawasim power was at every point suppressed and the Qawasim leaders widely disliked by the British, while the Nahyan through their seemingly cooperative spirit were generally more acceptable. Eventually the Qawasim were sidelined when with the advent of oil in Abu Dhabi territories in the twentieth century (with the minor exception of Sharja) they proved of little further interest to the British. A third difference was the nature of the prize that was at the core of the competition among members of both families. Many of the Qawasim territories were scattered across the Trucial States, far from their two main settlements and more difficult to defend. In many cases the residents of their dependencies had no direct blood or other connection to the Qawasim, and came under their control as a consequence of conquest rather than tribal affinity. The territories of the Nahyan by contrast were contiguous—not separated by holdings of other states, even though their centers were widely separated by expanses of desert. Most Abu Dhabi territories were inhabited by loyal tribes or ones with long-term traditional ties.

In terms of their personalities there were differences as well. Zaid I was widely respected and admired, while Sultan was thought petulant and not always trustworthy. One can not help but observe, however, that whatever his personal attributes, Sultan managed an almost miraculous recovery from the destruction of his fleet by the British and his vulnerability in the early days of his tenure. Whether he could have avoided the lows of Qawasim history if he had been more conciliatory is difficult to say.

In other matters, including succession, the rulers differed too. Whereas Sultan was a first son in a succession that passed to first sons for generations, Zaid I came to power in a succession that usually moved through brothers until it passed to one of their sons in the next generation. The Nahyan succession relied more on demonstrable leadership capacities, including whether the candidate had established a supportive group to back him. Lienhardt (2001) points out that primogeniture was not the invariable pattern in the Trucial States, and that other factors entered succession practices. If these two cases are taken as example, they suggest that all else being equal, earlier ruling families established fairly consistent expectations about the succession, the Qawasim based on a succession of rulers' sons, and the Nahyan on a pattern of brothers or their descendents. The first practice maintained control within the rulers' lineage, while the second required a more consensual, cooperative approach among extended family members, and, with the Nahyans, consultation with community elders. In these cases, the patterns may have been more coincidence than conscious intention. Often the choices were obvious when the ruler died, if his sons were too young or there were no sons, the ruler's brothers were established leaders of the community, or if a usurper established his right by removing the ruler.

Both patterns failed to produce stability after the death of these inspired leaders, largely for two reasons. First, the extraordinary power they amassed during their tenures made the ruler position an attractive prize worth a protracted struggle among lineage members. Second, both rulers left numerous sons with conflicting tribal connections through their maternal relatives. What was good in the father's generation proved disastrous in the sons. Qawasim family members soon started fragmenting their territories while the Nahyan, although competing for the position of ruler and killing one another to achieve it, never seriously sought to dismember their holdings.

CHAPTER 8

SHARJA AND RAS AL KHAIMA (RAK) SEPARATE UNDER QAWASIM RULE

Qawasim Rulers of Sharja (see below for RAK) from 1866 to the Present

- Khalid Sultan 1866–1868; son of his predecessor; died in combat with the Shaikh of Abu Dhabi
- Salim Sultan 1868–1883; brother of predecessor; deposed; (RAK ruler) 1909–1919; died naturally
- Saqr Khalid 1883–1914; nephew (BrSo) of predecessor; died of plague
- Khalid Ahmad 1914–1924; cousin of predecessor; deposed; died naturally
- Sultan Saqr 1924–1951; cousin's son of predecessor (FaBrSoSo); died of natural causes
- Saqr Sultan 1951–1965; son of predecessor; deposed by family decision
- Khalid Muhammad 1965–1972; cousin (FaBrSo) of his predecessor; killed by predecessor
- Sultan Muhammad 1972–present; brother of predecessor

Sultan Saqr was one of the most important figures in regional politics during the first half of the nineteenth century, despite efforts by the British to suppress him. After he died in 1866, the Qawasim empire began to crumble as his many ambitious sons took advantage of the power vacuum left by his death. The disintegration occurred on several fronts.

140

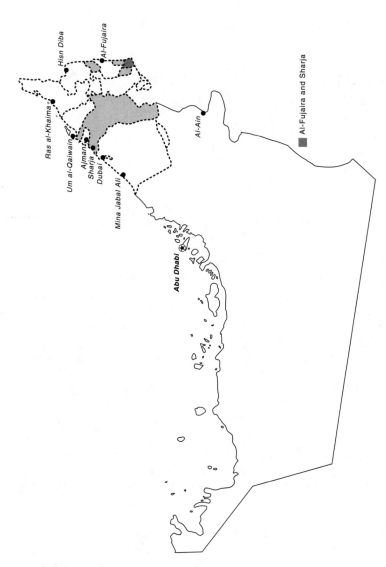

Hisn Diba

Al-Fujaira

Ras al-Khaima

Um al-Qaiwain

Ajman

Sharja

Dubai

Mina Jabal Ali

Al-Ain

Abu Dhabi

Al-Fujaira and Sharja

Source: http://lcweb2.loc.gov/frd/cs/united_arab_emirates/ae05_01a.pdf

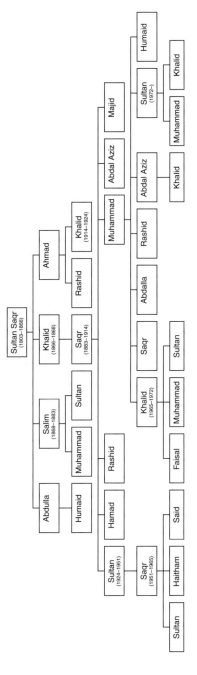

Figure 8.1 Qawasim Rulers of Sharja from 1866 to the present

On the northern Gulf coast, the Persians took advantage of divisions within the Qawasim family to extend their influence in the coastal area, so that by the end of the nineteenth century Qawasim rule in Persia was essentially over. Qadhib Rashid, the paternal uncle of Sultan, started the century as Shaikh of Linga (1805–1829).[1] He was succeeded by his son Muhammad for a few months until another son, Said, took over and ruled between 1829 and 1854. In 1854, Said's son, Khalifa, became shaikh and ruled for two decades. Up to this point the succession progressed in orderly fashion from father to son. But in October 1874, when Sultan's relative, Ali Khalifa (1874–1878), succeeded to the chieftainship, the Persians saw in his inexperience and the divisions within the Qawasim, a chance to seize Linga customs and impose high taxes on the inhabitants (Rush 1991: xviii).

In 1878, Ali was assassinated by a relative, Yusuf Muhammad (1878–1885), whom the family had appointed as his guardian. Seven years later, Yusuf was assassinated and replaced by another relative, Qadhib (1885–1887).[2] By 1887 with Qawasim influence in decline, Qadhib was taken prisoner by the Persians and deported to Tehran where he eventually died. The decline of the Qawasim on the Persian Coast as a result of family feuds was accelerated by the failure of Qawasim shaikhs in Arabia—who were also immersed in family feuds—to respond effectively.

By 1888 the Persians had brought Linga under their control (Rush 1991: xviii), and during the next decade many Arab families including numerous merchants deserted the Persian Coast for the Trucial States with their more liberal customs policies. In a final effort to regain control a decade later in 1898, Muhammad Khalifa Qassimi seized Linga and managed to rule for a year until he too was expelled by the Persians. Thus ended Qawasim rule on the Persian Coast that for most of the nineteenth century had been held by the Qassimi lineage of Qadhib Rashid.

Territories on the Persian side of the Gulf were one thing, but loss of territories on the southern Arabian coast was a more serious blow. The Qawasim had been the recognized rulers of Sharja, RAK, Ajman, UAQ, Dibba, Kalba, and other parts of the Shamaliya. Their main center had been RAK but as their interests shifted to other Trucial States, Sharja became a more convenient base. Up until 1820, Ajman and UAQ were dependencies of Sultan Saqr and thereafter held ambiguous status for a time. Within a short time after Sultan's death, Ajman became an independent state, and Fujaira and Kalba began a prolonged fight for independence. RAK became irrevocably independent in 1921.

Although the causes are complex, a main reason for the disintegration of the Qawasim state (beyond the part Britain played) was the failure of the ruling family to unite behind single successors. Sultan Saqr is a classic example of how strategies that bring leaders to power and help them achieve success, may work against stability in the next generation. Sultan's capacity to manipulate alliances and marriages made it possible for him to forge a powerful state out of diverse groups and interests. As long as he lived and controlled his sons, the state remained unified. But in the leadership vacuum that followed, the very kin that supported him scrambled to ensure their own positions.

The story of the Qawasim after Sultan Saqr's death centers on his sons' efforts to control Sharja and other lesser Qawasim territories. By the time of his death, four of his eleven sons had died, Saqr and Abdalla in battle, and Rashid and Saif probably in childhood. By the end of his life Sultan had long since given over administrative control of RAK and Sharja to his sons Ibrahim and Khalid (Rush 2 1991: 534). They continued to administer these units after his death (Rush 2 1991: 89).

At first Khalid (1866–1868) succeeded his father as overall ruler of Sharja and RAK (his mother, a Qassimi, gave him added legitimacy) but soon his half brother, Ibrahim, the administrator of RAK, declared RAK independent. Khalid responded by attacking RAK in May 1867 and was about to have Ibrahim brought to him in Sharja. But Ibrahim's captors, fearing retaliation, asked Khalid to promise Ibrahim's life would be spared. When he refused, they let Ibrahim escape to Ajman and RAK reverted to Sharja's control (Rush 2 1991: 94).

A year later, the Shaikh of Abu Dhabi led an expedition against Sharja, and riding ahead challenged Khalid to single combat. Khalid accepted and was mortally wounded. He died on April 14, 1868 and was succeeded by his 24 year-old, half brother, Salim Sultan (1868–1883) whose mother had been one of Sultan's slaves. Salim was quiet and unaggressive, and because he did not strongly enforce his orders, people tolerated but did not fear him. He adhered to the strict tenets of the Wahhabis and spent much time in the mosque. Most people in Sharja hate the tenets of Wahhabi *mullas* (religious functionaries) but not Shaikh Salim and his followers and relatives, said one report.

To give his brother Ahmad[3] and his nephew Saqr Khalid a way to make a living, Salim left the settling of legal cases to them where they received 10 percent on each claim. He however often reversed or changed their decisions. In his absences from Sharja he usually appointed these kin to take his place, and frequently sent them on official missions. British reports state that he seldom consulted other relatives or elders who he considered not to be men of stature. Because of his neglect, Bedouin who had been his allies discontinued relations with him or developed links with other rulers. An exception was Muhammad Ali Naimi, a nephew of the Ruler of Ajman, Humaid Rashid, whom Salim's sister had married (Rush 2 1991: 106, 108). This background explains events occurring later in his reign. They suggest what may have inspired his nephew Saqr Khalid to depose him and then reconcile several years later.

When Salim succeeded Khalid, he ruled over the reunified Sharja and RAK for a year, until a nephew Humaid Abdalla Sultan[4] (RAK 1869–1900) who had been administering RAK, declared it independent again. That same year, a Wahhabi agent from Buraimi went to Sharja hoping to seize and imprison Shaikh Salim, and restore the original ruler Ibrahim to RAK. The complicated plan involved transferring Humaid Abdulla from RAK to Sharja as ruler so Ibrahim could take his place in RAK. The plans failed when the agent was shot and killed. To appease the Wahhabi Amir, Salim resigned in favor of Ibrahim but they maintained such a close relationship that it is questionable whether a real transfer of power occurred. After a few years Salim resumed his position (Rush 2 1991: 71).

Salim and Ibrahim made a final attempt to remove Humaid Abdulla from RAK in May 1869, but the British Resident positioned a warship off RAK, halting their effort (Rush 2 1991: 72). One might wonder why the British intervened when earlier they showed little concern at Humaid's declaration of independence from Sharja. The likely reason was that any weakening of the Qawasim coincided with the British effort to suppress their influence in the Gulf. The British were therefore not interested in seeing Sharja retake RAK with its strategic location in the north.

Two years later in 1871, Salim and Ibrahim quarreled when the latter tried to assert his authority over part of Sharja. Salim called on his enemy Humaid Abdulla in RAK and the Shaikh of UAQ to defend his position in Sharja. Soon thereafter, Humaid retook villages on the island of Sir that once had belonged to RAK. Meanwhile defections were continuing from Sharja in 1875 or 1876, with the secession of Hamriya, under its chief Saif Abdul Rahman (Rush 2 1991: 72).

At the end of March 1883, Salim left Sharja to visit Abu Musa Island, and his brother Ahmad left for RAK. They left their nephew, Saqr Khalid (1883–1914), then 20 years old, in charge. Despite Salim's generosity in giving Saqr important responsibilities and providing him a means of livelihood, Saqr turned on his benefactor and proclaimed himself ruler. He was soon recognized by the Shaikhs of RAK, UAQ, Ajman, and Dubai and gained the support of a chief of the Bedouin Naim, and a sectional leader of the Bani Qitab. A British report in May 1883 claimed Salim only had about 25 supporters, "white and black," in addition to about 10 Bani Yas fishermen on Abu Musa Island, while the usurper, Saqr Khalid, was supported by all the people of Sharja, except Salim's wife's relatives and a religious leader and his followers. Even Salim's servants were supporting

Saqr (Rush 2 1991: 117). The only ones who remained loyal to Salim in other words were those who stood to gain if Salim remained ruler.

Saqr's support was related to the unpopularity of Salim as a leader. People objected to his closeness to the *mullas* and his indifference to his subjects. But, as reports note, Shaikh Salim was not any worse than his successor who soon showed that he was weak and did not keep his promises The new ruler stopped paying an allowance to his uncle Ibrahim who was living in Ajman on support given him by Salim and Humaid Abdalla (Rush 2 1991: 117).

In July 1883, Salim reached a settlement guaranteed by the Shaikhs of RAK and Dubai whereby he would acknowledge Saqr as ruler, and in return would receive an annual pension of 600 dollars and retain his properties in Sharja, Dhaid, and Abu Musa, while his debts at Sharja would be paid by Saqr. By the next year, both sides complained that the terms were not met. The guarantors believed the fault lay with Salim then living in exile on Abu Musa. Salim however complained that he had been forced to sell all he had to support himself, and would attack Sharja if Saqr did not give him his due. Already Salim had contacted Bedouins of the Bani Qitab and the Naim, and the Chief of Hamriya and they all promised to help despite their earlier support for Saqr (Rush 2 1991: 123). Salim and Saqr agreed to meet in June 1884 under the auspices of the Residency Agent and a new document was prepared whereby Salim would receive 400 dollars a year, the revenue of the island of Sir Bu Nair (about 200 dollars annually), and a sum of 250 dollars on account for the previous year (Rush 2 1991: 123).

Angered by the Hamriya Chief's support for Salim, Saqr launched an attack on Hamriya that failed in 1884 (Rush 2 1991: 73). The issue of Hamriya continued to fester until in 1904 it came to a head over a succession problem. Hamriya's Chief Saif Abdul Rahman died and his son, Abdul Rahman succeeded but soon resigned in favor of an older relative also named Saif. When Saif confiscated his personal property, Abdul Rahman took him prisoner and killed his son, and resumed the chieftainship. Shaikh Rashid of UAQ intervened and took the prisoner under his own protection (Rush 2 1991: 74).

After several attempts between 1886 and 1889 to obtain better terms from Saqr, Salim eventually reconciled with his nephew and returned from exile to become his *Wazir* (counselor). In 1900, Humaid Abdulla who had been ruling RAK independently since 1869, died of a paralytic stroke leaving no brothers and only a seven year old son, Jasim. With no obvious successor, Saqr reannexed RAK to Sharja without opposition. He put his cousin Hamad Majid Sultan in charge but not happy with this choice he replaced him a few months later with his own son Khalid (RAK 1900–1909).

When Khalid died, Saqr appointed the previously deposed ruler of Sharja, Salim, Governor of RAK where he governed until his death in 1917. He was succeeded by a son Muhammad who governed for two years (1917 to 1919)[5] until succeeded by Salim's second son, Sultan from 1919 until his death in 1948. During Sultan's rule (in 1921) RAK again became independent of Sharja and has remained so ever since. Sultan was succeeded by Saqr Muhammad Salim who ruled from 1948 into the twenty-first century.

As ruler of Sharja, Saqr Khalid was weak, but he was not without ambition as his bid for power proved. He contracted several advantageous marriages that enlarged his base of support, including one to his cousin (FaBrDa) the daughter of Humaid Abdalla, Shaikh of RAK. When Humaid died, he annexed RAK to Sharja. Among his other wives were Baluchi, Bahraini, and Qassimi women, and a daughter of Khamis Salim Huli.[6] Saqr made a living smuggling arms (Rush 2 1991: 133) and when he died left property worth 2 lakhs that was seized by his successor Khalid Ahmad (Rush 2 1991: 187).

Sharja's position continued to decline under Saqr. The British view of him was highly unflattering, as was often the case with Qawasim rulers: They said he was "weak, miserly, and uxorious" in his personal life and as ruler was "apathetic and seemed incapable of exertion." Most of his constituents and the tribes that had supporters were alienated by his "indifference to their grievances and requests." The other Trucial Shaikhs found him of little importance both personally and as ruler. However he was friendly and accommodating to British officials although from sheer laziness he sometimes did not enforce the claims of British subjects. They also complained that he depended too much on the British Residency for help with his political problems rather than solving them himself (Rush 2 1991: 75).

In 1904, Saqr's disgruntled subjects decided to overthrow him, but were thwarted when he received word of the attempt. He imprisoned the main instigator, Muhammad Khadim,[7] who escaped from custody and sought refuge in UAQ. By this time Saqr had turned over administration of Sharja to his son Rashid[8] while RAK continued to be governed by his son Khalid.

When Saqr died on April 20, 1914 from a plague sweeping Sharja, three of his sons, Sultan, Muhammad, and Majid,[9] were still infants. On his deathbed Saqr named his cousin Khalid Ahmad Sultan (1914–1924) to succeed him (Rush 2 1991: 79, 127). Khalid immediately aggravated Saqr's family by seizing his properties and refusing to give his sons their inheritance. Two of Saqr's sons, Sultan and Muhammad, went to live with their maternal grandfather, Khamis Salim Huli. The eldest Sultan married the daughter of Abdul Rahman Muhammad Shamsi who in 1920, tried to take Ajman from Humaid Abdul Aziz Naimi.[10] Sharja's Ruler and the British Residency Agent returned the Ajman fort to its ruler and Abdul Rahman went to Sharja to work off debts he owed there. He later tried to assassinate the Residency Agent in 1925 (Heard-Bey 1996: 213–215).

When Sultan's guardian expressed disapproval at his charge's marriage to Abdul Rahman's daughter, Sultan fled with his brother to the Ruler of RAK. Eventually Khalid invited both back to Sharja, whereupon Sultan tried to overthrow Khalid and become ruler himself (Rush 2 1991: 147). Sultan argued he had a right to the rulership because, although his father had deposed Khalid's paternal uncle Salim, he did so with the intention of restoring his own lineage to the rule. That meant Khalid Sultan's lineage had the right to succeed and not Khalid Ahmad's lineage. Since Khalid Ahmad's father had been governor of Dibba and not of Sharja, Saqr had only appointed him interim ruler of Sharja until Saqr's children reached their majority (Rush 2 1991: 157). Sultan Saqr also wrote to the Political Resident saying he and his brothers were subsidized by their maternal grandfather, Khamis Salim Huli, because Shaikh Khalid had withheld their inheritance, and added that Khalid's insulting treatment had forced them and their grandfather to go to Dubai where they were treated as guests for five years (Rush 2 1991: 157). He was establishing his grievances against Khalid before his next moves.

In the meantime, Sultan's maternal grandfather, Khamis, privately mobilized a group of Ali (the main tribe of UAQ), Hula, and Manasir tribesmen to assist his grandsons in seizing Sharja. They partially succeeded in 1924 (Rush 2 1991: 137) but Khalid kept control of the fort and retaliated. The British reported that Shaikh Khalid sent his men on November 4, to set fire to the town. They burnt 65 homes and "two hags who could not run away." Included was the house of Alia Khalid Saqr, paternal aunt of Shaikh Sultan Saqr (Rush 2 1991: 139). On November 12, a truce was signed whereby Sultan Saqr (1924–1951) became ruler of Sharja and would give Khalid Ahmad Rs. 30,000 in debt payment. Khalid would distribute the Rs. 60,000 he owed Sultan and Saqr's heirs to the rightful persons. State properties would be given to Sultan and he would not interfere with Khalid's personal properties. Sultan agreed not to demand return of his father's considerable properties (Rush 2 1991: 187). A tower built by Khalid was to be destroyed "because it overtops the people's houses" and invades their privacy. In the end the cost of the conflict was five casualties on Khalid's side and three on Sultan's (Rush 1991: 140). Khalid left for Dubai, and sent for his moveable properties (Rush 2 1991: 146).

Later difficulties between them required the mediation of the Chiefs of Dubai and UAQ. In a second agreement in 1927, Khalid and his brother Abdulla, were compensated for properties Sultan had taken and were given Dhaid where they and their families could live. They were allowed to visit all the Trucial States but Sharja (Rush 2 1991: 181–182). Shortly thereafter, a British representative visited the Shaikh of UAQ while Khalid was present, and learned that none of the conditions had been met, nor had Khalid tried to have them met. The Representative noted that it was clear he was not interested in having them fulfilled since he wanted to become ruler again (Rush 2 1991: 192–193) suggesting that his claims remained valid as long as the bargain was not kept. In 1928 or 1929 Khalid again visited Dubai from UAQ to ask about his allowance and when he got no reply collected 20 men and threatened to fight, after which his allowance was increased (Rush 1991: 308)

The British, in reporting the hostilities between Khalid and Sultan called Shaikh Sultan "young and headstrong." He had not satisfied the people and he was so uncooperative with the British Agent that "both my predecessor, in his time, and I, in mine, have considered the question of his disposition" (Rush 2 1991: 191). At the time he became ruler in 1924, he was 21 years old by his own calculation, 4 years older than the British believed him to be.

By the late 1920s, Sharja's economy was in a slump, partly because of the town's lack of security, but more importantly because of the decline in pearling. At the time there were about 45 pearling boats and 2,000 divers and pullers. There was also a major trade in Nubian and Ethiopian slaves between the interior Nejd and the Trucial Coast. They were brought from Riyadh to Hasa by Nejdi merchants and then through Qatar to Abu Dhabi and Dubai (Rush 2 1991: 190).

In 1930 Shaikh Sultan and his brothers Rashid and Hamad (or Humaid) quarreled and to avoid bloodshed Sultan gave his brothers allowances. The townspeople also were angered when Sultan fell in love with an Arab woman married to one of his subjects and forced her husband to divorce her so he could marry her (Rush 2 1991: 197).

Some tied an event of 1931 in Hamriya to the unresolved tensions between Hamriya and Sharja. During public prayers, the Chief Abdul Rahman Saif of Hamriya was shot by his 21 year-old nephew, Saif, the son of his elder brother. Shortly thereafter Saif's younger brother stabbed the guard at the fort, presumably so both brothers could take over the town. When the 14 year-old son of the deceased shaikh and his mother ran out of the fort they were both shot by Saif. Though Saif had seemed on good terms with Abdul Rahman, having been brought up in his house, he had recently been living in Sharja with his Qassimi mother who was a cousin of the Ruler of Sharja. Many years before she had argued with Abdul Rahman's wife and fled his house leaving her children behind. She was living there, presumably because as widow she sought the protection of her husband's brother. When Saif and his brother reached maturity they demanded their dead father's property worth Rs 10,000. Abdul Rahman at first denied their claim but then agreed to give them money once he sold some pearls. In the meantime, Saif became involved in a failed pearling venture, and perhaps to resolve his own financial difficulties, took revenge on his uncle. The British Agent put the fact of Saif's mother's connection to Sharja, and the good relations of the murdered Shaikh with the British together and concluded that the Shaikhs of Sharja and Hirah (Abdul Rahman Muhammad) were behind the murders. The rationale was that since Hamriya was a dependency of Sharja, the Ruler wanted to recover his territory.

Abdul Rahman's 35 year-old heir Hamad, had earlier been banished to Dubai after trying to take Hamriya from his father. Both Hamad and Saif now wanted the Hamriya chieftainship. Both had about equal support, but the outcomes would be different if Saif used his Qassimi connections to bring Hamriya closer to Sharja. The Political Agent asked the British government to become involved as they normally did with matters of succession. The Agent argued that the ex-Shaikh had been treated as if he had the same independent status as other chiefs. Only two years previously, the Political Resident warned the shaikhs they would not permit any more successions through murder and the shaikhs agreed, feeling that if the practice were not discouraged their own positions might be threatened (Rush 2 1991: 202–204). Nevertheless, despite having murdered his predecessor, Saif assumed the chieftainship. The Political Resident reported that Hamriya had reverted to being a fief of Sharja despite a letter the ruler of Sharja had given Abdul Rahman in 1923 recognizing Hamriya's independence (Rush 2 1991: 205).

In 1932 the ex-Ruler, Khalid Ahmad, again complained he was not receiving compensation from Shaikh Sultan of Sharja (Rush 2 1991: 183) and again he may have been keeping his claims to the rulership alive. In 1937, Khalid's wife Aisha, the daughter of Kalba's Ruler, Said Hamad, intervened and Khalid became Regent of Kalba for Said's underage son when he succeeded his father. When Khalid died 15 years later in 1952, the pension he received from Kalba's oil concession reverted to the ruler of Sharja, essentially returning Kalba to Sharja's control.

In 1949, Shaikh Sultan fell ill and was flown to London where he died after an operation on May 23, 1951. Two of his sons, Khalid and Muhammad, were at his side. In preparation for going to London, the Petroleum Company's head office planned to give him enough to pay his medical bills, providing their drilling concession was extended from 15 to 20 years (Rush 2 1991: 79, 209). In another self-interested report, the British agent wrote that Sultan was "pompous and negligent of the interests of his people," and that as far as they were concerned his main merit was that in 1932 he had offered them air facilities when other rulers had refused (Rush 2 1991: 79).

Sultan's brother, Muhammad Saqr, (both had Hula mothers) who had been acting ruler during Sultan's absence, declared himself ruler, but Sultan's son, Saqr contested his accession, and said that Muhammad had assumed the rule "by trickery and the contrivance of Sultan Salim and the Midfa[11] family," and against the desires of the rest of the ruling family and Sharja residents (Rush 2 1991: 217). Rumors spread that Levies with the help of Sultan Salim supported Muhammad, but when challenged by Saqr, the Agent denied Levies backed either side (Rush 2 1991: 218). The Agent agreed that Muhammad was under the influence of the Midfa family who controlled the finances of the country and were accountable to no one. When Sultan Salim proposed Muhammad for ruler in a family meeting, those present said they first wanted an accounting of the state's money. The British felt Sultan Salim's involvement was "inspired largely by an innate love of intrigue and desire to make mischief"(Rush 2 1991: 218).

The Rulers, Rashid of Dubai, Rashid of Ajman, and Ahmad of UAQ expressed astonishment at the succession of Muhammad to the rulership of Sharja, and asked the Agent to confirm whether the British had recognized him. When Shaikh Ahmad asked by what principles the succession was guided the Agent turned the question around to ask Shaikh Ahmad what he thought the principles should be. Ahmad replied that "where the son was of age and ability to succeed his father, as was the case with Saqr he would normally do so" (Rush 2 1991: 19). The rulers' interest was of course to establish a preference for sons rather than brothers, even though there was no clear existing precedent.

The dispute continued with family members unwilling to commit themselves to one candidate or the other. The British wanted to expedite matters, at least partly because they feared that their air landing facilities agreement might be held up indefinitely if there were no ruler to conclude the negotiations (Rush 2 1991: 221). Finally, Saqr asked the Political Agent to survey local notables and he agreed. Muhammad decided he lacked the support of his brothers and even if he became ruler would have a short and unstable reign. He agreed to withdraw his candidacy provided he received a pension. He was given Rs.15,000 a year—the same amount he received as acting ruler (Rush 2 1991: 224–225).

The British agreed to recognize Saqr once he accepted the usual conditions, which included that he agree to all treaties entered into by his father, spend his oil revenues in the interests of his people, and accept the advice of the Political Agent in matters related to governing the shaikhdom (Rush 2 1991: 79). Muhammad Salim, uncle of the new Ruler of RAK, was commended for his level-headed help during the negotiations (Rush 2 1991: 225). Possibly unbeknownst to the British, Muhammad's daughter was Saqr's stepmother. An ambitious woman, she may have preferred Saqr to a ruler from another lineage who might not be disposed toward helping her children. Muhammad Salim was therefore, not a disinterested negotiator. The contending candidate, Muhammad Saqr, later told the Resident that he only claimed the succession at first because his sister insisted, and since Saqr was like a son he would give him every support (Rush 2 1991: 227). Indeed Muhammad Saqr, his sister, and Saqr's father had all been brought up together in the same household of maternal Hula relatives. Assuming all details are correct, this scenario suggests the possibility of a quarrel between Muhammad Saqr's sister and Saqr's stepmother who was related to the RAK Ruler. From this, we would understand that Muhammad Salim ended on the winning side by supporting Saqr and his ambitious stepmother. Reports of the succession ceremony noted that along with the usual dignitaries there were "a large number of women who formed a black outer circle round the proceedings" (Rush 2 1991: 226). If this was indeed a power struggle between women played out by their male surrogates then the presence of the women is not surprising.

Saqr Sultan (Sharja Ruler from 1951–1965) was born in 1924, of a mother from the Hula tribe. The British felt he had a more modern outlook than other rulers because of his association with the Royal Air Force at Sharja during the war, and he also spoke some English. They also felt he had an "exaggerated idea of his own importance," but conceded that he seemed to take a genuine interest in the welfare of his people and thought he would prove to be a good ruler. Like many other rulers, he had difficulty with members of his family over their allowances. Saqr was 27 when he became ruler, and a third generation male of his line to marry, among others, a Hula woman. Soon after he came to power, Saqr told the Resident he had two requests—he wanted to establish a well-run school and be allowed to import 160 rifles (Rush 2 1991: 226).

The allowance issue remained contentious, but Saqr ultimately reached agreement with all his brothers. His uncle, the previous acting ruler of Sharja, Muhummad Saqr, however, complained to the Wahhabi Chief, Ibn Saud, that he received no support and eventually received money from him (Rush 2 1991: 79). Saqr meanwhile took steps to bring modern amenities to Sharja. He established a state school in a building provided by the British, began developing Sharja as a port, and permitted the Presbyterian Church of America Mission to open a hospital. He was on good terms with all his neighbors except Fujaira, whose independence he refused to recognize because of his own nearby dependencies.

Saqr had difficulties with the Bani Qitab who in the past usually sided with the Qawasim. When the Saudis took Hamasa in Buraimi, Saqr did not react, hoping to avoid offending Ibn Saud. However, a section of the Bani Qitab, led by Muhammad Ali who resisted Saudi solicitations for years, decided to submit to Ibn Saud at Hamasa. Their grievance was that their paramount Shaikh received money from Saqr but did not distribute it among them, a failure they held against Saqr (Rush 2 1991: 265). When they visited Hamasa, Saqr cut off their allowances entirely. Later Muhammad Ali and his Bani Qitab followers lived quietly near Dhaid, and the Political Agent asked the Ruler of nearby Khaur Fakkan to accommodate them there (Rush 2 1991: 267). Saqr controlled Dhaid which was the northern headquarters of the Bani Qitab and thus a place from where he could dominate them (Rush 2 1991: 81).

Meanwhile, the Saudis were attempting to gain influence with the Qawasim, as a prelude for taking Buraimi from Oman and Abu Dhabi. In 1951, Saqr's younger half brother Salim, went to Egypt to pursue his education at the expense of the Saudis. The British Resident noted that they were not happy to see "this evidence of Saudi interest in our Trucial Shaikdoms," but did not see that he could do anything about it. The Saudis also began demanding that the residents of the Trucial States use travel documents issued by their rulers, rather than the British in the Sharja Agency (Rush 2 1991: 237). The British Foreign Office suggested that perhaps their local agents could counteract Saudi influence by arranging educational courses in England and elsewhere for Trucial States' residents.

The education issue arose again in 1953, when Saqr's brother Salim wanted to go to England to continue his studies but knew his brother would not pay the costs since he had not paid other brothers the allowances he agreed to. The Resident suggested that British Council Scholarships paid for by the Kuwaiti Emir might be given in such a case (Rush 2 1991: 239–240).

Meanwhile, the widow of Sultan Saqr who had been involved in the succession conflicts, Mira Muhammad Salim, mother of Shaikh Saqr's half brothers Khalid, Muhammad, and Salim, decided to send Salim and a stepson, Abdulla, to Bombay with money from the Saudi government. This move may have been calculated to bring the boys—a year apart in age—closer together as sometimes was arranged with half siblings of ruling families. The Resident instead encouraged Abdalla (age about 13 or 14) to go to Bahrain, and Saqr promised to send another son, Saud there, if Abdalla proved successful (Rush 2 1991: 241), a move calculated this time to offset his stepmother Mira's influence. A return letter from the British Council said that although they had no information on Salim, "We very much doubt his aptitude for purely academic study or that such study would be of value to him in the future" (Rush 2 1991: 242). The British Council representative in Iraq felt Salim would do better with practical training, saying, "Presumably he must have some bent (though knowing the Arabs perhaps this is a great assumption)." In the end they recommended that Salim go to the American University in Beirut to keep him from too serious a break with the region. "This would have the advantage of disorienting Salim less, but he would, on the other hand, imbibe more of the pan-Arab than the British ways of thinking" (Rush 2 1991: 253). The Ruler of Doha agreed to support Salim at AUB (Rush 2 1991: 260).

Not wanting to be outdone, the Ruler inquired about sending his own son, Sultan, then about seven, to Harrow, but the Resident again thought the idea not suitable, and asked London for ideas about educating a child of that age, "taking into account that the home in which he has been brought up and to which he will return is not greatly advanced on the eleventh century!" (Rush 2 1991: 244). The report continued that the suitability of a British public school is "an entirely different matter; it would entail the complete anglicization of the boy and would probably mean that he would return to his home deracine and completely unsuited for the station in life which his father intends that he should fill" (Rush 2 1991: 246). The report recommended a sound British tutor and Victoria College in Alexandria, Egypt, at the age of 12 or 13 as the best solution, so as not to make a complete break with his background (Rush 2 1991: 246–247). These discussions about educating a new generation of ruling family sons suggests British attitudes about local families and their reluctance to take any responsibility for financially supporting their studies or providing education services in the local area. Meanwhile other shaikhs of the Gulf were playing a constructive role in financing education opportunities for residents of the Trucial States at a time when their ruling families still had few resources.

In 1952, Saqr had a canal dug to open up the waterway from Khan Creek to the open sea, but without proper advice, the British reported it "a sad and sorry affair." The station engineer was afraid to do more than lend shovels for fear his airfield might be flooded. Saqr was also preparing for his marriage to the third daughter of the ex-Ruler of Kalba, Hamad Said Hamad, who had been assassinated in 1951 (Rush 2 1991: 133). The bride's mother was from the Naqbiyeen tribe, the largest and most powerful in the Kalba area. No one from Saqr's family attended the wedding except his uncle Saif Abdul Rahman, who was Wali of Kalba

(Rush 2 1991: 231).[12] Most of the relatives had good excuses for not attending, while bad feeling between Saqr and his brother Muhammad explained the latter's absence (Muhammad was also believed to have had designs on the bride) (Rush 2 1991: 132). Meanwhile, Shaikh Muhammad Sharqi of Fujaira feared that Saqr might use the wedding as an excuse to retake Fujaira (Rush 2 1991: 234).

In 1954, Saqr's quarrels with his half brothers intensified. The problem centered on the half brothers' mother, Mira. She began agitating for her eldest son, Khalid, to become ruler and wanted Saqr to appoint her second son, Muhammad, as Wali of Khaur Fakkan. Her third son, Salim, she felt could handle accounts, revenues, and clerical jobs in the Sharja municipality. Salim spoke openly of murdering Saqr and making himself ruler but admitted he only had Muhammad's support. Khalid and Muhammad asked the ruler of Qatar for financial assistance and, at the instigation of Mira, he paid them Rs. 3,000 for summer expenses. She also encouraged her sons to sell travel documents to Persians bound for Saudi Arabia (Rush 2 1991: 260).

Saqr's resistance to their complaints broke down when he became embarrassed by their public appeals for financial support. A measure of Saqr's distrust of his kin was seen in his choice of deputy to act on his behalf while he was absent. His choice, Rahman Abdul Rahman, was a relative but not from paternal kin who might contest his rule. Saqr finally paid an allowance to his three half brothers and their mother of Rs. 9,000. In return they agreed not to interfere in Sharja politics and to recognize Saqr's son, Sultan, as his successor. Later he raised the allowance and sent Khalid to Abu Musa as Wali. The dispute over their uncle Muhammad Saqr's pension continued unabated (Rush 2 1991: 265–268) and Khalid still visited Qatar, Bahrain, Saudi Arabia, and Kuwait asking for money. Saqr's uncle, Majid Saqr, also received money from the Saudis and trafficked in slaves, much to Saqr's irritation, since he felt it defamed the family name (Rush 2 1991: 266). Similar, but not as serious, "brother trouble" also affected RAK during this time (Rush 2 1991: 257–259)

British documents later reported that dissident members of the Ruler's family (Mira and her sons) eventually settled in Saudi Arabia where they acted as agents for the Saudis. Once they were gone, Saqr's relations with his uncle Muhammad improved, and he continued his efforts to establish local schools and to secure places for local students in the Egyptian Al-Azhar University and a Syrian College. The school he established in Sharja was staffed mainly with teachers supplied through

Kuwait and Egypt. He also built a jetty for the harbor of Sharja (Rush 2 1991: 268).

An important issue for all the Trucial rulers was borders[13] especially as the British began defining boundaries in the 1950s. In some cases borders were arbitrary or vague. Sharja, for example, was to extend up to the Hajar range, including some Bani Qitab territories that had not always been in Sharja hands. When Saqr acquired Dhaid in 1952 at the death of the ex-regent of Kalba, Khalid Ahmad, he regained territory that had been surrendered to Khalid in 1928. Saqr's father had done little to control the Bani Qitab during his rule (1924–1951) and consequently they had committed numerous highway robberies. Saqr determined to use his possession of Dhaid to exert more control over the Bani Qitab. Apparently convinced of his control, the British included Dhaid and all areas in between as part of Sharja. Other important boundaries not defined until later were the borders between Sharja and Dubai, and the boundaries in the hills between Muscat and RAK (Rush 2 1991: 80).

In 1955 Saqr visited Kerbala and Samarra in Iraq, areas he claimed his family had come from originally (Rush 2 1991: 282). He also traveled to London in 1958 with his 11 year-old son Sultan and Sultan Ali Uwais, the son of a prominent Dubai merchant who was raised with Saqr and spoke some English, and apparently was brought along to help fund the trip (Rush 2 1991: 285). He created a good impression in England but Sharja residents complained he was away too much and did not spend enough on the people's welfare. In an aside in the same British report, the writer noted that the Petroleum Development Company had drilled 14,000 ft. without finding any oil (Rush 2 1991: 298). In February, Saqr rushed to Lebanon to see Muhammad Saqr who suffered a stroke. Later Muhammad returned to Sharja permanently paralyzed (Rush 2 1991: 296).

In December of 1958, a man named Sayyid Abdulla attempted to assassinate Saqr. Sayyid Abdulla claimed he was Chief of the Baluchis living in Sharja. Twenty years previous, in a revolt against Reza Shah in Iran, he and many others escaped to Sharja where he had been given a subsistence allowance of Rs. 200 a month. His dispute with Saqr involved a Baluchi man having difficulty with his wife. The man took the case to Saqr who referred it to Saif Abdul Rahman, overseer of the court in Sharja. Sayyid Abdulla had previously had the Baluchi man flogged, and when he heard the man had taken his case to Saqr, went to Saqr to explain that as the Chief of the Baluch, it was his prerogative to decide their disputes. Saqr embarrassed him by telling him to leave the audience area. Sayyid Abdalla pulled out a pistol but before he could do any damage an Egyptian teacher hit him from behind and took the pistol. Meanwhile Saqr seized a rifle and tried to shoot him but it misfired. Shaikh Saqr's followers seized Sayyid, beat him up, and imprisoned him. The Chief of the Baluch on the Batina Coast in Muscat had to come in to mediate the conflict (Rush 2 1991: 300).

Saqr was becoming increasingly unpopular. He failed to make payments on his debts and continued to spend his summers abroad. He feared plots against him from several sides—from the Rulers of RAK and Ajman, and by his half brother Muhammad, then a businessman in Dubai (Rush 2 1991: 273). Indeed it was around this time, that Saqr in a goodwill gesture, married his daughter to the Ruler of RAK's eldest son, Khalid, where, 40 years later, she figured in a succession dispute.

Saqr was finally deposed by decision of a family council in 1965 and his cousin, Khalid Muhammad (1965–1972), replaced him. Khalid was son of Saqr's uncle Muhammad who had earlier lost out to Saqr in his attempt to rule. Saqr went into exile in Egypt but later returned and killed Khalid in January 24, 1972 hoping to regain the rulership. This was the last time in the emirates that a ruler was assassinated. The governing council of the newly formed UAE federation sent him back into exile (Zahlan 1978: 196). Khalid's brother, Dr. Sultan Muhammad (1972 on) instead became ruler.

A coup was mounted against Dr. Sultan in June–July 1987 while he was on vacation in Britain. The instigator was Abdul Aziz Muhammad, Sultan's brother and designated Crown Prince. Shaikh Zaid of Abu Dhabi supported the coup because of what some said was his resentment over Sultan's arrogance. Sultan had received a doctorate in history from England and was better educated than the barely literate Zaid. Zaid felt he had not been treated respectfully by Sultan. The coup failed when Dubai and Abu Dhabi eventually decided not to support Abdul Aziz for the rulership of Sharja. The coup was over by mid-July and Shaikh Sultan returned to Sharjah. Abdul Aziz became special advisor to Shaikh Zaid with palaces in Al Ain and Abu Dhabi.

The Crown Prince and Deputy Ruler of Sharja is now Sultan Muhammad Sultan, who was appointed after the eldest son of the Ruler died in 1999 from a drug overdose. The young man Muhammad, was the son of Dr. Sultan's first wife whom he divorced in about 1976. His second wife, Jawahir Muhammad Sultan, was granddaughter of a previous ruler, Sultan Saqr (1924–1951) and his Huli wife. Dr. Sultan also has Huli grandmother. Jawahir bore several children including three daughters and a son. Her brother is current Crown Prince, a choice perhaps intended to reserve the position for Dr. Sultan's son by Jawahir once he is old enough.

Qawasim Rulers and Administrators of RAK from 1866

- Ibrahim Sultan — 1866–1867; Sultan Saqr's son; chief of RAK under father; deposed by brother
- Khalid Sultan — 1867–1868; brother of predecessor, reunified RAK and Sharja; died in combat
- Humaid Abdalla Sultan — 1869–1900; nephew (FaBrSo) of predecessor; first administrator and then independent ruler of RAK; died of paralytic stroke
- Hamad Majid Sultan — 1900; cousin (FaBrSo) of his predecessor
- Khalid Saqr — 1900–1909; cousin's son (FABrSoSo) of his predecessor; ruled RAK on behalf of Sharja; died of natural causes
- Salim Sultan — 1909–1919; grandfather's brother (FaFaBr) of predecessor; ruled RAK for Sharja;
- Muhammad Salim — 1917–1919; ruled jointly with Salim until the latter's death
- Sultan Salim — 1919–1948; son of predecessor; ruled RAK as part of Sharja and independently from 1921–1948; when he was deposed
- Saqr Muhammad Salim — 1948–present; nephew (BrSo) of his predecessor

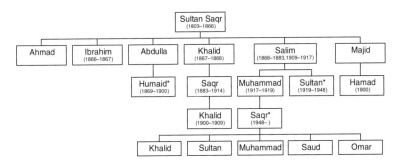

Figure 8.2   Qawasim Rulers and Administrators of RAK from 1866

* Independent Rulers of RAK; others governed under Sharja

RAK's complex relationship with Sharja requires a few additional paragraphs to give it coherence. Both emirates were controlled by Qawasim leaders during the two hundred year period described here. Sharja was continuously ruled by Khalid Sultan Saqr's lineal descendants from 1883 after

158

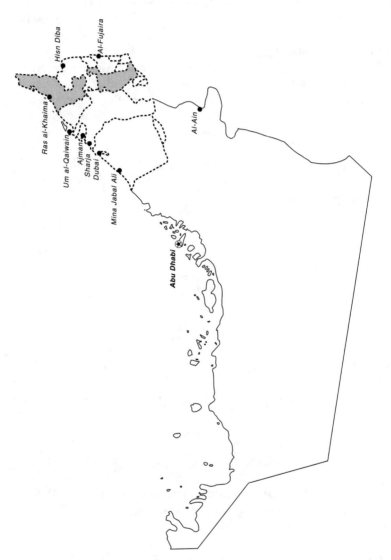

Source: http://lcweb2.loc.gov/frd/cs/united_arab_emirates/ae05_01a.pdf

Salim Sultan was deposed as ruler. After RAK became fully independent from Sharja in 1921, it came under the rule of Salim Sultan Saqr's descendants. Thus the lineages of 2 of the 11 sons of the nineteenth century Ruler Sultan Saqr "won" the Qawasim power struggles for the two main Qassimi centers, Sharja and RAK.

The modern history of RAK began with the death of Shaikh Salim in 1919. He ruled RAK as a Sharja-dependency after reconciling with his nephew, Saqr Khalid, who deposed him as Ruler of Sharja (see above). Salim's son, Sultan, ousted his brother Muhammad who ruled jointly with their father for the last two years of his reign and in 1921, managed to have RAK recognized as an independent state. He then ruled RAK until 1948. At one point Sultan offered his daughter in marriage to this disgruntled nephew who later overthrew him. Saqr accepted but was heard to ask whether the Shaikh thought he would sleep better as a result. A major issue was the lack of allowances Sultan gave his relations (Lienhardt 2001: 174).

The British only saw negative aspects to Sultan's rule. They said he was of a "wild and nervous disposition and was a thoroughly unsatisfactory Ruler." They felt he neglected the interests of his state and had an unsatisfactory attitude toward the British government on several occasions. Specifically, he caused problems about a Royal Air Force petrol barge in 1930, and sometimes did not call on British ships or representatives visiting RAK. At one point, in 1935, he took down his flag on Tunbs Island and seemed to be scheming with the Persians. He only replaced the flag when the British threatened to turn the island over to Sharja.

In 1947, trouble flared with the ex-Ruler Muhammad over Sultan's failure to pay him a share of oil revenues. In February 1948, Muhammad's son, Saqr (and Sultan's son-in-law), took over the fort when Sultan was absent, and was recognized as RAK ruler on July 16, 1948. The British reported that although Saqr was unimpressive, he had a forceful character, and cooperated well with the British. Soon after he became ruler, he took control of villages that had been essentially independent during the reign of his predecessor. His father, Muhammad, usually accompanied him and exercised a restraining influence over him. At one time, his older brother Humaid, had been proposed as Regent of Kalba (Rush 2 1991: 81).

Sultan soon intrigued against the new ruler to regain his position. To preserve the peace the Political Agent tried to remove Sultan to Bahrain, but when he was told to go to Bahrain, he started firing shots at those who followed him, including some that came close to hitting the Political Agent. Sultan fled to Muscat where the Sultan of Muscat arranged for him to pay a fine and remain in exile in Muscat for a year. After his exile he went to Manai near Wadi Qaur where the Sultan of Muscat paid him to protect his properties from raids. He also collected tolls from motor traffic using the valley route that was the only suitable way between the Trucial Coast and the Gulf of Oman. He established ownership of the western end of the road claimed by RAK and Sharja, and was able to control the Bani Kaab who grazed animals there without submitting to Qawasim authority.

In 1949 and 1950, Saqr Muhammad had trouble with his tribesmen and neighbors, probably again at the instigation of his predecessor, Sultan. These troubles involved the Khawatir tribe as well as tribes from the towns of Rams, Bakha, and Jazirat al Hamra who were paid allowances and owed allegiance to Saqr. Saqr was believed to have had no dealings with the Wahhabi Emir Turki when he arrived at Hamasa trying to strengthen his influence in Buraimi. However, to show his independence, the Chief of the Khawatir visited him before going on to Riyadh. Even though displeased, Saqr did not take any action against him. Sultan Salim however, saw the opportunity to increase his own support and irritate his nephew, and therefore made overtures to the Saudis by sending Emir Turki a present of camels. After this attempt, Sultan did not seem to have intrigued further against Saqr (Rush 2 1991: 81). But he continued to maintain his separate base in Wadi Qaur until attempts were made to reach an agreement on his allowance. In 1953, Sultan finally agreed to accept the status of subject to Saqr, and Saqr agreed to pay him an annual allowance of Rs.16,000 plus one-sixth of any future oil concessions (Rush 2 1991: 82).

The British commented that during these years RAK has "been the least orderly of the Trucial Coast Shaikhdoms and its Ruler has had neither the opportunity nor the resources to develop his State." Because of the numerous wells and irrigated gardens there was probably some potential to develop the area agriculturally (Rush 2 1991: 82). Clearly, Sultan's actions were one of the reasons Saqr was preoccupied with his own survival and unable to develop his emirate. In the meantime, Sultan's son Saqr, was agitating for his own fiefdom and in 1951, assassinated the Ruler of Kalba, hoping to gain control of that principality. There were suggestions that the assassination occurred with the collaboration of the Ruler of Sharja who by that time was Saqr Sultan Saqr, the usurper's distant relative (FaFaBrSoSoSo). Kalba had been independent of Sharja since 1936 and only reverted to Sharja's control after the 1951 assassination. The details of these events are in the Fujaira chapter.

Discussion

It might be argued that the collapse of the once powerful Qawasim family was inevitable once the British became their implacable foes and started restricting their power at the beginning of the nineteenth century. On the one hand, the ruler at the time, Sultan Saqr, deserves some blame for not recognizing the futility of challenging the British, or at least in not managing his relations with them better. On the other hand his remarkable comeback after his fleet was decimated, and his skill at controlling the disparate personalities of the Oawasim family attests to a remarkable ability in the annals of personal leadership. Once he was gone, no one possessed the personality to perform this valuable function. Although Abu Dhabi experienced a similarly contested succession in the period after Zaid I died, the difference was that the Nahyan family kept Abu Dhabi's territorial integrity intact and resisted the fragmentation that occurred with the Qawasim. A contributing factor in Qawasim decline was that besides their home base in Sharja and RAK, their influence at its peak extended over distant units that were difficult to defend. These units were surrounded by independent tribal groups with little affinity for the Qawasim of the kind that existed between the tribes of the Bani Yas and the Nahyan.

By the 1870s, only a few years after Sultan Saqr's death, the Qassimi Ruler, Salim Sultan, was reduced to controlling only Sharja. The Persians on the northern coast, taking advantage of Qawasim family's conflicts, erased most of the Qawasim influence there by the end of the nineteenth century. RAK became independent in 1869 under Salim's nephew Humaid Abdalla and retained that status until 1900 when for a short time it again became a dependency of Sharja. RAK became permanently independent in 1921 during the rule of Salim's son, Sultan. After this point, it is easier to treat the histories of Sharja and RAK separately[14] even though in reality their fates continued to be intertwined until well into the twentieth century. By the 1870s, Dibba and Kalba were being administered by two of Salim's brothers, Ahmad and Majid, and were only nominally under Sharja's control. By then, six of Sultan Saqr's sons were dead and two were still young. In the end, lineages of only three—Abdalla, Khalid, and Salim—secured the rule of the Qawasim emirates of Sharja and RAK. The fate of the remaining principalities, Kalba, Dibba, and Khaur Fakkan on the Shamaliya coast, appear in the chapter on Fujaira.

Throughout the century and a half covered by this chapter, as the British kept close watch over maritime interests on the southern coast of the Gulf, the decline of the Qawasim paralleled the rise of the Bu Falah in Abu Dhabi (Rush 1991: xviii). The Qawasim's primary involvement in maritime activities meant their containment was a higher priority for the British than states with inland interests. As the influence of the Qawasim diminished in Persia and the Persians exerted heavy-handed controls over commerce, Dubai's fortunes rose. Dubai's interest in a stable environment for commerce meant its maritime activities were viewed with approval by the British and by 1954, the British Political Agency moved its headquarters from Sharja to Dubai (Rush 2 1991: 277).

The brother-troubles in Sharja and RAK shed light on a persistent pattern in the history of the Trucial States. The issue is, why so many rulers cut off or reduced the allowances to their brothers when this was almost certain to provoke a break in their relationships, and in several cases brothers overthrowing rulers. Several reasons are likely. First and probably foremost, the rulers during this period only had limited funds to conduct the business of governing, including the priority of providing allowances to tribal chiefs. They probably felt the more immediate need of maintaining the loyalty of tribes than paying allowances to relatives who theoretically would remain loyal even if disgruntled.

A second probable reason relates to the often-intense competition among brothers for the position of ruler. This was especially true among half brothers, who grew up in the different households of their mothers. When these brothers or uncles showed an inclination toward overthrowing the incumbent, it made little sense for him to provide resources so they could carry out their plans. The case is essentially similar to those of Abu Dhabi and Dubai.

Finally, it may be just as likely that the complaints about allowances had other meanings. In several cases the complaints of deposed or thwarted leaders kept alive their claims to the ruler's position indicating they were not reconciled yet to supporting the incumbent. In other cases, the excuse of unpaid allowances provided a public rationale for disregarding kin loyalties and attacking the ruler. In effect, control over the purse strings was the main way a ruler concentrated power in his own hands and limited the ability of renegade kin to oppose him. In several cases one of the ruler's first acts in office was to confiscate the property of his predecessor. This ability to control resources made his position all the more attractive, allowing him to publicly manifest his dominance over others. In one case, the ruler succumbed to pressure only when his kin embarrassed him publicly for "not taking care of his family members." He expected that as kin, they would not air their disagreements so openly. Before oil revenues brought unimaginable wealth to some rulers, they all engaged in the balancing act of sharing and protecting assets. Political success depended on playing the game effectively.

During his lifetime, Sultan Saqr's sons freed him by taking on administrative duties to initiate adventures that extended his influence. After his death they focused on their own intrigues. To a certain extent, their political successes appear to be based on the circumstance of their background.

Three sons, Ahmad, Salim, and Majid had slave or Abyssinian mother(s), a fact that left them, in a structurally weak position, not so much because their slave mothers were of lower status but because they had no tribal backing beyond the recognized legitimacy as sons of the ruler. Saqr and Khalid both had Qassimi mothers putting them in the potentially stronger position of linking royal lineages but Saqr died early, leaving Khalid, the son in the strongest position within the family even though he was not the eldest. Unfortunately, although he succeeded his father, he died in battle before he was able to consolidate his rule. In his short reign he managed to rebuff attempts to make RAK independent. If he had lived longer and kept the territories united under one rule, the history of the Qawasim might have been different.

Khalid was succeeded by Salim, the son of a slave, who was acknowledged to be a weak ruler. He ruled for 15 years during which time Qawasim power made its most precipitous declines. At the end of this period he was overthrown by Khalid's son, Saqr, who argued that Khalid's line was meant to provide the rulers by being the first to succeed Sultan. Other than Salim's rule and a 10-year reign by Ahmad Sultan's son, all five of the other rulers of Sharja came from Khalid Sultan's line. The other son Saqr with a Qassimi mother also seems to have benefited from the extra legitimacy. He increased this legitimacy by continuing to contract marriages with Huli and Qawasim wives. Salim and Khalid Ahmad, the rulers whose mothers or grandmothers were slaves, were deposed with little opposition.

The remaining sons of Sultan with known mothers—Rashid, Ibrahim, and Abdalla had Bani Yas, Marzuki, and al Ali mothers, giving them influential backing during periods when their mother's tribes played strategic roles in Qawasim affairs. Abdalla was well established as Governor of Sharja during his father's lifetime but died early and his son, Humaid, went on to become the first independent ruler of RAK in 1869. Humaid's only son Jasim died young and although his daughters married the Rulers of UAQ and later Sharja this did little to advance his lineage that by this time was reduced to women. By the time of the Kalba incidents (see chapter 11) the fracture lines were becoming clearer and opponents on the Gulf of Oman had no difficulty playing one Qassimi group off against another.

CHAPTER 9

PRESERVING AJMAN INDEPENDENCE UNDER AL BU KHURAIBAN

Al Bu Khuraiban (Naim) Chiefs and Rulers

- Humaid Rashid
- Rashid Humaid   before 1820–1838; son of predecessor; natural death
- Humaid Rashid   1838–1841, 1848–1872; son of predecessor; deposed; natural death.
- Abdul Aziz Rashid   1841–1848; brother of predecessor; killed in Hamriya.
- Rashid Humaid   1873–1891; son of predecessor; natural death.
- Humaid Rashid   1891–1900; son of predecessor; killed by uncle (FaBr)
- Abdul Aziz   1900–1910;★ uncle of predecessor; killed by grandson of sister
- Humaid Abdul Aziz   1910 to 1928; son of predecessor; natural death.
- Rashid Humaid   1928–1981; son of predecessor; natural death
- Humaid Rashid   1981–present; son of predecessor

★ Lorimer (1986) says this date should be "to 1908" rather than 1910.

166

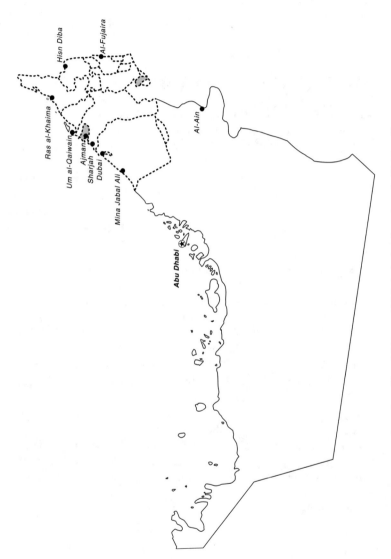

Hisn Diba

Al-Fujaira

Ras al-Khaima

Al-Ain

Um al-Qaiwain

Ajman

Sharjah

Dubai

Mina Jabal Ali

Abu Dhabi

Source: http://lcweb2.loc.gov/frd/cs/united_arab_emirates/ae05_01a.pdf

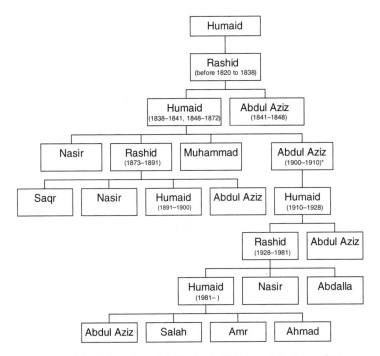

Figure 9.1 Al Bu Kharaiban (al-Nuaimi) Chiefs and Rulers of Ajman

* Lorimer says this date should be "to 1908" rather than 1910.

A jman gives yet another view of personal rule in the Emirates. As a small state, Ajman's history focuses on independence and surviving attempts to take it over. The town of Ajman was one of several coastal colonies established by the Naim in the eighteenth century. Subsequently it was annexed by the Qawasim of Sharja before becoming an independent emirate. The town sits on a piece of territory literally cut out of Sharja and only minutes away from Dubai.

Ajman is the smallest emirate with only about 100 square miles. Its modern population is roughly the same as RAK with 174,000 residents. Ajman's other units are Masfut, an agricultural village 110 kilometers to the southeast on the border of RAK and Oman, and Manama, a village 60 kilometers to the east on the border of Sharja and Fujaira. They lie on the two main land routes to Fujaira and Oman. Masfut is in Wadi Hatta and Manama on the route to Masafi and Wadi Ham. The rulers of Ajman are from the Bu Khuraiban section of the Naim, an independent tribe of settled and nomadic groups inhabiting areas of the UAE, including Sharja, Buraimi, and Oman. (Zahlan 1978: 15).

At the time the General Treaty for the Suppression of Piracy was signed in 1820, Ajman was still a dependency of Sharja. But by 1823, the Ajmani Chief Rashid Humaid (c.1820–1838) "exploiting Britain's unwillingness to recognize the full extent of the Qassimi domains . . ."(Rush 1991: xx), wrote a letter to the Resident complaining of aggressions against him by Sultan Saqr of Sharja and saying he could no longer submit to his authority. Sultan tried to substantiate his claim to Ajman with a paper signed by neighboring chiefs so "his jurisdiction was not altogether undisputed" (Rush 1991: 465). In 1827, Sultan punished residents of Ajman for maritime offenses without any objection from its chief, suggesting that Rashid still accepted the authority of the Qawasim. Later in the year he sought the help of the Wahhabi Chief, Turki Saud, to gain his independence from Sultan but Turki refused (Rush 1991: 465).

Sometime in the next few years Shaikh Rashid seems to have gained recognition from the British as an independent chief, for in 1835 he signed a truce on behalf of Ajman for the duration of the fishing season. Beside his name "Rashid ben Humed, the Shaik of Eyman," were the names of the Shaikhs of Abu Dhabi, Dubai, and the Qawasim (Lienhardt 2001: 231). In 1838, Shaikh Rashid died and was succeeded by the second of his three sons, Humaid Rashid (1838–1841 and 1848–1872). Humaid tried to win over the Qawasim by marrying the daughter of Shaikh Sultan of Sharja. Meanwhile Humaid's elder brother, Abdul Aziz, resenting the fact that he had been overlooked for the rule, took control of the fort of Ajman in 1841 and deposed Humaid. The majority of the residents supported his action and Humaid's father-in-law in Sharja did not intervene, deciding it was a family matter. When Humaid began building a fort nearby Abdul Aziz restored power to him temporarily until a better opportunity came for him to become ruler (Rush 1991: 466). He retook Ajman later that year ruling from 1841 to 1848.

The relations between Sharja and Ajman remained complicated throughout the reign of Abdul Aziz, revealing in several cases subtle British support for Ajman's independence. For example, in 1844, a boat from Sharja damaged a boat of Ajman. The matter was arbitrated by the British as though it were a maritime case between two states and Sharja quickly made restitution. Later two Sharja boats were blown into Ajman's port and the British praised Abdul Aziz for protecting the boats and their cargo (Rush 1991: 467–468), suggesting once again that the states were two separate jurisdictions.

In 1846, Abdul Aziz joined the Chiefs of Dubai and UAQ in an agreement to resist attacks by their common enemies, the Qawasim of Sharja
and the Nahyan of Abu Dhabi. But later the same year, under pressure
from Sultan Saqr of Sharja, Abdul Aziz withdrew from the agreement and
turned to Sultan for protection (Rush 1991: 468). The British felt that in
tribal matters Abdul Aziz was inconsistent but he usually adhered to the
maritime peace (Rush 1991: 473). In retrospect his behavior appears
entirely appropriate living so close to Sharja.

In 1848, a conflict arose between the Chiefs of Ajman and Hamriya, a
town claimed by the Qawasim. The problem started when the Hamriya
Chief died and another succeeded him. Abdul Aziz took advantage of the
transition to attack the village with the help of Humaid with whom he was
temporarily reconciled. The people of Hamriya won, killing Abdul Aziz
and wounding Humaid. Humaid recovered and became Chief of Ajman a
second time. Hostilities continued between the Chiefs of Ajman and
Hamriya and neither dared go pearling until the Chief of UAQ—whose
son was married to the Ajmani Chief's daughter[1] (Rush 1991 Annexure
No. 5: 776)—negotiated a peace (Rush 1991: 469).

Humaid Rashid ruled two more decades before he died of natural
causes, sometime before 1873. He was succeeded by his son Rashid
(1872–1891) whose mother was an Ali of UAQ. His sister was also married
to an Ali, Ahmad Abdalla Rashid Majid, the Ruler of UAQ (1872–1904)
during the time her brother was ruler, thus continuing the close ties
between the two small states. Although UAQ had little to offer militarily, it
had ties with other states that allowed it to play a useful role in mediation.

Near the end of Rashid's tenure in 1890, the residents of a Dhawahir
village in Buraimi rebelled against Zaid I of Abu Dhabi with the help of the
Naim tribe and the Chiefs of Ajman and Sharja. Eventually, Abu Dhabi,
with its allies in Dubai and with the help of the Saudi Ruler Sultan Faisal
Turki put down the rebellion (Abdullah 1978: 98–99) but this did not stop
Zaid from attempting to extend his influence along the Trucial Coast. In
1900, he supported his father-in-law, Sultan Nasir Suaidi, in colonizing
Zura Island near Ajman. The Ajmani chief complained to the British saying
anyone who lived on Zura ought to be a subject of Ajman and that, in any
case, a Hinawi like Sultan Suaidi should not be settling in Ghafiri territory.
Although he argued on Ghafiri grounds,[2] it was clear Ajman had no trouble
aligning with Hinawi groups when it was to its advantage.

When no action was taken, the Ajmani Shaikh built a fort across from
the island, and asked his relative, the Naimi Chief in the interior, to open a
front in Buraimi against Zaid if he continued to support colonization on Zura.

The Shaikh of Sharja was similarly alarmed that an adversary was establishing a foothold nearby and helped the Ajmani Shaikh by sending arms and supplies to Buraimi against Zaid. The Sultan of Muscat reacting to the instability in Buraimi predictably weighed in on the side of Zaid, as did Dubai and UAQ. UAQ, usually supportive of Ajman, in this case followed its Hinawi loyalties, probably because the issue was raised so publicly by the Ajmani Chief.

The Political Resident refused to support a settlement under these conditions and the standstill continued. In 1905, the Political Resident Sir Percy Cox again decided against settling the Zura issue unless all the Trucial Shaikhs agreed (Abdullah1978: 100). The case escalated until all the Trucial Chiefs felt forced to take sides. As with other matters of this kind, the implications went well beyond surface appearances. By establishing a base just off their coast, Abu Dhabi threatened the stability of Ajman and Sharja who saw Zura as a stepping-stone in Zaid's ambition to expand to the north and east. The Qawasim, mindful of their historic claims to Ajman, saw a larger danger if Abu Dhabi gained a foothold in the northern areas, and immediately cast their support with the Ajmani Chief. They also realized the usefulness of Ajmani connections with the Naim of Buraimi who could offset any future advances of Zaid. The Omanis, fearing for their Buraimi possessions, rushed to support their surrogate, Zaid. Although Ajman was a small and relatively weak emirate, it was able to mobilize an impressive array of allies on its side. The allies looked to Ajman's strategic location and Naim connections as assets in future contests. Characteristic of such events was the personal nature of the decision-making—a handful of chiefs determining who would side with whom, what would be done, and how they would do it. The unquestioned loyalty of their followers committed them to any action their chiefs decided upon.

After Rashid Humaid died in April 1891, his son, Humaid Rashid succeeded him as chief where he remained until murdered in July 1900 by his uncle Abdul Aziz Humaid.[3] The murderer and Rashid, the father of the deceased Humaid, were half brothers from different mothers. Abdul Aziz's mother was the daughter of Sultan Saqr Qassimi, and Rashid's mother was from the Ali of UAQ. Members of the ruling family agreed in advance to Abdul Aziz's takeover (Rush 1991: 496). He and his men attacked Government House while Shaikh Humaid was visiting a home in the area and fired on him as he reappeared. Members of the Ali tribe to whom Shaikh Humaid was related through his maternal grandmother rushed to Ajman to support him. They found to their relief that Humaid's condition was not serious although he remained in Abdul Aziz's custody. While they were deciding how to free him, Abdul Aziz, his son, and their followers strangled Humaid and put out the eyes of his younger brother Nasir. They imprisoned Nasir but did not kill him because of a chronic illness they believed would keep him from ever challenging Abdul Aziz (Rush 1991: 484, 485). Eventually he and another brother went into exile in Hamriya. Abdul Aziz meanwhile took the jewelry and property of the women in Humaid's family and evicted them from their homes (Rush 1991: 486). British reports claimed that no one sympathized with the deceased Shaikh Humaid who had alienated everyone in the family by not paying them regular allowances (Rush 1991: 473).

The British were unsure what to do. The ex-ruler Humaid had inherited his position legitimately, had respected British treaties, and had generally been law abiding. Now they had to contend with the wild and difficult Abdul Aziz.[4] Eventually, because there were no other logical candidates, they gave tacit approval to his becoming ruler despite his questionable character. They believed that under normal circumstances, murder should exclude a candidate from succeeding as ruler (Rush 1991: 491). A report of August 11 suggested Abdul Aziz felt he had been encouraged to take the rulership because of the active role his half brother Rashid had given him during his reign, and because he felt the Ajmani people liked him (Rush 1991: 492–493). The report noted that Rashid may have been partially incapacitated by the time Abdul Aziz assumed the deputy position which would explain his active role. The report said a close relationship existed between Abdul Aziz and the Ruler of Sharja (Rush 1991: 473) who was Abdel Aziz's maternal cousin (MoBrSo) so they probably spent time with one another as children.

Abdul Aziz ruled Ajman from 1900 until he was killed in February 1910. The murderer was his slave Yaqoor acting on the orders of Muhammad Rashid Ahmad, a relative of Abdul Aziz (his half SiSoSo) (Rush 1991: 523–524) and surprisingly the son of the UAQ Ruler, Rashid Ahmad Abdalla (1904–1922). Muhammad temporarily became Shaikh of Ajman (Rush 1991: 521, 524) despite his UAQ paternity. The case was unusual since Muhammad had no legitimate claim to the Ajmani rule. It is the only time in the history of the emirates that a member of a paramount family from one state attempted to take over the rulership of another state. Second, UAQ usually took Ajman's side in disputes with other states making the murder a decidedly unfriendly act between friends. Third, a niece may have encouraged the murder of her uncle-ruler. Finally, Muhammad, a claimant to the UAQ rule put his own life at risk when he already had a good chance of becoming ruler of UAQ. The best explanation for these bizarre events is that the murder was intended to avenge the death of the previous Ajmani Ruler, Humaid. Humaid Rashid had been killed by his "half" uncle Abdul Aziz. The man who killed Abdul Aziz was the grandson of Abdul Aziz's half sister who was the full aunt of his victim and married to a ruler of UAQ. She probably encouraged her grandson to avenge the death of her brother's son,[5] and to retaliate for her family's treatment by Abdul Aziz when he confiscated their property after Humaid's death. If this explanation holds, the fracture in the Ajmani family falls between progeny of different mothers, those descended from the Ali (UAQ) mother and those from a Qassimi mother. Whatever the explanation, the assassination of a ruler in another state was highly unusual.

When Abdul Aziz was killed, his son Humaid fled to Muscat, but by the third day when the slave Yaqoor and two brothers had been killed and Muhammad had been expelled from Ajman, Humaid returned and was appointed Chief in 1910 (Rush 1991: 524). He soon made a name for himself with the British by rudely returning their ceremonial presents two years in a row. Presented to him in 1911, these gifts consisted of a gold watch and chain, binoculars, and four yards of cloth, which he said were a joke that he would not accept (Rush 1991: 531). Later, he agreed to accept gifts and answer messages more politely in the future.

In 1911, a crisis that had been brewing for some time came to a head. A merchant family from India, the Bin Luta, with pearling interests in the Trucial States of Dubai, Ajman, and UAQ, angered the British by mediating differences among the rulers of these three states, a role the British reserved for themselves. At the same time the Bin Luta were having difficulties with Dubai and decided to take their divers to the more congenial environment of Ajman, thereby causing a problem because of unsettled debts in Dubai. The large number of boats in Ajman also attracted divers from UAQ. Instead of returning the divers as was customary when debts were involved, Humaid encouraged them to settle in Ajman and insisted the Bin Luta be considered Ajmani citizens. Before long, however, he began having problems with the Bin Luta when he started requiring their divers to work on his boats. Eventually in 1924, the British intervened to "safeguard the lives and property of British subjects" and restored the divers to the Bin Lutas that Humaid had taken. Of interest was the fact that the Residency Agent and his son had married Bin Lutas in 1890 and 1910 respectively (Heard-Bey 1996: 460n23). The British as usual focused on the adverse effects on their subjects, without considering the events that led up to the crisis. In this case the British also used the excuse of Humaid's "uncooperative" behavior (Heard-Bey 1996: 214).

In 1920, the Naim Shaikh in Buraimi suddenly decided to claim Ajman. The British rejected his claims based on past evidence, and explained that the Shaikhs—Sultan from Buraimi and Humaid from Ajman, were of the same Naim tribe, being related through their great grandfathers to a common ancestor Rashid.[6] They revisited the history of how the Naim (one branch in particular), came to control Ajman (Zahlan 1978: 46). Although the account is somewhat complicated, it helps understand the claims of the Naim Chief of Buraimi. According to the account, two brothers, Humaid and Khamis, were sons of an early ancestor Rashid. They lived in Buraimi when it was governed by a tribe called Baariya. One brother, Humaid Rashid, who later became the first Naim Shaikh of Ajman, governed a village called Asara. When Baariya rule weakened, Humaid helped his nephew Humaid Khamis, become ruler of Buraimi. On Humaid Khamis's death, his son Ali Humaid became Shaikh of Buraimi while Humaid Rashid continued to rule Asara. A dispute soon arose between Ali Humaid and Humaid Rashid and the latter left Asara to avoid bloodshed. He sought refuge with the Qassimi Chief of Sharja who let him stay in Hirah, a village near Ajman belonging to Sharja. The Shaikhs of Ajman then were from the Bu Shamis, a section of the Naim. Eventually Humaid Rashid expelled them and became Chief of Ajman (Rush 1991: 537–538). His descendents continue to rule Ajman to the present time. On the basis of this long rule, the British rejected the Buraimi Naimi Shaikh's claims.

Abdul Rahman Muhammad, then Shaikh of Hirah and a descendent of the Bu Shamis who had held Ajman originally, decided he also wanted to make a claim on the small emirate. At the end of Ramadan in May–June of 1920, he took over the fort of Ajman (Rush 1991: 537, Heard-Bey 1996: 46 1n. 36). By that time the rule had been in the hands of Humaid Rashid's family for more than a century. But Abdul Rahman calculated that the candidates in the Bu Khuraiban paramount lineages were weak and might be easily ousted. One, Nasir Rashid, had been blinded by Abdul Aziz in his bid for power while the other, son of then Chief Humaid Abdul Aziz, was only about 16 and not yet old enough to succeed his father (Rush 1991: 538). Therefore, the time seemed right for the Hirah Chief to seize power before Humaid's sons became old enough to defend their claims.

With the help of the Ruler of Sharja and the British Residency Agent, Shaikh Humaid convinced Abdul Rahman to leave the Ajman fort and nearby Hirah. But the British suddenly changed their minds when they learned Abdul Rahman had diving debts owed to British subjects, and instead made arrangements for him to return home for another diving season to pay off his debts. He failed to pay his debts and by the end of the year retreated to the fort at Hirah waiting for the attacks promised by the Shaikhs of Sharja and Ajman. Again the British fearing Abdul Rajman would escape his debts intervened to negotiate a settlement between him and the Shaikh of Sharja, whereby he would stay a short time in Sharja and then return to Hirah. He promised not to cause any more problems and the Shaikh of Sharja agreed to protect him. Humaid refused to attend the British mediation session and the British warned him to leave Abdul Rahman alone (Heard-Bey 1996: 215).[7] The British again put their interests first before considering the effects on regional stability. Humaid finally accepted British demands when they bombarded his fort (Rush 1991: 534,535; Zahlan 1978: 163).

Humaid Abdul Aziz died on April 20, 1928 and was succeeded by his son Rashid[8] (1928–1981), who was then 25. Rashid was recognized by the British after agreeing to the usual terms (Rush 1991: 541). They considered him a man of action, well respected among the Bedouin because of his suppression of bandits. They felt he managed "to resist the tendency to petty intrigue, apathy, philandering, and moral bankruptcy which has characterized the once proud families of Trucial Oman since the decline of the pirates . . ."(Rush 1991: 549), a strange comment coming from the British who had suppressed "piracy."

Rashid continued his father's feuds with Abdul Rahman, the Bu Shamis, and Sharja. In 1931, the Bu Shamis attempted to kill Rashid and he tried to kill Abdul Rahman three times. The British arranged an armistice between the rivals that lasted four months and eventually in 1934, Said Maktum of Dubai negotiated an end to the feud (Zahlan 1978: 63–65). This affair with Abdul Rahman shows how the very appearance of vulnerability in a small principality invites outside aggressions. In stronger states, the main challenges to the ruler came from within his own family.

In 1936, Rashid negotiated a two-year oil option with D'Arcy Exploration Company that paid him Rs. 500 a month. Shortly thereafter the British approved the transfer of D'Arcy options to Petroleum Concessions, a company with French, Dutch, British, and American interests. The India Office set up the conditions that all employees and geologists had to be British, that the British Political Resident would provide guidance to the company, that rulers would have to provide guarantees of safe passage, and that the British government would have to approve negotiations with any ruler and the concessions he agreed to (Zahlan 1978: 112). The British deliberately obtained their concessions first before tackling the issue of boundaries that they felt might upset the rulers (Zahlan 1978: 113). Rulers were told the British would only approve agreements with oil companies if they accepted responsibility for the safety of surveyors. If something happened, the rulers would have to pay compensation. Shaikh Rashid in Ajman ignored these admonitions until 1937 when he agreed to the security clause (Zahlan 1978: 113–114). At first the oil companies showed little interest in exploring either Ajman or UAQ, but finally granted an exploration permit for Ajman in 1939 and for UAQ in 1945 (Zahlan 1978: 124).

Despite documented differences, subsequent reports say that relations between Ajman and the British were always cordial. Eventually, a frontier was delineated, and although the Ruler tried to expand it by ordering his men to move the white-washed boundary stones overnight, this ruse was soon uncovered and the boundary stones returned to their former position. Rashid cooperated with other British projects including the establishment of a training camp for Trucial Scouts in Manama, and a British-built dispensary. Rashid's trade in passports that had become one of his main sources of income remained a contentious issue.

Rashid eventually became estranged from his eldest son Ali, who was considerably older than his brothers,[9] and was considered something of a playboy. Among complaints about Ali, were allegations about the morality of his mother whom Rashid had divorced. Before their estrangement, Ali had often served as acting ruler when his father traveled. According to reports, he financed a tour of the world by selling Ajmani passports (Rush 1991: 549). Ali later turned to exploiting the family monopoly over the Ajman-Dubai taxi service (Rush 1991: 550). Eventually his father cut off his allowances and countersigned his son's travel documents and Ali had to pawn his wife's jewelry to survive, much to the "enjoyment of his brothers, Humaid and Nasir, who hate him" (Rush 1991: 550).

Rashid's next wife was a daughter of the paramount chief of the Bani Qitab, who bore at least five of his ten remaining sons. According to British sources, she took every opportunity to "successfully intrigue on behalf of her sons" (Rush 1991: 550). In 1938, when geologists were having difficulty negotiating exploration access with Shaikh Sultan of Sharja because of opposition from the Bani Qitab who controlled the interior, Shaikh Rashid offered his help based on his wife's connections (Zahlan 1978: 145). The Bani Qitab had such strategic importance to oil exploration agreements that other rulers rushed to marry their women and conclude agreements with their leaders. The Sharqiyin of Fujaira tried to elicit their help against the Qawasim, and Shaikh Zaid of Abu Dhabi married a Bani Qitab daughter. Rashid's wife thus gave him a negotiating connection he used with his regional neighbors who needed links to the Bani Qitab. Furthermore, with his wife's Bani Qitab relatives located in the interior and his own land units at critical junctures along the main routes to the Omani Coast, Rashid was able to stage pincer-like pressure on adversaries like the Qawasim.

Shaikh Rashid died a natural death in 1981. He had been popular in Ajman where "his rule was just and his taxes low, all factors that contributed to a rise in the town's importance" He was however, not on particularly good terms with his neighbors (Zahlan 1978: 189). He was succeeded by his second son Humaid (1981 to the present) by his Bani Qitab wife. Humaid was about 50 when he ascended to the rule. He had three wives including one who died in 1980 before he became ruler. The first wife had several children including three sons, Abdul Aziz, Salah, and Abdalla.[10] Abdul Aziz (b. 1952, d. 1975) was killed in an automobile accident and the third son Abdalla in a motorcycle accident in 1993. His second wife Amna Ahmad Ghurair, was the sister of Maha Ghurair, the wife of the ruler of RAK. Amna died at the age of 15 in 1981. Her son Amr became Crown Prince and later married the RAK ruler's daughter (his MoSiDa). Humaid's third wife was Fatma Zaid Saqr Nahyan, granddaughter of Saqr who killed the father of Shaikh Zaid of Abu Dhabi, which explains the unusual marriage of a Nahyan woman outside the family group. Her family lived in exile in Saudi Arabia and Dubai. Fatima's mother, a Ghurair, grew up in Dubai and was connected to the Ghurair women married to the rulers of RAK and UAQ. These maternal relations probably facilitated Fatima's marriage. She bore Humaid a son.

Discussion

One need only note the number of powers lined up in a short stretch of the northeastern coast of the Trucial States to imagine the difficulties of a small principality like Ajman. Between Dubai and RAK, a distance of less than one hundred miles, lie the capital cities of Sharjah, Ajman, and UAQ. These states have small land units scattered across their hinterlands from which they can interrupt travel into the interior. Their populations reside mostly on the coast, while the nomadic groups that roam the interiors are either kin to or traditionally supported them in disputes. Ajman was particularly fortunate in its kin relations with the Naim, one of the largest and most powerful tribes of the interior. As opponents of Abu Dhabi's allies the Dhawahir, they supported Ajman by threatening Abu Dhabi property in Buraimi.

Ajmani shaikhs often married outside the family, seeking to link themselves with families who strengthened their positions with the major powers surrounding them. In the early 1800s as Humaid Rashid was seeking to assuage Qawasim fears about Ajman's independence from Sharja, he married a daughter of the Qawasim ruler. Later their son Abdul Aziz carried on friendly relations with the Shaikh of Sharja. A half sister married the Ruler of UAQ, another small emirate needing support in the region. Her son Rashid (Ruler of UAQ 1904–1922) married the daughter (Mohalf-BrDa) of his "half" uncle Abdul Aziz.

Rashid Humaid who ruled during much of the twentieth century married a woman from the Bani Qitab a tribe located strategically between Abu Dhabi and Dubai and therefore a necessary ally when they mounted aggressions against one another. Her son Humaid became ruler in 1981. His second wife, a Ghurair, was daughter of a wealthy nonroyal business-man whose other daughters married the Rulers of RAK, and UAQ. This marriage was probably contracted at a time when pearling had collapsed and rulers of the small emirates were experiencing financial hardship. Later he married a daughter of the outcast Saqr lineage of Nahyans. She was a niece of Shaikh Zaid's first wife Hussa. Fatima's mother was a nonroyal Ghurair and among her maternal relatives were members of Dubai, RAK and UAQ ruling families. Counting his wives, mother, and grandmother, Shaikh Humaid is linked to wealthy merchant families, the critical Bani Qitab, the Nahyans (albeit from a section that is not in favor), and the Rulers of RAK, UAQ, and the Bu Falasa of Dubai. In addition his sister married the Ruler of Fujaira, and her son is now ruler there. One could not be better positioned from the point of view of marriage relations to form political alliances with all parties in the area. Now, of course, these rela-tionships are not as important as they once were before boundaries were set. Another factor in Ajman's continuing independence was the British inclination to favor groups that limited Qawasim power.

Ajmani rulers were not immune to kin challenges that plagued the rulers of other states, but uniquely in Ajman's case, several challenges came from distant kin. These were based on purported historic claims to Ajman, as in the case of Abdul Rahman, and Sultan Naimi of the Bu Shamis and from a maternally related nephew avenging his uncle. The Ajman rulers also learned the same lesson other rulers learned, that family members require upkeep and attention. Humaid Rashid was assassinated for failing to give kin adequate allowances.

A final point requires comment, given the "duplicitous" acts of several Naimi rulers. These acts of "pragmatic dissembling," are similar to ones already mentioned for rulers of other states. They were accepted behaviors for a vulnerable person or group trying to hide some purpose, or gain some benefit. Changing boundary markers to increase the state's territories is appropriate for a ruler trying to improve the welfare of his people. So are the actions of a chief agreeing to and then disregarding a truce, or making and then immediately breaking an alliance. These acts are excused as a means of promoting the good of a state.

CHAPTER 10

UM AL QAIWAIN'S (UAQ) SURVIVAL UNDER THE MUALLA

Mualla (al Ali) Chiefs and Rulers

- Majid   1775–17??
- Rashid Majid   17??–ca.1820; son of his predecessor
- Abdalla Rashid   from before 1820 until ca.1854; eldest son of predecessor
- Ali Abdalla   ca.1854–1872; eldest son of predecessor
- Ahmad Abdalla   1872–1904; brother of predecessor; natural death
- Rashid Ahmad   1904–1922; son of predecessor
- Abdalla Rashid Ahmad   1922–1923; son of predecessor; killed
- Hamad Ibrahim Ahmad   1923–1929; cousin (FaBrSo) of predecessor; killed
- Ahmad Rashid   1929–1981; cousin (FaBrSo) of predecessor
- Rashid Ahmad   1981–present; son of predecessor
- Saud Rashid Ahmad,   Crown Prince and Deputy Ruler of UAQ; son of the ruler.

Like Ajman, UAQ was part of Qawasim territory until the British recognized its independent status. Soon after the British crushed the Qawasim in 1819–1820, they recognized UAQ and Ajman as independent states.[1] This meant two major coastal towns controlled by independent chiefs would separate the Qawasim ports of Sharja and RAK. Although these chiefs controlled their areas for some time, recognition meant they

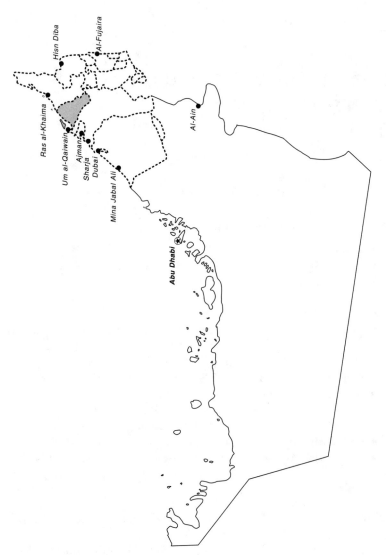

Hisn Diba

Al-Fujaira

Ras al-Khaima

Um al-Qaiwain

Ajman

Sharja

Dubai

Al-Ain

Mina Jabal Ali

Abu Dhabi

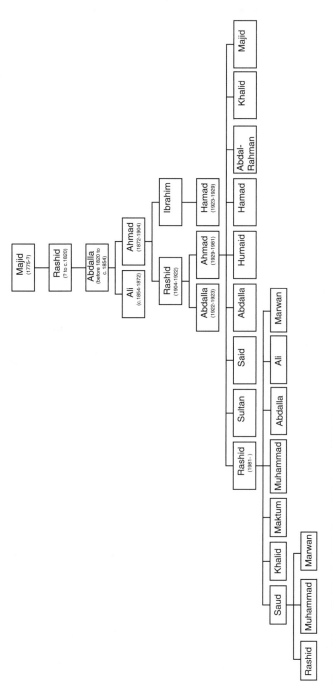

Figure 10.1 Al-Mualla Chiefs and Rulers of UAQ

could appeal to the British when threatened. Like the other emirates, UAQ had its main settlement on the coast near a protected harbor, and a less populated hinterland. UAQ is the second smallest emirate next to Ajman with an area of 300 square miles and the smallest population at roughly 46,000. Like Abu Dhabi it has a physically integral territory, extending in its case about 30 kilometers east into the rich oasis gardens of Falaj al Mualla belonging mostly to the ruling family. The rulers relied heavily on pearling until the industry collapsed, and now live on investments and subsidies from the UAE Government.

UAQ's settled populations were mainly pearlers until forced to revert to fishing and agriculture, unlike other emirates that turned to commerce and trade. UAQ has no oil or gas reserves although at one time it shared with Sharja the revenues of the small offshore Mubarak field. With few resources, the emirate and its ruling family have limited influence in the UAE. Most governing functions in UAQ are carried out by the ruling family.

The rulers of UAQ come from the Mualla, or Al Ali family.[2] From the end of the eighteenth century, there were seven Mualla chiefs with lengthy and two with short tenures. Lorimer (1986) wrote that so little happened in UAQ that there was virtually no internal history. The main events consisted of shifting alliances to defend against external aggressors. Like Ajman it was constantly buffeted by changes in the states surrounding it.

Perhaps the first notable event occurred in 1844, when Sultan Saqr of Sharja was driven to the shores of UAQ by a storm and enjoyed the hospitality of its Chief, Abdulla Rashid Mualla. They became friends and in October 1845, Abdulla supported Sultan in taking over a fortress near Ajman. But the following year Sultan tried to force UAQ to become his dependency and Abdulla quickly made an alliance with Maktum Butti of Dubai to resist the plan. They continued to resist Qawasim aggressions until all the Trucial State chiefs signed a general peace in 1847.

The following year, hostilities erupted between the Qawasim and the Bani Yas, and all the maritime shaikhs sided with the Qawasim except Abdulla who remembered the Shaikh of Sharja's designs on UAQ. He had meanwhile become friendly with the ruler of Abu Dhabi, Said Tahnun, and thus remained neutral (Rush 1991: 556). By 1850, Abdulla relented and sent a small force of fighters to assist Shaikh Sultan against Muscat. This time Sultan remembered the UAQ Chief's rebuffs and seized UAQ's date groves near Shinas and fearing an attack, the UAQ residents stayed home from pearling (Rush 1991: 557). All was quiet for two years until Abdulla joined Abu Dhabi in an alliance with the Dubai Chief, Said Butti, who was being challenged by Maktum Butti's sons, supported by the Shaikh of Sharja.

With the treaty of 1847 largely ignored, the British again focused on maritime peace. On May 4, 1853, Abdulla signed the Perpetual Treaty of Peace with the other rulers that called for cessation of all conflicts at sea (Rush 1991: 557). He died shortly after this and was succeeded by his eldest son Ali who served uneventfully until he died in 1873. His younger brother, Ahmad (1873–1904) then succeeded even though two of Ali's sons were of eligible age. In retrospect it was a significant moment since it shifted the rule from Ali's to Ahmad's lineage where it remains today.

Few events in Ali and Ahmad's rule were newsworthy enough to appear in British reports, other than as general comments on succession. When Ahmad died in 1904, his son Rashid succeeded[3] with the approval of his brothers Ibrahim, Said, and Nasir[4](Rush 1991: 563). The British Resident[5] wrote that the new Shaikh was "young and somewhat blatant." He has lots of money, is a good businessman and loyally supports his followers when they have problems Consequently, many of the Bedouin who were previously loyal to the Shaikhs of Sharja and Abu Dhabi, deserted "the former on account of his weakness and the latter on account of his distance," and have gone over to UAQ. He does not listen to the Shaikh of Abu Dhabi and takes advantage of Sharja's weakness to "annoy him through his wavering Bedouin adherents." The Shaikh of Abu Dhabi consequently was determined to bring UAQ into line (Rush 1991: 591).

In February 1906, after several years of troubles with the Bani Qitab in the hinterlands of Abu Dhabi and Dubai, Zaid I of Abu Dhabi decided to attack them. They appealed to Shaikh Rashid in UAQ who took their side. Fighting was only averted when the Trucial Shaikhs mediated an agreement between Abu Dhabi and UAQ. The Sheikhs agreed that the Bani Qitab, the Ghafalah, and the Bani Kaab would be considered UAQ dependents. Not satisfied with this, Zaid continued to press the Bani Qitab to pay restitution for the deaths they caused during the original crisis (Kelly 1964: 99).

In 1907, when Shaikh Rashid was excluded from an alliance of rulers, Zaid decided to take advantage of his vulnerability by destroying UAQ's forts and Falaj al Mualla where UAQ loyalists had gathered (Rush 1991: 591). He claimed Rashid had to be removed because of the mischief he was causing other states. If the British had not intervened Zaid might well have eliminated UAQ altogether. Zaid wrote Shaikh Rashid a friendly letter inviting him to visit so they could establish more cordial relations. But as soon as Rashid arrived in Abu Dhabi, Zaid imprisoned him. The Political Agent believed the alliance of the other Trucial Shaikhs—Dubai, Sharja, Ajman, and Abu Dhabi—encouraged them to take advantage of UAQ (Rush 1991: 579).

In answer to British letters requesting Shaikh Rashid's release, Zaid replied that he was only dealing with a man who caused problems all along the coast by supplying arms and refuge to exiles (Rush 1991: 586–588). The British increased their pressure and Shaikh Rashid was released on condition he refrain from acts that irritated other rulers (Rush 1991: 592). The conditions included that he should demolish his tower at Falaj, return camels taken from Ajman, and pay blood money for a slave killed in UAQ. He also agreed not to interfere in relations between the Shaikh of Sharja and the Chief of Hamriya, or between Fujaira and Sharja, or between Shaikh Saqr and his dependents in any area (Rush 1991: 594). These conditions suggest UAQ had been playing one group off against another. Since Zaid did not figure in these complaints, the suspicion grows that Zaid was using the discontent of other chiefs to take over a strategic location in the midst of Qawasim territory.

In 1912, Shaikh Rashid had a falling out with his half brother Nasir (or cousin, see footnote) whose mother was "an Abyssinian" (Rush 1991: 599) and therefore "not as popular as others" (Rush 1991: 600). The dispute arose over their father's property where Shaikh Rashid, according to Nasir, was not giving Nasir his full share. Rashid probably feared that if given more resources, Nasir might attempt a takeover. The crisis erupted when Rashid ordered a gardener on their adjacent land not to water Nasir's date trees, and Nasir's son Abdul Aziz made insulting comments about Rashid. Rashid had Abdul Aziz arrested and beaten. Rashid soon apologized but a month later the gardener was murdered, and Rashid blamed Nasir. Nasir took refuge in Rashid's mother's house (presumably because she had more influence than his own slave mother). Rashid eventually took Nasir and his sons to Sharia Court and then exiled his rival to Sharja even though he was not found guilty.

A while later, Nasir's mother asked for maintenance and the Political Resident encouraged Shaikh Rashid to grant it. Nasir had helped the British capture a cache of arms, and as reward they agreed to reconcile him with Rashid, or barring that, force Rashid to pay Nasir's claims. Rashid refused saying Nasir's mother was "only a negress" kept in slavery by his uncle Shaikh Ali and had "no legal or civil rights" (Rush 1991: 608). As for Nasir, Rashid said he had murders to account for, and the precedent set by other shaikhs was not to pay allowances to exiled opposition members. After numerous attempts to convince him to pay Nasir's claims, the British felt they would damage their relations along the coast if they did not take stronger action. Therefore, they sent warships to UAQ and demanded Nasir's money (Rs.10,000) along with an additional Rs.15,000 as fine. After the warships destroyed half of a defensive tower and were ready to demolish Rashid's house, he finally gave in. The restitution was made to Nasir along with Rs. 5,000 of the fine (Rush 1991: 595–644).

UAQ's relations with its nearest neighbor RAK were also less than amicable. In 1919, a Somali sailor was murdered in RAK and his murderers fled to UAQ. Shaikh Sultan Salim of RAK was reluctant to use military force to get them back, and relations between the two neighbors deteriorated. Sultan stationed men to watch his border in case the murderers returned. Meanwhile, Shaikh Rashid sent them to burn and pillage Jazirat al Hamra, a coastal settlement south of RAK. Shaikh Sultan complained to his cousin (FaBrSo) Khalid Ahmad of Sharja who was then nominal Ruler of RAK, but Shaikh Khalid was only too happy to weaken his RAK rival by collaborating with the UAQ Chief. Desperate, Sultan turned to Ajman and Dubai but they were unwilling to become involved. The British eventually warned UAQ to submit to mediation and the threat of war subsided. The British ordered Sultan to pay compensation for the Somali himself and threatened to send a warship if he refused (Zahlan 1978: 58). As Zahlan notes it was the ruler's responsibility to protect the rights of his people, but the British often restricted his ability to do so through their interventions. It became increasingly difficult to maintain his authority over his shaikhdom and win his people's respect (1978: 58–59).

The main exception to the largely peaceful succession in UAQ occurred in August 1922 after the death of Shaikh Rashid of pneumonia with only his mother and her slaves present. Many family members were already estranged from him and they soon split on who should succeed him, his son or a brother. Most UAQ men were still out pearling so Rashid's slaves took over his house and sent word to Falaj al Mualla to inform his eldest son Abdalla, who was about 18 or 20. They kept the news from Rashid's brothers, Ibrahim and Said. Abdalla returned to town with 20 Bedouin, and called for 100 more from the Bani Qitab. They prevented the uncles from entering the town and the townspeople, seeing this show of force, agreed temporarily to let Abdalla take control (Rush 1991: 647). One uncle, Ibrahim, stayed in Falaj while the other, Said, remained in RAK. The latter's son, also Abdulla, whose wife was the late Shaikh Rashid's daughter, was both brother-in-law and cousin to the new ruler. Because of his potential for trouble he was kept under house arrest in UAQ (Zahlan 1978: 39).

When the Political Resident tried to mediate, Abdulla Rashid refused to make peace with his uncles or resolve inheritance claims with the rest of the family. He remained on especially bad terms with Ibrahim's sons. By this time he had alienated most of his relatives, including his paternal grandmother who was his uncle Said's mother. Said left RAK for Ajman to stay with his ruler-cousin, and many UAQ residents secretly visited him there including his brother Ibrahim (Rush 1991: 652). The situation remained thus until the pearling crews returned.

A year later, the Political Resident wrote asking the Residency Agent whether the problems in UAQ were resolved. The Agent responded that Abdulla had gained the support of most of the inhabitants and only the two uncles, Ibrahim and Said, in RAK still opposed him, maintaining that they were owed inheritance from Rashid's estate (Rush 1991: 657). Rashid had been relatively wealthy, and enough may have been at stake to continue their resistance, or they were keeping their claims to rule alive.

Abdalla only survived a year in office before he was killed on behalf of his cousin (FaBrSo) Hamad Ibrahim (1923–1929). In a seemingly unrelated event on October 10, 1923, a slave of Shaikh Abdalla named Ashur Nubi stabbed a Nejdi man in the bazaar and the victim had complained to Shaikh Abdalla. When the Shaikh spoke angrily to Ashur, the latter attacked him. Shaikh Abdalla's younger brother, Ahmad who was only 14 at the time, ran to the spot and shot the slave and then placed guards in the towers of the house while his brother lay dying (Rush 1991: 663). According to reports of the Residency Agent, after burying Shaikh Abdalla, the cousin Hamad Ibrahim, managed to deceive Abdulla's young brother Ahmad and take over Government House. Seeing this and the fact that the slave Ashur recovered, married Hamad's slave, and went to live in his house, caused the family to suspect that the event had been organized by Hamad (Rush 1991: 664). By November, Hamad had made peace with Ahmad and his uncle Said (Rush 1991: 666) and ruled for several years.

In February of 1929, ostensibly because of a dispute between Shaikh Hamad and his blind uncle (FaBr) Abdul Rahman, the latter's servant Said, and another man killed Hamad and captured the fort of UAQ. Initial reports claimed Ahmad Rashid (brother of Hamid's predecessor, the murdered Abdalla) and Abdulla Said (paternal cousin of Shaikh Hamad) scaled the wall of the tower, entered it and offered Abdul Rahman and his men safe passage but they refused. During the night, they set fire to the fort and bombarded it until it was destroyed and some of the residents killed. Ahmad Rashid (age 18 or 21) was then appointed ruler (Rush 1991: 673), thus returning the rule to Rashid's line.

Later reports contradicted this earlier account although the results were the same. In the later version, Ahmad Rashid and his nephew Abdulla Said were joined by Abdalla Rashid of UAQ and the Shaikh of Sharja. A UAQ resident admitted that Abdul Rahman and his servant were burnt to death intentionally to keep them from revealing the real story. The involvement of the Shaikh of Sharja was suspected because upon hearing of Hamad's death he went to pay condolences to Ahmad—surprising everyone because he was not related to the UAQ rulers and therefore would not be expected to attend the condolences (Rush 1991: 675). People interpreted his visit as an effort to persuade the new ruler to expel Khalid Ahmad, the ex-Ruler of Sharja who by then had taken up exile in UAQ. It eventually became clear that Ahmad had orchestrated the death of Hamad as revenge for the death of his brother. Because the British strongly disapproved the killing of rulers, Ahmad tried to cover up his involvement. The British Commander of the Lupin reminded the new UAQ ruler that he was expected to abide by earlier treaties where the Shaikh of UAQ and Khalid Ahmad agreed not to intrigue in Sharja (Rush 1991: 675–677).

By the mid 1930s, after the decline in pearling, most rulers of the Trucial States were looking for other avenues to increase their earnings. In UAQ the main options were fishing and agriculture. Shaikh Ahmad was interested in expanding agricultural production and asked the oil companies to look for underground water in his territory, but the companies failed to find water. By 1936, oil concessions had been signed with five of the Trucial States but UAQ and Ajman were considered of so little importance they were ignored. When they were ignored in a second round of negotiations, the Resident complained to Petroleum Concessions that others might come in with agreements to undercut their influence. Subsequently in March 1939, Petroleum Concessions made exploration agreements with Ajman and in 1945 with UAQ (Zahlan 1978: 124). Like the other rulers, Shaikh Ahmad resisted British efforts to build an airfield on his territory and the British responded by threatening the destruction of his fleet. However, before this happened, he let them survey for the facilities and was pleased to learn that the UAQ was unsuitable for a landing strip (Rush 1991: xxi).

Overall, Shaikh Ahmad was a good leader, gradually winning the respect of his people. He reportedly consulted with members of his *majlis* before making any major decisions. Those who were influential in these discussions were his brothers-in-law, Abdalla Said (who was also his cousin—FaBrSo) and Abdalla Nasir (also his FaFaBrSoSo), his brother Ali Rashid and the brother of his predecessor, Ahmad Ibrahim (his FaBrSo). These individuals represented the lineages of all the remaining contenders for UAQ rule, including the more distantly related Abdalla Nasir who was grandson of the final ruler (Ali Abdalla 1853–1872) before the rule shifted to the lineage of Ahmad Abdalla (1872–1904). The fact that they all attended his *majlis* suggests their general satisfaction with and willingness to identify with his regime. He managed to bring to an end the violent overthrows that followed Rashid Ahmad's death.

By the 1930s, UAQ's main source of wealth in pearling had been severely curtailed and the rulership probably was not the key prize it had once been. A British report of 1958 noted that UAQ was a small state, governed simply by its Ruler, Shaikh Ahmad and members of the ruling family who had been assigned various functions in the government. The state caused few problems and other than poverty had few difficulties. "The Ruler is a man who combines piety with good living and, as well as being the gourmet of the Trucial Coast, he is looked up to and respected by all the other Rulers for his personal qualities, which have enabled him in the past to settle many disputes between them" (Rush 1991: 697).

Shaikh Ahmad's 52-year reign ended with his death by natural causes in 1981. He was succeeded by his son, Rashid Ahmad, who ruled into the 21st century. Rashid's eldest son Saud is the designated Crown Prince and Deputy Ruler of UAQ.

As usual, marriage strategies give us an insight into the political thinking of the UAQ chiefs. The first known marriage was that of Ali Abdalla (1853–1872) who married a daughter of Abdulla Sultan Qassimi, the Governor of Sharja (1848–1855) under his father Sultan Saqr, the Ruler of Sharja. Her brother, Humaid Abdalla, was ruler of RAK (1869–1900). Although the exact date of this marriage is unknown, we do know Ali Abdalla was born before 1828, and therefore was probably ready for marriage around the mid- to late-1840s. In 1844 (see above) Sultan Saqr of Sharja and Abdulla Rashid of UAQ had become acquainted when Sultan's boat washed up on the shores of UAQ. In 1845, Abdulla supported Sultan in a military foray near Ajman but the following year their relationship deteriorated when Sultan tried to take over UAQ. With the exception of short periods in 1847 when there was a general peace, and 1850 when Abdalla supported Sultan against Muscat, their relations were tense. It is likely therefore, that Abdalla married his son Ali to the granddaughter of Sultan either during their short friendship during 1844–1845, or a few years later in an attempt at reconciliation when their relations were strained. This one marriage conveniently linked the UAQ ruling family to Qawasim neighbors in RAK and Sharja.

Ali's brother Ahmad (1872–1904) also married a sister of the RAK ruler Shaikh Humaid (1869–1900) but he later divorced her in 1882 (Rush 1991: 558). It is not clear whether she was the same sister of Humaid who married Ali, or whether the British reports confused Ahmad with Ali. Ahmad was also married to the daughter of Humaid Rashid (Ruler of Ajman 1838–1841, 1848–1873). Her brothers, Rashid (1873–1891) and Abdul Aziz (1900–1908) were both rulers of Ajman. Ajman usually sided with UAQ on issues of common interest and therefore these marriages would be a natural way to maintain close ties. In the unstable situation created by the fragmenting of the Qawasim empire, the smaller emirates benefited from joining forces to maintain their independence. This Ajmani marriage added the third small emirate[6] to the list of UAQ allies. If we look at these marriages as Shaikh Abdalla's choices, the two sons alone brought him connections to the ruling families of all three northeastern Gulf emirates: Ajman, RAK, and Sharja, in some cases through more than one linkage and over more than one generation of rulers. It would be difficult to find marriages that in theory at least would have positioned UAQ better in its neighborhood. They were not as well positioned however with Abu Dhabi and Dubai. At the time, Abu Dhabi was trying to extend its influence up the coast and was unlikely to have wanted any binding alliance with UAQ to interfere with its designs. In any case, the Nahyan did not normally marry their daughters into families of lesser chiefs.

Ahmad's son Rashid (1904–1922) was the next to became ruler, at the age of 29. His mother was the daughter of the Ruler of Ajman who died in 1872, and the sister of the Ajmani ruler during part of Rashid's tenure. Probably with his mother's encouragement, Rashid married the daughter of his mother's brother, Abdul Aziz Humaid, Ruler of Ajman (1900–1908) and sister of Humaid, Ruler of Ajman (1910–1928) during the rest of Rashid's tenure. These links to the Ajmanis were well established by the time Rashid took office and he simply continued to maintain them. However, their "close relationship" did not prevent the Ajmanis from siding with other Trucial State rulers and almost obliterating UAQ in 1907 when Rashid provoked them.

After first marrying a royal wife—albeit from another state—Rashid married a Baluchi woman from the serving classes who bore four of his five sons.[7] This was a less threatening second marriage for the first royal wife and her family, since a servant would not have been considered a serious competitor. However, as happened in this case, the blue-blooded heir from the royal wife did not survive long, and a younger brother from the Baluchi mother ruled for a half century. The violent period in UAQ history (see above) occurred during this period after Shaikh Rashid's death.

Abdalla succeeded his father for a year until killed by Hamad Ibrahim (1923–1929) who ruled for six years. The succession then returned to Rashid's lineage with the ascension of Ahmad Rashid (1929–1981), son of the Baluchi wife. At 14, he had shot the slave who killed Abdalla, and a few years later participated in the plot to kill Hamad. Ahmad married his uncle Nasir's daughter, probably before the death of Hamad around the mid-1920s based on the date of birth (1930) of his second child. By 1923, when his brother Abdalla was killed, Ahmad was the main hope to restore the rule to the Rashidi branch. Although only 14 then, he could have been married in the next few years. Indeed it is likely that his marriage to Nasir's daughter and his sister's marriage to Said's son were a calculated strategy to coalesce three branches of the family behind Ahmad. The Nasir and Said branches with Ahmad were the only ones left with the legitimacy to oppose an incumbent.

Shaikh Ahmad died in 1981 of natural causes after a long reign, and his second son Rashid Ahmad (1981 to the present), born in 1930, succeeded him. Rashid would have been about 50 when he became ruler. Shaikh Rashid married twice. One wife whom he must have married in the late 1940s or early 1950s when he was around 20 years old was Shamsa, sister of Juma Majid, one of the five wealthiest Dubai merchants. Shaikh Rashid has seven or eight sons and four daughters. One daughter married Faisal, the son of Rashid's elder brother, Abdalla, who was skipped over in the succession. Abdalla held prominent positions including Chairman of the UAQ Municipality. Another daughter married Butti Maktum, whose father remained close to the Dubai rulers through his wife's connections as the sister of the ruler. This marriage filled in the Dubai gap in UAQ's network of relations with neighboring ruling families. Only Fujaira and Abu Dhabi were missing and members of these ruling families were married into the ruling family of Ajman and therefore had indirect marriage links to UAQ.

The marriages of Shaikh Rashid's daughters to a paternal cousin and to a branch of the Dubai ruling family conform to conventional wisdom that women should marry within the family or to outsiders with the same or higher status.

The eldest son of Shaikh Rashid, Saud, born in 1952, is Crown Prince and Deputy Ruler of UAQ and more typical of a younger generation of ruling family males received considerable schooling outside the country. He went to Shuwaikh boarding school in Kuwait, Shouaifat school in Beirut; Oxford, and then the University of Cairo. In 1987, he married Somaya Saqr Qassimi, daughter of the Ruler of RAK. He is reported also to have married a Syrian but that marriage is not usually mentioned. He has at least four sons: Rashid, Muhammad, Marwan, and Ahmad. His mother, Shamsa Majid, and his wife's mother, Mahra Ghurair are related.

A number of marriages in the smaller emirates have recently involved maternal relatives. According to conventional wisdom, these marriages accentuate affectionate private ties, and strengthen the position of the bride and her maternal relatives over the strategic, public interests of the husband's family. These marriages are appropriate in periods of stability when strategic, political, and military links are not as essential. The other perhaps more important reason is that the pool of preferred candidates tends to be limited in smaller emirates, and families would rather strengthen their ties with known outsiders such as maternal kin as opposed to "unknown" outsiders. Finding marriage partners for royal women is a major concern for reasons noted before. The situation is exacerbated when a particular royal family is over-supplied with females in relation to males. A complicating factor is the growing understanding that health risks may be associated with generation after generation of close-kin marriage. Some smaller paramount families now debate whether royal women should be given a chance to marry even if it means a nonroyal husband. The situation is particularly acute in RAK where an overabundance of daughters causes a problem but it is also important in other small emirates where the pool of marriage candidates is limited. The tendency to marry children in age rank from oldest to youngest means the candidates often run out before younger women marry.

Discussion

The situation of UAQ is similar to that of Ajman. The rulers of both emirates were continually preoccupied with maintaining their independence from the more powerful states surrounding them. Both were one-tribe states—the Naim in Ajman and the Mualla in UAQ, and were consequently unlikely to assimilate willingly into the populations inhabiting neighboring states. Their locations made them vulnerable to the ambitions of more pow-erful emirates and more positively for them, coveted allies of rulers having issues with other states. Fortunate for them also was the fact that the British intervened frequently to protect them from other states. Indeed, early British recognition of Ajman and UAQ, a byproduct of wanting to weaken the Qawasim, served importantly to maintain their independence. In what seems contradictory to its welfare, UAQ went out of its way to cultivate its nuisance value with neighbors by giving sanctuary to their opponents and carrying out raids against their property. This however guaranteed them a presence at almost every bargaining table where they used their ability to provoke as a negotiating point in exchange for other advantages. Finally, UAQ rulers like rulers of other small emirates used marriage as a key strategy in establishing political relationships with ruling families around them. They contracted three main types of marriage: those that allied them with other ruling families on the Persian Gulf coast, those that consolidated ties within the branches of the Mualla family to support specific contenders, and those that garnered more revenues for the ruler in the face of the disastrous decline in pearling. Over their history, they continually linked themselves with most of the ruling families of the northern emirates. These links provided quick channels of communication when they needed help.

UAQ's location between the Qawasim towns of Sharja and RAK and its large protected harbor made it a logical stopping point on the coast.

When Zaid of Abu Dhabi was hoping to extend his influence north, UAQ became a natural focus of his attention. In recent times UAQ and RAK have had good relations largely because of the kin connections between the two rulers' wives and the intermarriages between the two families. Adding to this is the empathy developing among rulers of emirates financially dependent upon the UAE Federation and Abu Dhabi's largesse.

The largely peaceful succession of the Mualla rulers can probably be explained by four factors: (1) The small and relatively unimportant role they played in regional politics; (2) The homogenous nature of the residents who with few exceptions were all members of the same tribe; (3) the limited resources they possessed during much of their history; and (4) The external threats by their neighbors that encouraged internal cohesiveness. Removing the two rulers who were killed in office, each of the remaining six rulers served for 30 years on an average.

The succession was contested violently only during the 1920s after Rashid Ahmad died and his sons, and his brothers and their sons disrupted the smooth transition. Several factors explain why this period was so contentious: (1) There were a number of legitimate contenders for the throne of UAQ—always a dangerous situation—who may have seen their chances slipping away; (2) The British were unlikely to recognize any new emirates on the western coast, and therefore the recognized rulers occupied a finite number of influential positions; (3) At that time, Shaikh Rashid was fairly prosperous through his pearling ventures and thus the property implications of becoming UAQ's ruler were considerable; (4) By the end of Hamad's rule, as pearling declined, any source of stable income looked attractive including the potential for oil revenues that only rulers received. No one knew at the time that oil would not be discovered in UAQ.

CHAPTER 11

THE SHARQIYIN AND PURSUIT OF FUJAIRAN INDEPENDENCE

The Sharqiyin Chiefs and Rulers

- Matar
- Muhammad Matar
- Saif
- Abdalla Saif★
- Hamad Abdalla   Chief between 1888–1932; son of predecessor
- Saif Hamad   Chief between 1932–1938; son of predecessor
- Muhammad Hamad   Chief between 1938–1952; ruler 1952–1974; brother of predecessor
- Hamad Muhammad   Ruler 1974–present; son of predecessor

★ Various sources call him Abdalla Khamis or Abdalla Saif

Fujaira is a small emirate with 3 percent of the population and 1.5 percent of the landmass (440 square miles) of the entire UAE. It is relatively poor because of the absence of oil resources. In some ways it is unique, including that it is the only emirate located on the Gulf of Oman. Its territory comprises four noncontiguous land units including Fujaira and small towns located on the Shamaliya coast, north of Oman. The Shamaliya stretches from Dibba in the north to Khaur Kalba in the south and includes inland valleys that empty from the Hajar mountains into the Gulf of Oman. The mountains trap rainfall that makes agriculture possible. Its economy is based on fishing, trade, maritime services, agriculture, and some tourism.

194

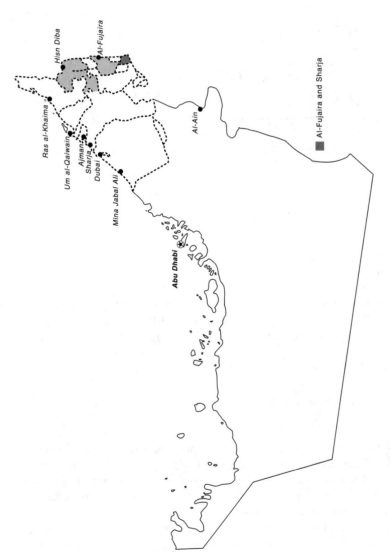

Hisn Diba

Al-Fujaira

Ras al-Khaima

Um al-Qaiwain
Ajman
Sharja
Dubai

Al-Ain

Mina Jabal Ali

Abu Dhabi

Al-Fujaira and Sharja

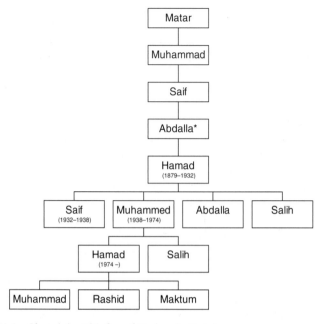

Figure 11.1 Sharqiyin Chiefs and Rulers in Fujaira

* Different sources call him Abdalla Khamis or Abdalla Saif, but this seems to be the accepted version.

Fujaira's strategic advantage is its location as the only emirate outside the Persian Gulf where shipping can be controlled by the straits of Hormuz. Overland Fujaira controls the entrance to Wadi Ham, a major route between the coasts. For most of its history the overland routes have been difficult and dangerous to traverse. An asphalted road was completed only after the UAE was established in 1971.

For over a century and a half, the chiefs of Fujaira pursued the single-minded effort of gaining British recognition for their independence. Unfortunately they were of little interest to the British in establishing maritime peace in the Persian Gulf or in frustrating Qawasim hegemony there. In seeking their goal, the Fujairan chiefs attempted to expand their control over as much of the Shamaliya as possible. They exploited their nuisance value with powers like Sharja, RAK, and Ajman that controlled towns of the Shamaliya, and developed links with others who supported them. Above all they tried to remain a factor in the affairs of the Trucial States to show that although they occupied a remote location they were still an important presence. Virtually all the ruling families of the other states had properties in the interior or along the coast of the Gulf of Oman—some given to them by chiefs of the area. The pleasant valleys, orchards, and unusual plant life made it an agreeable place for residents of the Persian Gulf Coast to go for vacation, away from the monotony of the desert.

The ruling family of Fujaira comes from the Hafaitat section of the Sharqiyin, one of the largest tribes in the Trucial States. The Sharqiyin resided exclusively in territories controlled by the Qawasim. At the start of the twentieth century, they constituted the largest group to inhabit villages of the Shamaliya, although two-thirds of the residents belonged to other tribes (Heard-Bey 1996: 73). The Sharqiyin trace their origins to Yemen and to the Azdite group of Arab tribes descended from Fahim Malik who migrated to the Shamaliya over 2,000 years ago following the collapse of the Marib Dam. The Shihuh, a tribe living in the remote mountainous interior north of RAK, are descended from a brother of the Sharqiyin's ancestor, Shahha Malik. The Sharqiyin belong to the Hindawi as opposed to the Ghafiri faction that divided the tribes of Arabia (Hellyer 1994: 34). Thus it aligns with Abu Dhabi and the Muscati Omanis rather than the Qawasim. The Sharqiyin are Shafi as opposed to other Sunni schools of Islam followed by the other emirates.

The earliest recognized Sharqiyin chief[1] was a man named Matar who is believed to have had at least one son, Muhammad Matar. Lorimer notes that in 1808, this son assisted the ruler of Muscat in taking Khaur Fakkan, a village north of Fujaira, but that their forces were quickly expelled. Muhammad had a son Salih about whom little is known, and possibly a son, Khamis, who may have been father of the next chief, Abdalla (Khamis, or according to other sources, Abdalla Saif). Over the nineteenth and first half of the twentieth centuries, the Sharqiyin chiefs fought for control of the main Shamaliya towns—Dibba, Kalba, and Khaur Fakkan. Their powerful neighbors, the Qawasim and the Omanis, at different times supported them as allies or adversaries in their efforts to control these areas.

Fujaira's location on the Gulf of Oman isolated it for centuries from much involvement in the affairs of the Trucial States. Compounding its isolation was a mountainous range that prevented easy access between it and the other emirates. At times its isolation proved advantageous in fending off aggressors from the western coast, especially the Qawasim who controlled several settlements of the Shamaliya. The agricultural character of the interior and its polyglot seafaring communities made Fujaira's interests more akin to those of Oman. Together they challenged Qawasim control over towns of the coast until their authority was stabilized after Fujaira gained independence in 1952.

The Shamaliya region went through an especially troubled time during the nineteenth century. The regional powers with sizeable forces—the

Omanis, the Qawasim, the Wahhabis and the local Sharqiyin—vied for control over the main Shamaliya towns with their rich commercial and trading potential and villages on the strategic passes to towns of the Persian Gulf. The Shamaliya's location north of territories claimed by the Chiefs of Muscat or Sohar made it particularly important as an entry to the eastern Gulf, since Oman was largely unassailable because of British support. At the start of the nineteenth century, the northern Shamaliya was claimed by the Qawasim who were often at odds with the Omanis. In 1798, Sayyid Sultan of Muscat attacked holdings of the Qawasim Shaikh at Dibba but the Sharqiyin and the Naqbiyin (the second largest tribe) joined the Qawasim to prevent Dibba from falling into Omani hands. The Qawasim retained control to the displeasure of the local people.

Several years later, the Qawasim also took control of nearby Khaur Fakkan and established a base from which to launch attacks on shipping in the Gulf of Oman. Worrying that this takeover might signal further aggressions on towns to the south, including Fujaira, in 1808, the Ruler of Muscat, with his uncle in Sohar, and the local Sharqiyin Chief, Muhammad Matar, captured the Qawasim stronghold in Khaur Fakkan. But Sultan Qassimi immediately retook it (Rush 2 1991: 449). The following year, the Wahhabis decided to extend their influence into the region by taking the forts of Fujaira, Bitna, and Khaur Fakkan and Shinas, further south. Alarmed at the incursion into Omani territory, the British assisted the Omanis in 1810 in recapturing Shinas. The other forts were less important to Muscat.

The Ruler of Muscat must have recovered the rest of the Shamaliya from the Wahhabis sometime later, since by 1831, the Qawasim Shaikh Sultan Saqr was demanding either Dibba or Khaur Fakkan as his price for assisting the Muscat Chief in attacks against the Chief of Sohar. The constant pressure from the Qawasim was part of their effort to reestablish themselves after Britain's humiliating destruction of their fleet in 1819–1820. Muscat rebuffed Shaikh Sultan and a year later in 1832, the latter took advantage of the Muscat Chief's absence in Africa to seize Dibba, Khaur Fakkan, and Kalba. By 1835, Qawasim attacks from those towns on Omani boats caused the British to retaliate, and eventually Khaur Fakkan and Kalba were returned to Muscat. The Qassimi Shaikh however continued to claim the towns, and joined forces with the Chief of Sohar in 1850 to seize Shinas, Kalba, and Khaur Fakkan. When the Chief of Muscat returned from Africa in 1851, Sultan withdrew his support from the Sohari Chief and Shinas and Sohar fell again to Muscat. However, Sultan continued to hold areas of the Shamaliya he had won with the Sohari Chief's support (Rush 2 1991: 450). What is striking is the extent to which towns passed back and forth among the powers of the region with supportive roles played variously by the British and local tribes. The aggressions were largely aimed at capturing strategic locations from which to strike at enemies. The Shamaliya thus became the battlefront for maritime control, waged in this case between the British and Omanis on one side and the Qawasim on the other. The Sharqiyin in Fujaira, as pawns in the struggle, sought opportunities where possible to advance their interests.

The Shamaliya continued to be held by the Qawasim. In 1855, a tribe related to the Sharqiyin, the Shihuh, attempted to overthrow the Qassimi Governor of Dibba, a grandson of Sultan Saqr. He suppressed the uprising and the Shihuh retaliated by murdering him as he traveled between Dibba and RAK. This led to a general war between the Qawasim and the Shihuh taking some pressure off the Shamaliya towns.

When the Qawasim leader died in 1866, Abdalla Saif, then Sharqiyin headman of Fujaira village, took advantage of the weaker leadership under Khalid Sultan and refused to pay the customary tribute to Sharja. His act is recognized as the first major step on the road to Fujaira's independence (Zahlan 1989: 105). Abdalla was the first Sharqiyin chief to effectively mobilize the warring groups of Sharqiyin in defense of Fujairan independence. Indeed, some reports say the whole Shamaliya rose up in revolt and the Qawasim may not have recovered the area until after Shaikh Khalid's death in 1868.

Khalid's successor in Sharja, Salim Sultan immediately reestablished a garrison in Dibba to defend the region. Meanwhile, the Chief of Fujaira allied with the Shihuh and when the Qawasim garrison plundered the Shihuh, they besieged the fort and prevented the Qawasim from traveling through nearby passes.

In 1876, the Shaikh of Sharja sent 50 armed men by boat around Musandam Pennisula into the Indian Ocean to recapture Dibba. Salim defended this incursion by claiming that sending reinforcements to his own territory by sea did not technically violate the maritime peace. The British Resident reported testily that every time armed bodies of Arabs went to sea they quickly forgot the original object of their voyage and committed depredations on any unprotected boats they met. The Shihuh and Sharqiyin retaliated by attacking Dibba and the fighting stopped only when a British warship appeared on the scene. The Qawasim meanwhile, mounted a force of 800 men who approached from the Shinas side and captured the fort, killing 36 persons and taking 30 prisoners (Rush 2 1991: 559). A peace was arranged by the Shaikh of Sharja's brother and the Sharqiyin returned to paying tribute to Sharja (Rush 2 1991: 561).

In 1879, the Fujaira inhabitants expelled the Qawasim representative, and appointed Hamad Abdalla Sharqi, chief without consulting Sharja.

When a party informed Shaikh Salim in Sharja he imprisoned them and sent a garrison of Baluchi troops to Fujaira. Several local inhabitants were seized and exiled to Abu Musa Island. Hamad fled to Muscat and in April 1879, asked the Sultan for protection (Rush 2 1991: 561). Although tempted because of his animosity toward the Qawasim, the Sultan equivocated and eventually refused. By the end of the year, Hamad returned and led an uprising that ousted the Qawasim from Fujaira (Rush 2 1991: 452).

In January 1880, reporting on these events, the Political Agent in Muscat said Hamad had retaken Fujaira "partly by treachery." The Qassimi Chief requested British permission to retake Fujaira through an expedition by sea, later changing it to "by land" to allay British sensitivities, and asked that a British vessel be sent to keep the Sultan of Muscat from siding with Hamad (Rush 2 1991: 561). The British, as always suspicious of the Qawasim, replied that the Qassimi Chief needed to explain how Fujaira had originally been taken, what were their rights there, and whether seizing the territory in the first place had not been a breach of the maritime truce. They asked why they should allow him an exception to recapture the town (Rush 2 1991: 560). The Qassimi Shaikh did not pursue the matter further.

Meanwhile, the Sultan of Muscat countered Qawasim claims to Fujaira by saying that the area was not, nor had it ever been, a territory of the Qawasim and that it was an independent tract between two countries. He admitted that although he had drafted an agreement with Hamad Majid, the Qassimi appointed governor, he said it had gone no further than that. The Sultan did not claim Fujaira himself but wanted to prevent his Qawasim enemies from controlling a town so near his borders. He offered a concession that appeared to contradict his previous statements when he said he thought the tribute that Fujaira normally paid the Qawasim was still their due. He also felt that the attack on Fujaira by Shaikh Salim of Sharja had not been justified. The British decided there was no compelling reason to change Fujaira's status (Rush 2 1991: 559–560) since it would only increase Qawasim influence in the area.

In another account, the Sultan, Sayyid Turki, wrote the Political Agent to explain that the Fujaira fort was built by his ancestor, Sayyid Sultan Imam Ahmad, who had given it to the local inhabitants to defend. He, Sayyid Turki, did not claim a right over the people or the place, and appealed to the British not to allow Sharja to claim it. The Sharja Ruler produced an 1871 paper sealed by Sayyid Turki stating that all territory west of Khaur Kalba, except Khasab on the Musandam Peninsula, belonged to the Qawasim. Sayyid Turki answered that he had already repudiated the document written before he became Sultan, because it had been given in understanding of an exchange of services, and the Qawasim had not honored their side of the agreement (Rush 2 1991: 561).

In May 1881, the Political Resident summarized the status of Fujaira saying that the coast where Fujaira was located extended about 45 miles from Dibba to Kalba, and appeared to have been part of Muscat before it was taken by the Qawasim 50 years previously. Although the British had earlier sent a naval force to preserve the integrity of the Sultan's lands, they had not compelled restitution of the territory, even though there was no flaw in Muscat's claim. The Resident concluded that Muscat had a dormant claim and the Qawasim an active claim to its possession. He noted that the local people played one power off against another in trying to achieve independence from both. He ruled there should be no question of complete independence for Fujaira since it would "be undesirable in the general interest." In subsequent reports the British explained that they did not favor a proliferation of states in the area and therefore saw no need to recognize Fujaira.

The unwillingness of the British to recognize Fujaira meant a solution had to be found for the problem of jurisdiction. The people of Fujaira eventually submitted to arbitration by the Qassimi Shaikh of RAK, and the Political Resident approved as long as the settlement would result in the submission of Fujaira to Sharja, and payment of customary tributes (Rush 2 1991: 562). In 1881, the Fujairan Chief agreed to his dependence on Sharja, and Colonel Ross officially recommended against Fujairan independence (Rush 2 1991: 453).

In 1883, when Saqr Khalid became ruler of Sharja, he found the Shamaliya coast divided into two fiefdoms, one adjoining Dibba governed by his uncle (FaBr) Ahmad, and the other, Khaur Fakkan, governed by his uncle (FaBr) Majid, both appointed by their brother, the previous ruler. It was not in Saqr's long-term interest to let these potential rivals establish a power base but he was afraid to challenge their authority directly. So he encouraged the "turbulent character" (Lorimer 1986: 781) Hamad Abdulla of Fujaira to capture Gharaifa on the Coast, and Bitna in Wadi Ham on the only direct route to the Shamaliya from the Persian Gulf. However, instead of turning the territories over to Saqr as was intended, the Fujairan Chief approached Saqr's rival, the Chief of RAK for support. The Sharja ruler backed down for fear of offending his RAK cousin, but did not try to regain the towns.

Hamad[2] succeeded his father Abdalla as Chief of Fujaira in 1888.[3] He was chief during Fujaira's expansion between 1888 and 1932 or 1938.[4] In the early part of this period, between 1888 and 1901 when Fujaira temporarily gained independence from Sharja, there were several efforts by outsiders to take control of Shamaliyan towns (Rush 2 1991: 453). In 1893, at the instigation of the Shaikh of Abu Dhabi, Shihuh tribesmen of the Musandam attacked and destroyed the Qawasim fort at Hair, and in the following year, when the Qawasim Shaikhs of Sharja and RAK wanted to rebuild Hair, the Shihuh tribesmen prevented that from happening. During 1896–1897, a Qassimi was murdered at Fujaira and the Shaikhs of Sharja and RAK sent an expedition to collect blood money.

In 1900, when the Shaikh of RAK died, Fujaira was left without protection against the Ruler of Sharja and the town was absorbed again into Sharja. At the time, the Shamaliya was being administered by sons of the two original Qawasim grantees, in the north by Rashid Ahmad and in the south by Hamad Majid.[5] In 1901, the Shaikh of Sharja sent the Chief of Fujaira Shaikh Hamad, to deal with the Shihuh over a murder that occurred in Dibba. But Shaikh Hamad took advantage of the situation, and made an agreement with the Shihuh to foment disturbances that would put the relative of the Shaikh of Sharja, the Governor of Dibba, in danger. Hamad claimed he was retaliating for Shaikh Saqr's rebuff in solving the robbery of visitors to Fujaira committed by Qawasim allies, the Awamir and Bani Qitab. Saqr told Hamad he should solve his own problems, so Hamad turned to the Shaikh of Dubai. With Saqr's permission, the Dubai Chief helped Hamad retrieve the plundered property.

Although by 1901, Fujaira had successfully asserted its independence from Sharja (Rush 2 1991: 83) Hamad still could not obtain recognition from the British. The following year, when Saqr Khalid was preparing to send Bedouins against Fujaira and the Rulers of Dubai and Ajman were indicating their support for Hamad, the Political Agent in Muscat decided to pay Hamad a visit. Hamad told him the agreements executed in 1881 did not apply to Fujaira and he therefore would not accept the suzerainty of Sharja. The British meanwhile restrained the Chiefs of Dubai and Muscat from supporting Fujaira (Rush 2 1991: 454). The Residency Agent convened a conciliation council in Sharja but Hamad refused to attend. Shaikh Saqr took a harder line and in November 1902, ordered two Fujairan residents killed as they returned from Ajman. He complained to the British that the Fujairan Chief had reasserted his independence and was being protected by the Dubai Shaikh (Rush 2 1991: 570).

The Political Resident counseled patience but Hamad remained angry because he had received no compensation for his murdered friends (Rush 2 1991: 586). The Shaikhs of Dubai and Sharja discussed the issue and decided the problems between the Qawasim proxies, the Mazari tribes, and the people of Fujaira should be settled through mediation by Shaikh Maktum of Dubai (Rush 2 1991: 575). In December 1902, the Political

Agent tried to effect a reconciliation onboard a British boat off Fujaira, but Hamad would not attend. The British abandoned their efforts, saying that as long as there were no problems at sea, the two sides could do what they wanted. Shortly thereafter, in early 1903, the British abruptly changed their minds and decided to recognize the Shamaliya from Dibba to Khaur Kalba as belonging to Sharja making clear it was not an independent state or connected to Oman. In April of the same year, the emboldened Saqr moved against Fujaira, and Hamad sued for peace, but little changed (Rush 2 1991: 455).

In a new effort to win independence from Sharja in 1905, Hamad claimed a large area of the Shamaliya by adverse possession, including the villages of Bitna, Gharaifa, Marbab, Qaraiya, Qidfa, Saqamqam, and Sufad, as well as Fujaira. By that time, the Ruler of Sharja was getting older and had lost interest in Fujaira. A year later in 1906,[6] when Zaid I of Abu Dhabi arbitrarily claimed Fujaira as his dependency, there was no objection from Saqr (Rush 2 1991: 456).

Shaikh Saqr died in 1914 and was replaced in Sharja by Khalid Ahmad. The Sharqiyin leader Hamad, saw it as an opportunity to press his case again, and in 1916 asked the Ruler of UAQ to help him reconcile with Khalid. Khalid's father had governed Dibba and his brother had governed Kalba, and Khalid himself had been Regent of Kalba from 1907 under Saqr. Hamad thought he might therefore better understand the region. However, the British became suspicious when Hamad decided to visit UAQ and warned its Shaikh not to get involved. When Hamad asked to visit Sharja, the Resident Agent refused, saying that if he did so the Shaikh and his ally in UAQ might arrest him (Rush 2 1991: 590–591). One can speculate from previous actions that the British prevented this reconciliation because: (1) They reserved for themselves the role of mediator between states and may have feared the unpredictable consequences of the meetings; (2) They wanted to discourage Fujaira's hopes of independence; and (3) They may have wanted Fujaira's challenges to Qawasim hegemony to continue.

During the 1920s, Fujaira's fights with the Qawasim intensified, and eventually the Fujairan Chief took over much of the Shamaliya that Sharja had claimed, although again he did not gain British recognition. Angry at their position, he refused to board a British vessel in 1925 for talks with the Political Resident about Kalba and other coastal villages he wanted to control. He remained defiant even after the British demolished his fort at Fujaira, ostensibly because of a slavery case. During the bombardment, Hamad's daughter-in-law died but Hamad remained obdurate and when the British imposed a fine on him, he forced the people of Kalba to pay it (Rush 2 1991: 83).

Hamad died in 1932 but before we move on, we need to look more closely at Kalba.

The Fight for Kalba

Kalba deserves special attention for the fact that it was one of the most contested towns of the eastern coast in the nineteenth and twentieth centuries. Located at the southern end of the Shamaliya near Oman and close to Fujaira, it was a difficult town to defend, yet one of the most strategic in controlling the region. Kalba's story is additionally interesting for the unabashed role the British played in its politics and for the unusually detailed account of one of its critical successions.

As was their practice, the rulers of Sharja appointed family members to serve as administrators of Kalba. In this capacity, Majid Sultan Qassimi (Kalba 1871–1900) was Wali under his brother Shaikh Salim, while his son Hamad (Kalba 1900–1903) succeeded him and also governed RAK in 1900 for his cousin (FaBrSo) who was then Ruler of Sharja. At Hamad's death in 1903, his son, Said, governed Kalba, and became its first independent ruler in 1936.

The story starts at a time when the British were urgently seeking landing facilities on the Coast, and suddenly relented on the issue of refusing recognition to states of the Shamaliya. In 1936, Britain decided to recognize Kalba as an independent state (Rush 1991: xxi) with Said Hamad Qassimi as its ruler, and agreed to support Said if other shaikhs threatened him. They also accorded him the important status symbol of a three-gun salute in recognition of his independence and his positive attitude about the landing facilities. Shaikh Said agreed to abide by all agreements binding upon other Trucial Chiefs, to provide land for the facilities, permit a godown for petrol, a house for airmen and passengers, and moorings for flying boats and a beacon, and in return he received rent, a subsidy for himself, and payments for guards and protection (Rush 2 1991: 457–465). For Said, these payments were no small achievement at a time when chiefs had few steady sources of income.

This arrangement was a blow to the Sharqiyin who had unsuccessfully fought for Fujaira's independence. The Kalba agreement not only gave independence to the town closest to Fujaira, making it off-limits to Sharqiyin influence, but also put a Qassimi who was Hamad's bitter enemy, in charge. At one point, to mollify those affected by Kalba's new status, Said married a daughter to the Fujaira Chief and another daughter Aisha, to Khalid Ahmad, the deposed Ruler of Sharja (her FaFaFaBrSo). Said himself was married to the sister of the Ruler of RAK. These marriages connected three Qawasim branches that were rivals of the Shaikh of Sharja, and gave them a mutual connection with Fujaira's Chief who wanted independence from Sharja. These links became important in events that unfolded.

Even after he became Chief in 1903, Said lived in Ajman, leaving the administration of Kalba to a trusted slave, Barut. In the 1920s, he went to live in Kalba (Heard–Bey 1996: 91). In April of 1937, while visiting Khaur Fakkan, he fell ill from a boil on his neck and by the next morning was dead. On seeing her father nearing death, Aisha took two slave women and traveled to Kalba. There she gathered the slaves and guards and posted them in towers of the fort to prevent the news from spreading and to defend against anyone trying to take over by force. She appointed Barut who had been running Kalba, as acting Emir. After consulting with family members and town elders she sent a party of men to notify her husband Khalid Ahmad, visiting his brother in RAK. Although they were cousins of the Shaikh of Sharja, they kept the news from him. In notifying her husband who was a distant relative, Aisha in effect bypassed her younger brother. There are several possible explanations but the most likely were probably personal. Her husband had earlier been deposed as Ruler of Sharja (1914–1924) and his position taken over by Sultan Qassimi. Aisha wanted to keep the news from the Sharja Ruler, knowing he might ask for Kalba's return to Sharja. She may have seen the death as an opportunity for her husband to secure a fiefdom, one that eventually would benefit her children. She may also have felt that as an ex-Ruler, her husband possessed the prestige to maintain Kalba's independence.

Khalid Ahmad immediately sent his brother and several followers to determine whether the inhabitants of Kalba would accept him as ruler. He awaited the answer in Ajman since he was forbidden from entering the town after its independence because of his previous connections there (Rush 2 1991: 474). Meanwhile Khalid's brother Rashid, Governor of Dibba, heard the news and left for Kalba hoping to become ruler. When he reached Khaur Fakkan the Naqbiyin Chief told him he could stay one day if he was planning to pay condolences, but should leave immediately if he wanted to take over Kalba (Rush 2 1991: 470). Rashid replied that he only came for condolences and would return to Dibba.

The Shaikh of Sharja, Sultan Saqr, soon heard the news from the crew of a fishing boat and sent a message to his cousin (FaFaBrSo), the Shaikh of RAK Sultan Salim, asking for confirmation. The British wrote that the Shaikh of RAK had intentionally kept the news from the Shaikh of Sharja in order to get a first chance at gaining the shaikhdom of Kalba himself, since the wife of the Shaikh of Kalba was his sister. On May 5, 1937, the Shaikh of RAK arrived in Sharja, and the British commented that the two Shaikhs would do their best to make trouble for anyone who became Shaikh of Kalba (Rush 2 1991: 470). The Shaikh of Sharja sent his clerk and another aide to Kalba but they were stopped at Hair.

In May of the same year, the people of Kalba choose the 12 year-old son Hamad, of the deceased Shaikh to succeed him. The RAK Shaikh, hoping to gain influence in Kalba through his sister's connection, encouraged the local Naqbiyin Chief to oppose Hamad's selection. The Naqbiyin as rivals of the Sharqiyin had been key players in gaining Kalba's independence. The RAK Chief told the Naqbiyin Chief he would appoint him Emir of Khaur Fakkan and Kalba, and would send Rs.150 to the servant Barut to make an inventory of the estate of the deceased and keep it safe. The Shaikh received three polite but firm replies: one from the family of the deceased saying the inventory could be deferred until the summer, the second from the minor son saying he had succeeded his father, and the third from the Naqbiyin on behalf of the people of Kalba saying Hamad had succeeded his father (Rush 2 1991: 473).

Meanwhile, Khalid Ahmad left Ajman and with the help of the Shaikh of UAQ, secretly began gathering a force to enter Kalba (Rush 2 1991: 474). On May 19, 1937, he camped with his men outside Kalba where he planned to wait until the people demanded he become Shaikh. The idea was not so preposterous since Khalid was generally liked by the local people (Rush 2 1991: 475) and his candidacy by that time was supported by the Shaikh of Sharja whom the people of Kalba had rejected in June.[7] As a result, the Shaikh of RAK was rebuffed in his efforts to gain a foothold in Kalba. Under the guise of helping young Hamad (his sister may have been Hamad's mother) he set about gaining influence in the town (Rush 2 1991: 476–477). When the British were informed that young Hamad was the people's choice, they insisted that a regent needed to be named to approve treaties on his behalf, but they refused to accept Barut because he was a servant and not a notable. The people of Kalba replied that there being no suitable notable available they had elected Barut (Rush 2 1991: 479–480).

On September 13, the Residency Agent went to check on the situation and found that the Naqbiyin had brought Khalid Ahmad to Khaur Fakkan, given him an oath of allegiance, and then surrendered the town to him. After hearing this, the notables in Kalba told the Residency Agent they wanted to make Khalid Ahmad Regent of Kalba. He was summoned from Khaur Fakkan and on September 17, 1937, the Kalba notables pledged their allegiance to him (Rush 2 1991: 483–484).

However, before turning the town over to him, the notables made him agree to the following:

1. To recognize Hamad Said as legal Shaikh of Kalba
2. To turn Kalba over to Hamad when he attained a satisfactory age
3. To pay a monthly allowance to him of Rs.150
4. To bear house expenses and pay all gifts to the Bedouin and others as during Shaikh Said's lifetime
5. To accept Barut as Wali and not interfere with the slaves or family of Shaikh Said
6. To not impose any duty or tax that had not been imposed by Shaikh Said and to treat all the people—Naqbiyin, Zaab, and Kalba people— with the same privileges they enjoyed during Said's lifetime
7. To not allow deported people back into Kalba or encourage people hired by him to do anything detrimental to the people's rights
8. To keep accounts of all income and expenditures
9. To take actions only with the approval of the notables (Rush 2 1991: 485–486).

The agreement ended the crisis and Khalid became Regent, making him the most influential authority on the coast—in charge of Khaur Fakkan and Kalba, and supervising Dibba—while his rivals in RAK and Sharja no longer held influence in these towns (Heard-Bey 1996: 89). Meanwhile, the Sharqiyin kept a low profile as their rivals, Khalid and the Naqbiyin, solidified their hold over Kalba.[8]

As Khalid became increasingly infirm, he left the affairs of Kalba and Dibba "in the hands of a dissolute nephew," Humaid Abdullah, while he resided in Khaur Fakkan. In 1948, the people revolted against him and pro- posed that another member of the Qawasim family, Humaid Muhammad Salim, be appointed regent. In January 1948, this action was precipitated by a rebellion in Khaur Fakkan against Khalid that ended when Khalid's men reoccupied the town in July (Rush 2 1991: 499). By September, Khalid and his nephew also regained control of Kalba (Rush 2 1991: 500). The notables' proposal to reach into a third Qawasim lineage for a regent sent a clear message to Khalid. Members of the proposed lineage had previously caused Khalid's overthrow as Ruler of Sharja, and consequently the Kalba notables were signaling support for a similar action when he did not deal with his nephew's mismanagement. The forcible recapture of Kalba put this idea to rest.

Following the death of Khalid's dissolute nephew, Hamad Said, now 24, forwarded letters in February 1950 to the British from Kalba notables asking that he become ruler of Kalba and Khaur Fakkan (Rush 2 1991: 506). The British Representative, arriving in Kalba, found a strong dislike for Khalid among the people. Hamad was willing to work out an arrangement to govern under Khalid's supervision, but the notables were afraid that because of Khalid's senility he might appoint another disastrous person like his nephew with the same results. The nephew had "squandered such income as the shaikhdom possessed, had sold the rifles of the fort guards, had extorted money from the merchants, and in return, had given neither security nor justice." He did not prevent many of the residents from being kidnapped by Bedouins and sold into slavery (Rush 2 1991: 511).

The British representative took Hamad and Khalid Ahmad on a trip to Fujaira to show that they were willing to work together (Rush 2 1991: 511). But Hamad still claimed the people were threatening to desert Kalba if Khalid remained regent. The Representative called together four notables chosen at random to hear their opinions. They all complained that Khalid was responsible for Kalba and Khaur Fakkan falling into decay during his regency. He had taken PCI oil payments (Rs. 24,000 per year). and the community's taxes and had not given the inhabitants good government. They wanted the British to recognize Hamad. Khalid could not find notables to argue his case and said he anyway preferred to return to Sharja (Rush 2 1991: 512–513).

The Political Resident visited Kalba in April and saw no "personal defect" that would justify refusing Hamad the rulership (Rush 2 1991: 514). Therefore on June 7, 1950, Hamad was given his letter of approval based on the Resident's satisfaction that this was what the notables wanted and that he was fit to perform his duties. The Resident reported that Hamad was "physically fit" and intelligent and was capable of good government even though the Resident was cautious about guaranteeing his moral character or predicting that he would prove to be a good ruler (Rush 2 1991: 515). The terms of the agreement (Rush 2 1991: 517ff) included an annual pension from the oil concession for Khalid of Rs.10,000 or nearly half—somewhat surprising given his poor service to the towns.

In the following year (1951), Hamad was assassinated by Saqr Sultan, son of the deposed Ruler of RAK (Zahlan 1989: 105). According to the Political Agent, on July 4, Saqr, his brother Khalid Sultan, Ali Amir (Secretary to the Shaikh of Fujaira), and Ramis, a slave of Saqr's father followed Hamad to his room. While he was preparing to sleep they killed him along with his secretary and a young slave. Four men waited outside to take over the fort. Saqr immediately declared himself ruler and had local notables sign that they agreed. The Political Agent Mr. Wilton heard of the affair on July 9, and left for Kalba with some Levies and Saqr's father as security. Mr. Wilton asked Saqr to come talk with him, which he did, accompanied by around 70 followers. At this point, Saqr's father walked out of the camp "going in the opposite direction." At first Saqr explained that he had been forced to murder Hamad because of Naqabiyin complaints against Hamad. The British felt Saqr was not suitable for the rulership since, among other faults, he bribed the men who helped him kill Hamad. The Agent concluded that it would have a bad effect on the local tribes, the Saudis, and the other rulers if the British did not take strong actions to resolve the issue. He suggested that they mount an expedition to expel Sultan Salim and his sons from the Coast (Rush 2 1991: 528).

Meanwhile, Saqr began explaining Hamad's death somewhat differently. He said that when he went to Kalba to visit his cousin he found Hamad was treating the people badly. The people asked Saqr to counsel Hamad, "as we are of one family and the sons of one father (metaphorically) . . ." Although Saqr counseled Hamad, he refused to refrain from his negative activities and threatened Saqr, at which point Saqr "took prior action and killed him . . ." (Rush 2 1991: 25).

The Political Resident and Mr. Wilton disagreed about what to do (Rush 2 1991: 526–529). One believed Saqr should remain Shaikh of Kalba, while the other disagreed and believed he should not be allowed to consolidate his position. In the meantime they both refused recognition and withheld the oil revenues usually given a ruler (Rush 2 1991: 531). By November, there was still no resolution. One issue was a lack of obvious successors since there were no more males in Hamad's line (Rush 2 1991: 534). Four generations of the same lineage had occupied the Kalba position from the time Shaikh Majid was appointed by his father, Sultan Saqr. An active presumption existed that this line was entitled to rule the town. Selecting Saqr would reward the perpetrator of an assassination, while selecting anyone else would show favoritism. The Resident suggested Saqr's father, Sultan Salim, as a candidate but the Foreign Office felt him undesirable because of his past history (Rush 2 1991: 532–533).

In an attempt to resolve the impasse, Saqr sent letters in May 1952, asking the Sultan of Muscat to intervene. Saqr wanted the Sultan to invoke British sympathy by saying that his (Saqr's) and his brother's wives were sisters of the late Shaikh Hamad, and would become destitute if asked to leave Kalba since they depended on the oil revenues halted by the British (Rush 2 1991: 544). The Sultan dutifully followed Saqr's instructions and wrote "that the family is poor and that once Saqr leaves Kalba neither he nor the deceased Shaikh's sisters whom he and his brother have married will have a penny, and they hope that the two ladies at least will get an allowance" (Rush 2 1991: 535).

A few days later, the Ruler of Sharja confirmed that none of the sisters of Hamad were married into the family of Shaikh Sultan Salim. One was married to the Ruler of Sharja's uncle, Humaid Saqr who had died recently. The second was married to Humaid Saqr's son and the third was unmarried. Saqr's creative dissembling failed (Rush 2 1991: 424). He probably counted on the privacy surrounding women to keep the correct information from either the Sultan or the British. All three women in fact lived in their late brother's house in Kalba (Rush 2 1991: 423, 553).

With the concurrence of the Council of Trucial States rulers, the British decided to revoke Kalba's independence and return it to Sharja. They sanctioned force to remove the usurper (Rush 2 1991: 79). With the threat of a British warship, Saqr left Kalba on May 12, 1952 for Muscat. The next day the Ruler of Sharja (Saqr Sultan Saqr)[9] took over Kalba. That day, Kalba's principal spokesman told the Political Agent that the townspeople preferred the exiled Saqr and would resist attempts by the Ruler of Sharja to enter the town (Rush 2 1991: 551). The Agent suggested the spokesman meet the Ruler of Sharja in Fujaira and when he did, he reiterated the people's refusal to accept him as ruler.

Meanwhile the Sharja Ruler's advance force secured Kalba and he entered the town without difficulty. The Agent found most people in the bazaar pleased with the outcome, though one said that since the decision was already made by the British they had no alternative. Apparently one problem they had in accepting the Ruler of Sharja was that the late Shaikh's sisters accused him wrongly of being implicated in their brother's murder (Rush 2 1991: 552).

Shaikh Saqr of Sharja proposed his uncle Rahma Abdul Rahman as Wali of Kalba, a man the British had problems with over slave trading (Rush 2 1991: 552). The British noted wryly that, Shaikh Saqr sometimes had "an unfortunate inability to rise to the level of the occasion, and he frequently appeared more pre-occupied with the fact that the retiring Shaikh (the other Saqr) had taken with him the late Ruler's motor car, rifles, and most of the household goods and chattels, than with the immediate problems of instituting a good and stable government in Kalba." The Agent appended a list of confiscated items and stated that this constituted a valid reason not to give the exiled Saqr a pension (Rush 2 1991: 553). Afterward the two Saqrs reconciled their differences. On October 6, the exiled Saqr Sultan Salim married the sister of Sharja's Saqr Sultan Saqr. A terse note in British reports said the couple would live in Dhaid until his crime was forgotten and then go on to Dubai (Rush 2 1991: 267, 554).

Why had Saqr murdered Hamad and taken over Kalba in 1951 when there was no reason to suggest he was entitled to the position?

One possible explanation was that Saqr's father, the Ruler of RAK, was overthrown in 1948 and replaced by a nephew, Saqr Muhammad. This event seriously diminished the 24 year-old Saqr's hopes of becoming RAK ruler. The ambitious young man may have seen Kalba as an easier target. There were no heirs-apparent and no logical candidates once Hamad was gone. In this scenario, Saqr may have hoped to secure an independent emirate. In personalized rule, only one person at a time achieves the ultimate authority of becoming ruler. Thanks to British actions, by that time, there was a major gap in status and finances between rulers and local chiefs. Kalba had attracted the similar attention of the deposed Ruler Khalid Ahmad, when he was looking for a fiefdom.

Fujaira Reemerges

Even during Kalba's short independence in the late 1930s, its power was limited by Sharqiyin control of surrounding areas (Heard-Bey 1996: 94) and Naqabiyin influence in Khaur Fakkan. During his chieftainship, Hamad Abdalla expanded Fujaira's influence to the west of the Hajar mountains and northward to areas controlled by RAK. When Hamad died in 1932, his son Saif Hamad (1932–1938) succeeded him. Saif's mother was the daughter of Hamad Majid Qassimi, the Governor of Kalba from 1900–1903. Saif died six years later and was succeeded by his brother, Muhammad Hamad, aged 30.

During the 1940s, Fujaira became more influential than Kalba under Muhammad's rule. In 1950, Muhummad again asked the British to recognize Fujaira's independence, this time saying he needed independent status to contract oil leases. A description of Fujaira at the time shows its strengthening position. The report says that the area controlled by Shaikh Muhammad included Fujaira town and its surrounding areas with the mountains and valleys of Wadi Ham and Wadi Najdiyayna, the coastal towns from Kalba to Khaur Fakkan with the villages of Ghuraifah, Mirbah, and Gidfah, and the coastal strip from Bidyah to Diba-Ghurfah and the mountains to the west, including the town of Habhab. As the report notes, all these areas were previously controlled by the Qawasim family who were the main power "until our suppression of piracy early in the nineteenth century" (Rush 1991: 599). Now, none of the Qawasim rulers "even claim to exercise any control over Fujaira territory," and although the Muscat Ruler claimed the Shaikh as his subject the British did not recognize the claim nor did he actually control the area. Quoting experts, the report believed that this part of the coast was not likely to find oil. However, it proposed recognition and noted that Shaikh Muhammad had been cooperative, was generally respected, and had a good influence over local tribesmen.[10] At 650 square miles, Fujaira was larger than some of the existing Trucial States. The report concluded that the current situation was unsatisfactory since it left a substantial part of the coast outside the supervision of any recognized ruler. However, it was unlikely that any oil company would be interested or even that the Saudis would want it (Rush 2 1991: 599). Despite his arguments for granting independence, the Resident reported he was against increasing the number of Trucial shaikhdoms and felt it was better to let things remain as they were for as long as possible (Rush 2 1991: 600). None of the boundaries of Sharja, RAK, and Muscat had been defined as yet (Rush 2 1991: 83) and there seemed no need to grant Fujaira a status that might be contested later.

But soon Fujaira gained so much influence the British feared that if they refused it independence the Chief might seek protection from Ibn Saud or "otherwise embarrass the British" (Rush 2 1991: 83). The Political Resident noted his favorable impression of Shaikh Muhammad as being quiet and having "excellent manners." The Resident informed Shaikh Muhammad that in principle, the British Government was willing to recognize him and they were only awaiting instructions about the documents to sign (Rush 2 1991: 601). In March 1952, Muhammad accepted British terms and on March 23, Fujaira became the seventh Trucial State (Rush 2 1991: 602, 608).[11] Shaikh Muhammad requested assurances that he could deal with oil companies and was told he could do so as long as the British concurred (Rush 2 1991: 611). In turn, he agreed to the free passage of Levis through his territory (Rush 2 1991: 604).

The Sultan of Muscat had no objection to Fujaira's recognition but the Shaikh of Sharja, repeated his historical claims to Fujaira and said the British decision disappointed him (Rush 2 1991: 613). He was supported by the Shaikh of RAK (Rush 2 1991: 615). The British replied that 50 years had passed since they agreed to protect Qawasim claims and in an aside the Political Agent said he felt the Qawasim chiefs would do nothing to oppose Fujaira's recognition (Rush 2 1991: 614). Shaikh Muhammad received a three-gun salute (Rush 2 1991: 613) to recognize his status, and Fujaira finally achieved the full independence it had been working toward, for almost a century.

A report commented that independence had been achieved both as a result of the weakening of the Qawasim in Sharja and the persistence of Shaikh Hamad in Fujaira who pushed for this outcome until his death in 1938. He mobilized the Sharqiyin against the Qawasim in Sharja and Kalba and defied the British "whom he held in undisguised contempt" (Rush 1991: xx). The expansionist efforts of the Sharqiyin did not stop with recognition, nor did their relations with the Qawasim improve. In 1954, the British reported an incident at Masafi instigated by the Ruler of Fujaira (Rush 2 1991: 621). Shaikh Muhammad explained to the Political Agent that he simply built a wall across a road many miles inside RAK territory. The Agent added sarcastically that Muhammad covered the wall with pill-boxes and constructed defenses in depth back as far as Masafi with the "sole and apparently laudable object of shooting at the Ruler of RAK." Muhammad said he had no intention of shooting the British state's representative and would issue strict instructions that only the Ruler of RAK should come under attack. The Political Agent told Shaikh Muhammad that his behavior required drastic change (Rush 2 1991: 623) and before he left the interview Muhammad agreed to withdraw his men, to open the road, to demolish the towers in the hills, and to pay a Rs. 3,000 fine (Rush 2 1991: 622). In an aside during the interview he admitted to being mistaken in his handling of the affair. The Political Agent commented that it was dis-turbing to think any ruler would believe such behavior was normal but then added that Fujaira's remoteness and recent independence had to be taken into consideration, since such methods were only recently "quite fashionable on the coast" (Rush 2 1991: 623). Shaikh Muhammad felt so abject about his behavior that after returning from Pilgrimage he consid-ered abdicating and putting "a popular anti-Qassimi landowner" in his place (Rush 2 1991: 625).

During the period 1952–1959, British reports dealt mainly with Shaikh Muhammad's health problems, his travels for medical services, his efforts to obtain oil concessions, and his continuing problems with the Shaikh of Sharja in the Khaur Fakkan and Kalba areas. Muhammad attempted to lure the Musaid, the largest subsection of the Bani Qitab, away from their chief's allegiance to Shaikh Saqr to bolster his position, but failed (Rush 2 1991: 629–631). With the border settlements, Muhammad's claims to parts of the Qawasim empire were secured and he made considerable effort to ensure the loyalty of residents there. The reports said he continued his dis-putes with the RAK Ruler, Saqr Muhammad (Rush 2 1991: 631) after he seized power in 1948.

Shaikh Muhammad remained independent ruler until his death in 1975. Although he was illiterate, Muhammad knew the communities of his emi-rate well. He consolidated his ties with the Ruler of Ajman by marrying his daughter, but remained on bad terms with the Ruler of Sharja who con-trolled Kalba, and continued to intrigue against him (see Rush 2 1991: 234). His older son Hamad succeeded him at the age of 27 and has contin-ued to rule Fujaira into the twenty-first century. He is a graduate of Henon Police Academy in London, and served as the first UAE Minister of

Agriculture and fisheries from 1971–1974. During his youth (in the 1950s and 1960s), he lived with his maternal grandfather, Shaikh Rashid of Ajman. He married Fatima Thani Maktum from a lineage related to the ruling Maktums of Dubai. They have several children including at least three girls and three boys. The current Deputy Ruler of Fujaira is from another branch of the Sharqiyin family (Hamad's great-grandfather's brother's grandson), Hamad Saif Surur Saif. The ruler's younger brother, Salih, is chairman of Fujaira's department of industry and economy and other posts.

Discussion

For Sharqiyin leaders the main interest over a century and a half was expanding control over the coastal towns of the Gulf of Oman and gaining British recognition for Fujairan independence. Recognition was essential to legitimize territorial claims and eliminate costly challenges to the chiefs' control. In the 1950s, legitimacy also brought with it the authority to make oil exploration agreements and contract other commercial ventures. Why was it so difficult for Fujaira to gain recognition? There are several reasons: (1) Other regional powers were also interested in preserving their strategic and commercial interests on the eastern coast. Sharja and RAK claimed many coastal towns and villages between the two coasts. Oman claimed prior rights, but took no steps to exert direct control. Even Abu Dhabi and the Wahhabis tried at various times to annex the Shamaliya; (2) The Naqbiyin who were rivals of the Sharqiyin sided with outsiders when it was to their advantage, and with the Sharqiyin when outsiders were gaining too much influence; (3) The arbitrary policies of the British meant they were unwilling to grant independence to Fujaira when they saw no political or administrative advantage to themselves, and possibly a disadvantage in setting a precedent others might emulate.

Kalba's case illustrates the arbitrariness of British actions. In 1936, after long refusing Fujairan independence, the British suddenly granted the status to Kalba, making the Qassimi governor there, ruler. The main reason was British desire for landing facilities. Later in 1952, when they disapproved the candidate for ruler, they revoked Kalba's independence and it reverted to Sharja. The British recognized Fujaira only in 1952 when they feared Wahhabis or others might be attracted to the growing importance of the Shamaliya and worried they might lose their influence there. They also finally conceded that without recognizing Fujaira there would be no satisfactory authority to take responsibility for the actions of local residents. By that time, the Qawasim had withdrawn, boundaries lines were being defined, and there was no group other than the Sharqiyin actively seeking control. British involvement in the internal affairs of the Trucial States that had been gradually increasing, reached an all time high in the political maneuverings in Kalba.

As a small state battling major powers, Fujaira possessed several unique features that differed from the other small Trucial States. The first—its isolated location far from the Persian Gulf proved both an advantage and a disadvantage. An advantage was its distance from the home bases of its main Qawasim adversaries, over difficult-to-traverse mountain tracks. The Qawasim might send overwhelming force to take over a town of the Shamaliya but when they left behind small garrisoned forts to defend the towns, local people frequently overran them. The second advantage was that the Sharqiyin comprised the largest tribe in the area with significant numbers residing in many of the contested towns of the Shamaliya. Third, they could usually count on the Qawasim's enemies, the Shihuh who lived conveniently on the Musandam Peninsula just northeast of RAK to help defend the towns of the Shamaliya. The Shihuh had common albeit distant blood links to the Sharqiyin that gave a basis for their cooperation. In certain dire cases, the Sharqiyin could also count on their local rivals the Naqbiyin for help. Finally, the Sharqiyin had far-sighted early leaders like Abdalla Saif who coalesced the dispersed Sharqiyin and focused their attention on independence.

On a broader front, Sharqiyin leaders elicited support from allies like Oman, Dubai, and Ajman who were usually happy to see the Sharqiyin engaging the Qawasim on distant territory. The Omanis proved useful allies when it came to determining rights to the Shamaliya. They were so occupied by internal conflicts between Sohar and Muscat, and the Muscat Chiefs' lengthy trips to Zanzibar that their most valuable assistance was verbal support for Fujaira's claims. Even though Fujaira helped Omani factions in their conflicts, the Omanis were less ready to engage forces on Fujaira's behalf, unless Qawasim aggressions becoming a direct threat to their own interests.

The Sharqiyin also benefited both from Qawasim infighting and British efforts to suppress their influence. But frustration over independence caused the Sharqiyin chiefs to rebuff British attempts at mediation several times in order to indicate their displeasure at not being treated well. The rebuffs ultimately showed the British that as regional players they were too important to ignore.

Sometimes their physical remoteness also stalled Sharqiyin ambitions. Much of the time Fujaira simply did not concern the British who were focused on maritime stability along the Persian Gulf. They saw little reason for Fujairan independence when administratively it was easier to work through Qawasim chiefs to control the towns of the Shamaliya. Even when oil exploration became an issue, no one believed commercial quantities would be found in Fujaira. Furthermore recognition of Fujaira was likely to raise issues the British were reluctant to tackle, such as the legitimacy of Qawasim claims to the Shamaliya, the status of other nearby principalities, and the question of borders that had not yet been fully defined. These reservations became less important later when Qawasim control over the Shamaliya weakened and the British felt the Sharqiyin might turn to other powers in frustration.

The Sharqiyin crafted long-term relations with rulers of other Trucial States. By the end of the twentieth century, the Fujairan Ruler had marriage links to the Ruler of Ajman through his mother, and to the Maktums of Dubai through his wife. Both marriages strategically connected Shaikh Hamad to rulers located on either side of his major competitor in Sharja. Shaikh Hamad grew up in Ajman with his maternal relatives and thus was well versed in the politics of that coast. In addition, Ajman had and still has links to the Naim in Buraimi/Al Ain and possesses land units on the main routes to Fujaira (Masfut and Manama). The Naim are an independent tribe with contacts in Sharja, Buraimi, and the coast of Oman (Zahlan 1978). Shaikh Hamad benefited from the ties of his Ajmani relatives to the rulers of UAQ through the Ruler's mother who is a Mualla of UAQ. At several points UAQ support for the Sharqiyin proved critical. The network of Sharqiyin relationships surrounding the Qawasim, made it difficult for the latter to act with impunity. Even more important, was the visibility these links gave the Sharqiyin on the "main" coast to keep their political interests alive.

The cases of Fujaira and Kalba throw light on the personal networks and trust relations that cause some groups to be seen as better mediators than others. Sharja asked Fujaira to mediate with the Shihuh since the Shihuh were distant relatives of Fujaira. Sharja asked their Qawasim relatives in RAK to negotiate with Fujaira. Although Sharja and RAK had their own problems, the fact that Fujaira for a time was a dependency of RAK meant it might have some influence there. The Sharqiyin asked the Qawasim to negotiate with the Awamir and Bani Qitab who for a time had been allied with the Qawasim, but when they refused, the Sharqiyin turned to Dubai where their influence was increasing. The pragmatic nature of these arrangements is striking—even enemies may be asked to perform favors when they have a special influence. Past alignments leave behind so little long-term hostility that these negotiations can be carried on in good faith.

This leads to a related observation that chiefs are reluctant to let bad feelings persist or get in the way of long-term relationships. A chief who mends his fences has more latitude to act than a chief with enemies waiting to take advantage of him. If the Shaikh of Sharja wants to start a fight with the Shaikh of Fujaira, he thinks twice when his neighbors Ajman and Dubai declare support for Fujaira. Adversaries at the end of a conflict commonly make gestures of reconciliation, as for example, when the Shaikh of Sharja who undermined his cousin's effort to rule Kalba, married his sister to his cousin.

Similarly, chiefs move with alacrity to connect themselves with a newly recognized ruler, as happened when Kalba became independent and later when Fujaira was recognized. This is consistent with rulers' interest in maximizing their influence. It also fits with normative expectations for marriages of royal women. A newly independent ruler becomes technically equal to other rulers and therefore it may suddenly become more comfortable to marry daughters into his family.

Finally, the Fujaira/Kalba case suggests that reputation and standing depend more on achieving political results than on the way they are achieved. Much craft including untruths, broken promises, and treachery[12] went into achieving political aims in Kalba, but they seem to have been excused (except by the British) as a normal means by which leaders, especially the vulnerable Qawasim, were expected to achieve their ends.

CHAPTER 12

THE POLITICAL CULTURE OF LEADERSHIP

I am like an old father who heads his family and takes care of his children. He takes
them by the hand and supports them until they have passed through adolescence
—Shaikh Zaid April 25, 1977

This book set out to answer four questions: What is the political culture
of leadership in a tribal society like the UAE? What were the external
factors that transformed the shape of personal rule? How were rulers able to
shift so rapidly from egalitarian rule to a rule requiring hierarchy and
authority? And finally, does a similar political culture exist today and if so
how is it expressed?

The cases showed the political actions of chiefs and rulers during the
nineteenth and twentieth centuries as tribal governance changed from
egalitarian to centralized rule. Throughout this period the political goals of
the various states differed: from Abu Dhabi's expansionism, to Qawasim
efforts to restore their empire, to smaller Ajman and UAQ trying to maintain their independence, to Fujaira's search for recognition. Each pursued
different aims but the strategies they used were roughly similar. We will
start with the changes that transformed leaders' relations with their people.

What Transformed the Shape of Personal Rule?

The three external factors that most impacted personal rule were: (1) The
increasing British involvement in the affairs of the Trucial States;
(2) Urbanization; and (3) The acquisition of huge amounts of wealth by
some of the rulers after the discovery of oil.

Chapter 1 describes how the British substantially increased the power of a handful of chiefs by doing business exclusively through them. Chiefs who had previously ruled through consultation, consensus, and cajoling, but with limited authority, suddenly had to enforce maritime agreements. Once-loyal tribesmen often fled to other chiefs to avoid punishments and fines.

Simultaneously the British limited many traditional functions of rulers such as the ability to wage war, to deal with foreign powers, to raid commercial boats, and to engage in lucrative slave trading. They discouraged the deposing and murder of rulers, a prerogative of ruling families to rid themselves of unwanted incumbents. The British reserved the right to approve successions, requiring candidates to agree to all previous treaties and conditions as well as to accepting British advice. When oil exploration started, the British established the Trucial Scouts manned by locals but commanded by British officers with the job of suppressing conflicts and protecting commercial interests, especially those of British citizens. Also in pursuit of oil, the British fixed territorial boundaries by identifying which tribes had paid taxes to which rulers. Tribes' traditional *dirahs* (the lands where they had rights) came under the jurisdiction of specific rulers making flight an abandonment of territory. Nor did it make sense for rulers to expand their influence by wooing independent tribes on their peripheries. Consultation and consensus were supplanted by British force and the needs of oil exploration. British demands created an awkward position where the chief's subjects, with not much to gain from loyalty and often more to lose, began exerting their independence on issues from Buraimi to removing themselves to economically more lucrative jurisdictions.

The British failed to recognize how rulers used military engagements as a show of strength and support. They also failed to see how overthrowing rulers was a means of removing unpopular incumbents and sharing power among several lineages of paramount families. When oil revenues were eventually channeled through rulers, these super leaders became even more powerful. Their supporters, whose taxes previously kept rulers accountable, soon became dependent upon gifts doled out by the ruler. This situation solidified a paternalistic role for the ruler who decided what was best for his "children-subjects" and punished their infractions. Many of the conflicts that arose in the transition involved kin or tribesmen complaining they did not receive sufficient support from the ruler. Rulers like Shakhbut of Abu Dhabi found it difficult to adjust to the super-father role of doling out allowances and providing social services.

The second factor contributing to authoritarian rule was the growth of settlements along the coast. As long as people were nomadic with trans-portable property, rulers could do little to prevent disgruntled sections from moving to other chiefs. Also when families were scattered in small groups across the desert, they were less likely to come into conflict. If problems arose, tribal elders resolved them on the spot usually without recourse to paramount leaders. Tribal law was invoked upon request rather enforced by authorities.

On the other hand, town residents acquired property that tied them to a location. Even when residing in tribal or ethnic quarters, close contact with people from other tribes as well as other Arab and non-Arab countries, inevitably led to conflicts. Rulers found themselves taking on more authoritarian roles to curb disruptions, especially after the British held them accountable for maritime infractions and damage to British's citizens property. Other elements in settlements that encouraged this authoritarianism were concentrations of wealth, standing militias,[1] protective fortifications, and the fact that towns became the locus of attacks by opposing leaders (Lienhardt in Serjeant and Bidwell 1975: 68–69).

Even so, the older rulers continued to see themselves in their tribal roles where legitimacy derived from the reflected power of satisfied citizens (Heard-Bey/lecture 2004). With time these roles took a paternalistic turn when chiefs like Zaid Sultan of Abu Dhabi with enormous wealth anticipated the needs of his people with public works and social services. Zaid was careful to extend his influence to potential rivals by sharing his wealth, assigning them positions of power, and arranging marriages to encourage closer relations with them.

A third factor—economic change—also forced adjustments in rulers' ways of relating to people From a tax-based system that brought early leaders in contact with many groups, to an intensifying involvement in pearling and slave trades, to the collapse of both these industries and a need to identify other sources of income, rulers were constantly on the look out for revenues to support their activities, until in the case of some of the rulers, oil and other stable sources of revenues made them independently wealthy.

One of the main effects of these forces was a change in the balance of power from Qawasim to Nahyan family superiority. From the eighteenth century, the British were intent on suppressing the Qawasim and were suspicious of any move to regain their pre-eminence as a maritime force on the southern coast of the Gulf.[2] They countered Qawasim moves to expand, while largely ignoring similar efforts by the Bani Yas whom they saw as a useful counterweight. The Qawasim further exacerbated their problems by openly confronting the British while the Abu Dhabi sheikhs pursued their course with greater diplomacy.

By the end of the nineteenth century, several dependencies of the once great Qawasim empire were administered separately by Qawasim branches.

When Sharja's ruler attempted to consolidate them he was rebuffed by the British who saw fragmented power as a positive development. Nahyan history similarly contains conflict among family members over the succession, but the contenders never sought to fragment their holdings as did the Qawasim. Another difference was in the way rulers of the two families related to tribes within their jurisdictions. The Qawasim formed a weak connection with the tribes of the hinterlands and indeed were often at odds with them, while the Nahyan claimed blood links to the Bani Yas tribes and had well-established relations with the independent tribes of their area. When oil was found in small quantities in Qawasim territories and in large quantities in Abu Dhabi, the power differentials between the two became irreversible.

What is "Political Culture" in a Tribal Society Like the UAE?

If governance is based on personal relations more than on formal institutions, what are the characteristics of tribal political systems? Do general social expectations apply to political behaviors, or are rulers judged by a separate set of expectations? This study assumed that patterns of political behavior could be identified from recurring actions of leaders. The patterns should suggest, with reasonable confidence, behaviors likely to appear again under similar circumstances.

Ibn Khaldun explains how the concept of *asabiya* (group spirit) underlies all social relations, and in particular political affairs. Group spirit, he says is a feeling of "affection and willingness to fight and die for one another" (1967: 123). The job of the leader is to inspire in his followers this sense of group feeling so they will fight and die for his causes. This kind of rule works best when two conditions exist: (1) The ruler can engage in face to face contact with people having the authority to commit larger groups in the community; and (2) The players have assets—strategic location, resources, personal contacts, or sizeable groups—to complement partners' assets and give them weight in negotiating exchanges.

Chapter 2 presented three models for personal relations—tribal, family, and outsider—that are familiar to most members of Arab society. They are premised on the assumption that people in a moral society have obligations toward one another. The morality comes from a belief that responsibilities are God-given[3] and not man made as are rights or entitlements. The emphasis on responsibilities rather than rights, gives a qualitatively different feel to personal relations—a straining to contribute to the group, rather than taking from it. It fits nicely with Ibn Khaldun's concept of group spirit.

The tribal model has discrete units—families, tribal sections, and tribes—that at each level are treated equally. Circumstance may require units to aggregate or disaggregate to strengthen the group against enemies or lessen their damage when land capacity is limited. In becoming more powerful or more adaptive, the units keep the essential ability to group and regroup. Strategy comes in assembling appropriate size groups for special purposes.

The family model is authoritarian and hierarchical and thus different from the egalitarian tribal model. Each family member's sets of responsibilities are unique to their age, sex, role, and so on. Older members have authority over younger people who are expected to be more obedient and subservient. All have **fixed** responsibilities—a father's obligations toward his son are different from those toward his daughter, and both are different from those of the son and daughter toward him. The responsibilities of family members in relation to one another are therefore **unequal**. The responsibilities are also **required**—they cannot be redefined under normal circumstances. They are **enduring** because they are expected to last forever. Together they form a tightly-knit fabric of personal relations where the withdrawal of any set of responsibilities, such as the death of a son or a mother leaves a gap.

These tribal and family expectations accomplish two missions. They establish the group feeling that Ibn Khaldun believes is so important to society and rule, and they create clear boundaries. Tribal and family boundaries are in fact boundaries of personal obligation. As members of tribes and families, people have obligations in both circles of relationship. Once the context is set people know what is expected and know also that they will be judged on the extent to which they meet those expectations. People consequently have frequent opportunities to practice being members of tribes and being members of families without any sense of contradiction even though they call for very different behaviors.

The third set of expectations, the outsider model, is protective of the basic units of society—again family and tribe—by distinguishing between insiders and outsiders—between an "us" and a "them." These boundaries again mark sets of responsibilities. From the family or tribal perspective, any relationship beyond its boundaries constitutes an "outsider" one. Outsider obligations differ from "insider" ones in that they are mutable—they can be made closer or more distant. To become closer, the parties settle on mutually understood obligations, such as. treaties, alliances, or understandings to define their relations, or they redefine the context, as when marriages are contracted to encourage outsiders to act more like kin. They can also distance themselves by breaking agreements, failing to reciprocate, or by divorcing a spouse. Agreements with outsiders do not carry the same weight as ones within the tribe or family. It is advantageous for leaders to break agreements with impunity when they are no longer beneficial, since then they can focus on relationships that are more productive. By redefining the boundaries of obligation, leaders can organize their investment in relationships more efficiently. Rulers can, for example, create relationships with outsiders that stress warmth and affinity—more like kin relations—and they can drop them when they want. Leaders' broken agreements and marriages are accepted as sometimes necessary to advance the welfare of their families and communities.

The three models seem contradictory. The tribal model sees society as discrete units organized horizontally with obligations to aggregate or disaggregate according to need. The family model imposes vertical controls and coordination through designated authority figures. The outsider model permits discretionary boundaries that draw people closer or distances them. The first model stresses egalitarianism (tribal), the second hierarchy and authoritarianism (kin), and the third flexibility and options (outsider). In practice, the models complement one another. The tribal leader depends on family patriarchs to commit their well-disciplined groups to tribal goals, and to control their members' behavior so conflicts do not disrupt community life. This gives tribal leaders the space to focus on external concerns. The limited number of patriarchs makes possible the face to face negotiations so essential to personal rule. Families in turn preserve their dignity by being treated equally.

Rulers can select from this flexible tool kit of models to shape personal relations to their will, as long as they frame the context so their behaviors make sense to others. They can activate "tribal" expectations to increase or decrease the weight of their support. They can evoke hierarchical relations if they want cohesive "family-like" relations stressing authority and obedience. They can form alliances with outsiders for longer-term commitment. They can basically define their relationships in ways that meet almost any challenge. By incorporating outsider tribes or rulers into their circles, they can make them insiders as long as they want. Or they can relocate kin to outsider status when they want to retaliate.

The models discussed so far are heuristic abstractions. The section below looks at four practical applications: rulers' relations with various groups, succession, official appointments, and marriages, to show how they are shaped by cultural expectations.

Practicing Personal Rule

The first job of rulers during the 200 years covered by this book was to mobilize supporters for various contingencies, similar to the backgammon strategy described earlier. The needs were modest when leaders were still first among equals and political challenges were limited. A leader's networks could be visualized as a set of concentric circles reaching out as far as his personal relations extended. At each level of inclusiveness, he dominated groups of acknowledged leaders who made decisions for their followers. It is Ibn Khaldun's image of politics, where leaders first dominate groups surrounding them, and then more inclusive groups until they dominate the main groups of the society. A short-cut developed in the tribes, whereby certain families established themselves as paramount families with the privilege of providing leaders. A leader then only needed to dominate his paramount family to be accepted as chief or ruler. The legitimacy of these families was so well established in the emirates that in the period covered here, there were only two times when individuals outside the legitimate branches tried to take over. In both cases a maternal kin relation to the incumbent explains their audacity.

Membership in a tribe, subsection, or family means accepting the obligations implied by membership, just as pledging loyalty to a ruler meant accepting obligations of support. Once a ruler accepted suzerainty, he was obligated to protect and look out for his supporters' welfare. Nonroyals also might put together groups to pursue business and trade but few juggled as varied a network as a ruler. The Nahyans for example, developed relationships with a variety of groups. There were: (1) Their kin who, in theory but often not in practice, should have been the most loyal;(2) The Bani Yas with "automatic" obligations to their paramount Nahyan family coming from purported "kin relations" that were almost certainly fictive; (3) Several independent tribes residing in the greater Abu Dhabi state whose interests often coincided. Although usually loyal, their lack of permanent connection meant they had no long-standing obligation to support the Nahyan. The Nahyan kept their loyalty by including them in decision-making, appointing them to status positions, and in some cases marrying their daughters. These tribes included the Manasir and the Dhawahir; (4) Other tribes with more tenuous links included the Awamir, Bani Qitab, Bu Shamis, and Naim; (5) Rulers of neighboring states who were drawn into short-term agreements when it suited the need. The price of sustaining these links tended to be high with often the need to provide reciprocal support; and (6) Finally, the Nahyan drew in numerous groups through techniques to involve "outsiders," such as hospitality, favors, or marriage. Because of their many permanent and quasi-permanent links, the Nahyan held an advantage over the Qawasim whose more tenuous relations with other groups required them to expend more energy wooing temporary allies and fending off attacks.

People accepted the impermanence of rulers' links to outsiders. Rulers could drop alliances with impunity, or shift sides in a conflict, or deliberately undermine allies with whom they had recently agreed. They fought battles with relatives of in-laws even when marriages had been contracted with the intent of solidifying their interests. "Deceptions" were excused as "pragmatic dissembling" in the belief that a higher morality attached to protecting constituents, pursuing political goals, or saving oneself as the one responsible for the group. The deceptions were viewed as a necessary strategy against the rulers' powerful enemies.

Rulers' relations with kin turned out more problematic than theory would suggest. Kin should theoretically submit to family authorities, but in paramount families kin were the main competitors and it was often not clear whether age or position determined who was the ultimate family authority. Rulers who did not give kin the attention, positions, and allowances they expected, invariably found themselves challenged. Kin complained that rulers spent resources on distant groups and forgot about their nearer kin. The ruler faced a dilemma: if he neglected his kin he was almost certain to face a challenge, but if he gave them resources they might use them against him Most rulers at one time or another experienced the discontent of kin. Often with their limited resources they sacrificed the needs of immediate kin to appease distant groups who seemed a greater risk. Few rulers were skillful at satisfying all the demands. Only after Hamdan Nahyan's brothers killed him did they realize he was not as wealthy as his generous gifts to tribal visitors made it appear.

The most successful Nahyan and Qawasim rulers had large families. Through multiple marriages, they were able to draw diverse, often hostile, groups into closer relation and produce multiple children. As their sons matured they assigned them administrative and military responsibilities thereby extending their own power. Sultan Saqr for example, put his sons in charge of the many principalities belonging to the Qawasim, and thus maintained control over these "city-states" despite British efforts to contain him. The very semblance of power sons gave a ruler was often enough to prevent would-be challengers from attacking.

The key lay in the ruler's ability to control his sons. If he failed, a cycle of deposing or killing rulers might precede his death, as happened with the earlier Shakhbut. After the ruler died, the common pattern was for multiple sons to begin an intense battle for their father's position. During a lengthy reign, there was also likely to be a long period of tension between the rulers' brothers and his sons who would be positioning themselves for succession. In both cases these paternal kin in theory should have had close, supportive relations.

Taking the example of Nahyan rulers (12 cases with complete information), the more sons a ruler had the longer his reign. Rulers with no sons averaged 5 years in power; those with fewer than average (four sons) reigned on average 12 years, and those with more than the average, 25 years. One aspect is of course that the longer a ruler reigned the more time he had to produce children. But it was also the case that the more sons he had, the more likely he used them strategically to stabilize his reign. Conversely rulers with fewer wives and children had fewer strongly committed supporters.

A second association found among Nahyan rulers is that the more brothers a ruler had the shorter his rule. Those with fewer than the average (5) brothers averaged 30 years in power while those with more than the average only remained 7 years. Thus, while large numbers of sons help to consolidate the ruler's power during his lifetime, large numbers of brothers undermined his rule. Brothers who wanted to rule, often sought a strategic moment to attempt a coup before the incumbent consolidated his position and while his sons were still too young to offer help.

Even though these data are limited, they raise interesting questions with respect to the succession after Zaid Sultan of Abu Dhabi. Zaid possessed all the characteristics of an epochal ruler: he ruled for a long period, consolidated Nahyan influence to its highest point, married many women, and had many sons. He had only one living brother after he deposed Shakhbut, and that brother Khalid, lacked the personality to challenge Zaid. Zaid had the largest number of sons (19) of any Nahyan ruler, and he took care to connect them strategically through marriage to potential supporters. He also gave them important responsibilities in government when they became adults. Zaid's dilemma was how to ensure a peaceful transition after his death, so as not to repeat the conflicts of history.

But history may now have only limited bearing on future successions. The main differences between the past and present are that: (1) Killing an opponent has been essentially eliminated as an option and even if a murder were committed it is unlikely the murderer could become ruler; (2) Deposing a ruler requires family consensus and that is now more difficult to organize and keep secret from a ruler; (3) Oil wealth has permitted the creation of military and security forces that make unseating a ruler more difficult; and (4) Crown Princes are now appointed before a ruler's death, giving them a clear advantage over others.

The formal appointment of a Crown Prince is relatively new in the Emirates.[4] His appointment takes the succession decision out of the hands of community notables and ruling family members and puts them in the hands of the ruler. The ruler almost always prefers his own son (if he is old enough) in order to keep the rule in his own lineage. All else being equal, selection of an eldest son is the best way to achieve an orderly succession, assuming younger sons see this as a fair choice that does not eliminate them in the future. However, a ruler's candidate is only as viable as his family's willingness to honor his choice. If sons are dutiful as convention expects, they will accept their father's wishes. But nothing prevents a new ruler from appointing his own choice once a suitable period has passed. These points illustrate the difficulty when no precise rules for succession exist other than the general presumption that sons of a ruler have an advantage in rough age order.

In the cases (contrary to the experience of Saudi Arabia) when the rule opened to a succession of brothers, the result was controversy and competition. A succession of brothers raises expectations in many people including the brothers' eldest sons, their nephews, and cousins all hoping the musical chair of rulership settles in their branch. The rulership only confers secure benefits on a single person and his close kin. Potential contenders therefore are under intense pressure from their own close kin to attain the position as quickly as possible. Most are aware of how swiftly lineages can become consigned to the political margins. The example of Kalba shows the importance of even a small fiefdom and the lengths to which ambitious candidates will go to acquire one.

Despite the violent conflicts among kin, most notably in the Qawasim and Nahyan families, the ideals surrounding kin relations continue to exert strong emotions. As Lienhardt noted in the 1950s, the murders in the generation that succeeded Zaid I were "remembered with pain" by succeeding sheikhs since killing brothers was "considered only less shameful and disastrous than to kill a father" (2001: 179). When practice violates norms, it does not mean the norm does not exist. People still suffer from its breach.

Marriage proved too important a political tool to relegate to the private sphere of life. Indeed one can say almost categorically that royal marriages were always contracted with a political purpose in mind. They were at all times a public indicator of the ruler's political thinking. Society at large preferred marriages between brothers' children to consolidate political, economic, and emotional ties. However, for rulers, other marriages often produced greater political benefits. For example, it might be more advantageous for a ruler to marry into the family of a reconciled enemy who could then be encouraged to maintain cordial relations, or into a family that controlled an area where the ruler hoped to increase his influence. Even marriages to kin often had a larger political motive such as drawing certain lineages closer at the expense of others. The reason might be to reward a lineage for its loyalty or exclude one for its treachery. Or it might be to co-opt a lineage's support when they might otherwise challenge the rulership, as was certainly a rationale behind the multiple marriages between Zaid's children and the Bani Muhammad.

The marriage strategy was used variously by different rulers. The Nahyan rulers, Zaid I, and Zaid Sultan, themselves married women of various tribes. Zaid Sultan married his children mainly to cousins. Zaid I married his daughters conventionally "with honor" to classificatory paternal cousins. Few Nahyan married outside Abu Dhabi. The Qawasim used marriage to increase their support internally, and were more willing than the Nahyans to contract marriages with families of outsider chiefs where they hoped to gain influence. At one point, after an intense period of family feuds over the rulership, Dubai's rulers married their children within branches of their own family to reward loyalty or heal enmities. Several more distant Bu Falasa families married into families of other rulers. The chiefs of small, vulnerable emirates such as Ajman, UAQ, Fujaira, and RAK used marriage to other rulers' families and merchant families as a way of strengthening their position against potential aggressors. The spouse pool in small emirates was often limited, and therefore ruling families there had to broaden the search for marriage partners so royal women could marry men from appropriately high status families. Several never married when appropriate men could not be found.

Zaid Sultan's marriages are a classic example of marriage used as political tool. "His" marriages include his own, those of his children, and those of his grandchildren where as the family patriarch he played a significant role in deciding marriage partners. His choice of partners evolved as his political needs changed. One of his first wives was a conventional classifactory paternal cousin (FaBrSoDa)—preferred as a choice for early marriages. Second he married tribal women from groups with importance to the Nahyans. The number of these marriages increased rapidly when he became the main candidate for the rule after his older brother Hazza died. Third, after his children became adults, he began marrying them into the families of his main competitors, the Bani Muhammad. Fourth, as the Bani Muhammad threat subsided with the death and infirmity of its patriarchs, he began marrying his children into nonthreatening influential families such as his and his wives' maternal relatives. Finally, late in his life, the marriages contracted between his grandchildren consolidated power and influence within Zaid's own family lineage. In other words, Zaid moved from developing broad support among the tribes, to appeasing his potential opponents, to consolidating power in his own family as external dangers vanished.

Two cautions are necessary when using marriages as indicators of political thinking. The first is that each set of marriages is unique to a person— Zaid Sultan's network is unique to himself and the influences he was developing. Khalifa, his eldest son, has a different set of connections that only overlap in part with his father's. The second point is that each marriage takes place in the specific political context when it was contracted. The factors that made it a good marriage at the time may no longer be valid some years later. Thus Zaid's early tribal marriages had little political relevance near the end of his life.

After the establishment of the UAE, another way that rulers cemented their relationships was through appointments to advisory councils, federal cabinet positions, heads of organizations, and other highly visible positions. Barring other circumstances, these positions were assigned in recognition of family or tribal loyalties. The positions in effect co-opted future commitment and provided access to influence for the group's members—a patronage system of sorts.[5] The jobs were assigned according to a group's importance and to lesser extent the appointed individual's position in the group. Once assigned, the group knows roughly where it stands relative to other groups. The criteria might be the group's relation to the ruler, paternal or maternal relatives, a mother-block of the ruler's own sons, a request of an influential that a supporter be given recognition, and so on. Until recently these "relationship" criteria overrode any special capacities of the assigned individuals. When the person "representing" the group leaves the position, another member of the same group may be appointed to communicate that the group is still important. There are relatively few prominent positions and therefore appointments constitute a sensitive barometer of politics.

The composition of the local executive councils and the Federal Cabinet provides a clue to rulers' political vision. Rulers, especially in smaller emirates, fill the most influential positions with family members to keep control in their own hands. Dubai however with its more technocratic interests assigns prominent businessmen to committees that determine commercial and trade policies. Abu Dhabi's Executive Council is perhaps the most politically sensitive in terms of representing groups within the royal family and within the Emirate as a whole. The councils in effect indicate who outside the ruling family are currently being given "insider" status.

As with marriages, a ruler's political appointments are a public acknowledgement of his network. Once he dies, his network dies with him and a new ruler with his own network comes to power. The new network may contain some old personalities, but their social distance relative to him will be different—with some groups closer, some more distant, and some putting in a first appearance. Each person wanting connection with the ruler will reevaluate his or her group's position, since in subtle ways it has changed. For example, even though members of the Dhawahir tribe might retain positions in the new Abu Dhabi Council, their personal relations with the ruler are no longer based on a shared history of troubles in Buraimi as with Zaid and instead depend on how close Khalifa has become to members of the Dhawahir clan. He may appoint them to important positions based on their historic relation to the Nahyan, but their relations may not have the same emotional content that infused relations with Zaid.

Women's roles in politics are not easy to discern from public evidence. However, one must assume from the incidents that do come to light that their role is important. Strong women like the two Hussas of Dubai and Abu Dhabi who held their own *majlises* and advised their ruler husbands and sons, are just one manifestation of the wife/mother role in politics. The Dubai Hussa reportedly put on men's clothing and led the defense of the city against attackers when she became frustrated by the inaction of her men. Others such as Salama the mother of Shakhbut and Zaid were consulted, people say, on an almost daily basis by their sons. Salama and Maitha, the Mansuri wife of Zaid I, extracted oaths from their sons not to commit fratricide in one case and not to accept the rulership position in the other. Mothers also influenced the candidacies of their sons with their ruler-husbands. They sought refuge for their children with maternal kin when their ruler-husbands were assassinated, and became deeply involved in seeking out and lobbying for specific marriage partners for their children. Aisha rushed to inform her husband when the ruler of Kalba died, thereby sacrificing her brother's chances in favor of her husband and children. Today, in virtually every emirate, rulers' wives have established associations and clubs for women, and have otherwise worked for women's welfare. To know the strong personalities of the UAE women leaves little doubt that their influence is felt behind the scenes.

The actions of royals even when departing from the norm are usually within the cultural understanding of commoners. They justify many behaviors by a ruler's expanded obligations. His larger number of wives and children (uncommon in most families and now even in younger members of ruling families), for example, are not a sign of depravity but rather a need to cement important connections. His broken agreements are not duplicitous; his nonkin marriages not an avoidance of preferred marriages, his pragmatic dissembling required in the interests of a higher morality, and so on. Commoners are more likely to be judged critically on behaviors that diverge from the cultural ideals. But they too may use strategies similar to those of a ruler when co-opting business or other connections. It is now probably fair to say that as tribal significance wanes in political life, royals and nonroyals alike refocus on family commitments—attending to economic and domestic issues and meeting appropriate kin obligations.

Does Tribal Culture Exist Today and, If So, What Form Does It Take?

To answer the question, this section describes two recent events in RAK and Abu Dhabi. The example from RAK describes a kin dispute in the ruling family that erupted into public. The next from Abu Dhabi shows how Khalifa as new ruler is securing his own position.

Changing the Crown Prince in RAK: The RAK story illuminates how personal relations are still fundamental to governance in the UAE. Roughly 40 years ago the Ruler of RAK Saqr Muhammad, appointed his eldest son Khalid to the position of Crown Prince, and in 1999 when he was more than 80, he turned the day-to-day administration of RAK over to Khalid. Suddenly in June 14, 2003, Saqr made a surprise announcement that he would replace Khalid as Crown Prince with his fourth son, Saud. Khalid's supporters responded by encircling his residence and forcing the Ruler's Emiri guard back to the Ruler's palace. Calm was restored only when Abu Dhabi intervened with armored cars.

Press accounts reported that Shaikh Saqr's dispute with Khalid came from a dispute over the conduct of Khalid's wife, Shaikha Fawaji.[6] Saqr had encouraged the marriage of his son to Shaikha Fawaji since at the time the marriage linked the two Qawasim lineages ruling Sharja and RAK. The first of Fawaji's six sons and an unknown number of daughters, was born in 1964 suggesting that by the time of the crisis in 2003 she must have been around 60. Newspaper accounts called her a playwright and women's rights activist. Shaikh Saqr felt she was becoming too outspokenly aggressive and interfering in the affairs of RAK. He wanted Khalid to banish her from the UAE and abolish the local women's club she had founded. The reports said that Shaikh Zaid[7] of Abu Dhabi disapproved of her public activities as well as Khalid's public stand on certain policy issues. These included Khalid's desire to restore the Tunbs Islands claimed by Iran to RAK, a contentious issue that Abu Dhabi did not want to raise at a time of much turmoil in the Gulf. Khalid had also permitted the RAK radio station to air pro-Saddam Hussein and pro-Palestinian commentaries and express anti-American opinions. After the 2003 invasion of Iraq, Khalid openly joined a demonstration in RAK against the American occupation. These actions amounted to public criticism of Shaikh Zaid's low-key foreign policy approach and this is probably the main complaint against Khalid. Shaikh Zaid's disapproval reached Saqr, probably indirectly. It is unlikely he would have asked Saqr directly to remove Khalid, but probably hoped Saqr would control him.

Local observers felt Khalid might have salvaged his position if he had handled the crisis better. But he refused to banish his wife and instead of reconciling with his father, did not speak to him—an extreme act of disrespect. He should also have paid Shaikh Zaid a visit to ask for his forgiveness. Instead he went off to Oman where he remained for several years at the expense of Sultan Qaboos—ignoring his father's requests to return. This action made the conflict public, announcing in effect that the ruling family of RAK could not settle their problems privately. It was an action designed to humiliate Shaikh Saqr.

Meanwhile the appointment of the new Crown Prince was greeted warmly by many, including Shaikh Zaid whom Saud visited regularly. Besides having a very likeable personality, Saud as a graduate of the University of Michigan was well-educated and a businessman. He was the eldest of the three sons of Saqr's third wife Mahra Ahmad Ghurair, daughter of a wealthy Dubai businessman and related to the wife of the Ruler of UAQ. Saud's wife, Hana Juma Majid, the daughter of another wealthy Dubai businessman, also held advantages. The deposed Khalid had been the eldest son of Saqr's deceased wife Nura Sultan Salim, who was Saqr's paternal cousin (FaBrDa) and of tribal background. Khalid had therefore not enjoyed the education and opportunities that the much younger Saud experienced. Soon after the change, people remarked on the better relations that were developing with Dubai through the Crown Prince's interest in business and his mother's and wife's connections to merchant families.

In this episode one sees both conventional and "modern" behaviors. The first surprise is the activist wife who took her leadership in women's organizations beyond accepted boundaries, and her husband's defiance of his father's instructions to exile her. Second was the Ruler's selection of a new Crown Prince from another mother-block of sons rather than by birth order, and the likelihood that the more recent wife influenced the choice of her son over older sons of a long-deceased wife. Finally; there is the advantage people see in business connections. Indeed two years later Crown Prince Saud had established several important new industries in RAK and was hoping to create a world-class university that would attract students from all over the region.

The episode illustrates what is becoming commonplace: rulers reaching beyond eldest sons to select Crown Princes more technically suited for the job. The birth order system may be more orderly when many candidates of roughly equal qualification are vying for the position—giving an acceptable rationale for the choice—but its weakness is that the chosen candidate may not be as well qualified as younger sons, especially now that rulers need more than just tribal skills. Changing the succession from a ruler's brother to a ruler's son as the latter grows older is considered normal but changing the succession from son to son is more surprising. The first is rationalized as the "natural" desire of a ruler to put his own son in the position, while the latter implies a problem with the merits of the original candidate. Recently other cases have occurred where an expected candidate has been bypassed in favor of a "better suited" younger candidate—in Abu Dhabi, Dubai, and Jordan.

After Zaid: Zaid died of natural causes on November 2, 2004. By the time of his death he was acknowledged as perhaps the greatest leader the region had known. At his death, he was Ruler of the largest emirate, Abu Dhabi, and President and prime mover of the UAE Federation. It is too early to know what the future holds for Abu Dhabi, but two announcements shortly before and after his death suggest how things might change. The first announced the restructuring of the UAE federal ministries and the naming of a new slate of ministers. The second announcement, coming 40 days after Zaid's death, restructured the Abu Dhabi Executive Council and named new members. Because Abu Dhabi is the most prominent state in the Federation, the two slates are important in revealing the political vision. Of the two the Abu Dhabi Executive Committee is more important than the ostensibly more powerful federal body.

The Federal Cabinet was named on the morning of the day Zaid's death was announced. The timing struck people as unusual, but the careful composition of the slate and the thoughtful restructuring of the ministries suggested to knowledgeable people that it was not the product of last minute planning. By announcing the slate at this time, the Cabinet appointments carried the weight of Shaikh Zaid's approval[8] and undoubtedly his thinking. The swearing-in ceremony on November 21, added the approval of important Abu Dhabi and Dubai dignitaries who were present. The new Abu Dhabi Ruler and President of the UAE Shaikh Khalifa, presided over the ceremony in the presence of the Ruler of Dubai. Khalifa's recognition as UAE President suggests that the position belongs permanently to Abu Dhabi. Originally, in a verbal agreement, it was to have rotated among the seven rulers on a yearly basis (Al Nabeh 1984: 33), but in practice Zaid was re-elected every 5 years.

Dubai's ruler Maktum filled the Vice President/Prime Minister position, and Abu Dhabi filled the Deputy Prime Minister position. The Cabinet consisted of 19 members, including 12 who were in the previous Cabinet although sometimes in different positions. Two sons of Zaid appeared for the first time: Saif Zaid the eldest son of Zaid's wife Muza, "representing" her block of five sons that until now had played a minor role in Abu Dhabi politics and Mansur Zaid, son of Zaid's wife Fatima and brother of Crown Prince Muhammad. Two members were from the Bani

Muhammad: Hamdan Mubarak and his brother, Nahyan Mubarak, long time Minister of Higher Education whose portfolio was expanded in the new Cabinet to include Primary and Secondary Education. Hamdan Mubarak previously held the Civil Aviation position on the Abu Dhabi Executive Council. By moving him "up" to cabinet level, a position opened on the Executive Council for a Bani Muhammad closer to Khalifa. Lubna Qassimi from Sharja was the first woman ever appointed to the Cabinet. As Minister of Economy and Planning she replaced an RAK Qassimi Fahim Sultan, whose father was deposed by the present RAK ruler. A long time member of the Cabinet, Fahim was moved to Minister of the Supreme Council and GCC Affairs. The three other new members—a Hamili, a Mansuri, and a Kaabi—were from prominent tribal families.

Perhaps equally as important as those who were new to the Cabinet were those who left. They included two royals, from UAQ and Ajman, three "tribals"—a Dhahiri, a Nasseri, and an Awamir[9]—three "merchant" families (from Dubai), and one from RAK. The UAQ "representative" was not replaced, one Ajmani remains, a Dhahiri remains, and the businessmen were not replaced. Overall, the new Cabinet increased the number of Nahyan family members at the expense of "royals" of smaller emirates. It diversified "tribals" while eliminating merchants. Putting aside any special competencies of members, the picture was one of increasing tribalism, a characteristic long associated with Abu Dhabi and Zaid.

In theory, ministerial positions are apportioned among the emirates according to a scheme agreed upon at the establishment of the UAE.[10] The December 1971 Cabinet gave Abu Dhabi 6 appointments, Dubai 3, Sharja 3, UAQ 2, Ajman 2, and Fujaira 1 (RAK joined two months later). Between 1971 and 1997 Abu Dhabi's share of Cabinet members rose from 6 to 8 members and Dubai's share from 5 to 7 at the expense of smaller emirates that started with 2 or 3 and ended with 1 or 2.

The earlier 2004 Cabinet was restructured down to 19 from 21 members by merging ministries and adding one. Not counting the President (Abu Dhabi) or the Prime Minister (Dubai) Abu Dhabi had 12 positions, including 5 of Zaid's sons, 2 Bani Muhammad, and 5 tribal families loyal to Abu Dhabi. Dubai had 3 positions and the Qawasim had 3: 1 from RAK and 2 from Sharja. Ajman had a distant relative of the ruling family as nominal Foreign Minister while Zaid's son Hamdan served more prominently in the foreign affairs position. Fujaira had 1 position and UAQ no members. Overall Abu Dhabi dramatically increased its presence while Dubai and the smaller states lost members. This undoubtedly reflected Abu Dhabi's frustration at paying most of the federal budget, while depending on ministers from other emirates to make decisions.

Zaid's 2004 Cabinet was again replaced in early 2006, following the death of Dubai's Shaikh Maktum. Muhammad Rashid took Maktum's place as Ruler of Dubai and as Vice President and Prime Minister in the Federal Government. He also retained his previous position as Minister of Defense. Known for his active role in Dubai he began his tenure in the federal government by making unannounced visits to hospitals, offices, and schools across the country to check on how well they were being run. The announcement said the new Cabinet slate was proposed by Muhammad Rashid, who seemed on several counts to be initiating a more active role for Dubai.

The 2006 Cabinet was billed as one that promoted economic growth and accountability, and more participation by the citizenry. Of the 23 ministers, 10 remained either at the head of the same or reorganized ministries. The number of new faces added were 8, including 1 woman (making 2 women ministers) most of whom could be called technocrats. Zaid's 6 sons, 2 Bani Muhammad, several from other ruling families, and at least 4 tribals also made up the Cabinet. Abu Dhabi retained its 12 members, Dubai increased to 5, Sharja had 3, RAK 2, and Ajman 1. UAQ and Fujaira were not represented. While the 2004 Cabinet had preserved the strong tribal presence of Abu Dhabi, the 2006 Cabinet showed more active involvement by Dubai and its focus on economic progress. Over time the 2006 Cabinet may be seen as a transition to more technocratic cabinets.

A month after Zaid's death Khalifa announced the restructuring of the important Abu Dhabi Executive Council—the first public sign of his intentions as ruler. Would it be business as usual, or would he try to strengthen his position against his rivals? As in the federal cabinet, departments were merged to make a leaner organization. The announcement listed 11 members including the new Crown Prince, Muhammad Zaid, as chairman, and Muhammad's long time manager, Muhammad Ahmad Bowardi, as secretary-general. The rest of the line-up included 2 sons of Zaid who with the Crown Prince, make equal representation for the three main "mother blocks" of Zaid's sons (Fatima's 6 sons, Muza's 5, and Aisha's 4). Fatima also has 3 sons and Muza 1 son on the Federal Cabinet, and Muza a son appointed director of the important Abu Dhabi Investment Authority (ADIA). In addition, both of the new Ruler Khalifa's sons, Sultan and Muhammad, joined the Abu Dhabi Council, as did his Bani Muhammad nephew (MoBrSo) who is also brother of Sultan Khalifa's wife (i.e. Ruler Khalifa's daughter-in-law). The rest of the members include 3 "tribals," a Muhairbi (Bani Yas), a Dhahiri, and a Suwaidi, and finally a member of the nonroyal Mubarak family. The last is the grandson of a now deceased chief justice of the Sharia Courts.[11]

The new appointments suggest Khalifa was indeed strengthening his position in Abu Dhabi by appointing people he trusts—one son is in the

Crown Prince's Court and the other in the Department of Finance. Having only two sons and no full brothers, Khalifa has little depth among close kin to fill critical positions, and has had to go further afield to find trusted people. His main competitors, the Bani Fatima, occupy three positions at the less influential federal level. Khalifa therefore filled the Council with half brothers from two other mother-blocks, his Bani Muhammad nephew (MoBrSo), and several tribals probably proposed by his half brother ally, Sultan. With the exception of Crown Prince Muhammad and his associate, the entire Abu Dhabi council now consists of Khalifa's supporters.

The tribal system, as described by Ibn Khaldun and Khuri, where rulers dominate groups of increasing inclusiveness to counteract opponents, is alive in the largest emirate of Abu Dhabi. Abu Dhabians still admire and honor (albeit in modified form) the ideals of tribalism: egalitarianism, reputation, consensus, accommodation, long genealogies, disdain for commerce, access to rulers, and at least a semblance of consultation and consensus. Because Abu Dhabi dominates the UAE, tribalism still has an important bearing on the way politics are conducted at the federal level and in the smaller single-tribe emirates. Only Dubai has altered its focus substantially to rely on technocrats to create the systems and policies that allow modern commerce to thrive. The extent to which the UAE evolves from a tribal to a more commercially oriented society will depend on the extent to which the influence of the new Rulers of Abu Dhabi and Dubai are felt. The largesse handed out by Abu Dhabi still has a significant hold on several of the emirates while the commercial successes of Dubai also create a compelling model.

Where tribalism flourishes, its diverging lineages and segmental power makes competition among sons of a former ruler inevitable, especially where separate mother-blocks of sons exist. As history demonstrates these sons only have a generation or two to establish their claims, or their lineage fades into political oblivion. Muhammad as Crown Prince of Abu Dhabi will certainly try to ensure a place for his lineage in the succession. But given Khalifa's moves to strengthen his position since Zaid's death, there may still be opposition.[12] The question for Abu Dhabi still remains, "Who will be the next Crown Prince?"

How Did Leaders Adapt So Quickly to the New Conditions in the Trucial States?

If culture helps sustain systems for personal relations, how did rulers move so quickly from egalitarian forms with little inherent authority to ones where power was concentrated and centralized? The answer may lie in the models for personal relations described above. Rulers were practiced in being both tribal leaders in their communities and father-figures in their families. When changing political and economic conditions suddenly demanded hierarchy and authority, the ruler already occupied a role—father patriarch—that matched the requirements. He understood the role of distributing support and services, coordinating members' activities, setting and enforcing standards, and quelling internal disturbances. Indeed the father role felt comfortable to both rulers and their constituents in a society that, as Khuri (1990) says, idealizes family and likes to generalize kin values to all aspects of human relations.

It should not be surprising to find rulers making statements like the one that heads this chapter where Shaikh Zaid framed his role as father to the citizens. Such statements are not meant for effect but rather express a heartfelt desire to serve the people. Zaid saw his power as derivative, valid as long as he met his responsibilities as leader. Nationals on their side felt obligated to honor Zaid as a father by showing appreciation for his efforts.

It will be interesting to see how younger rulers operate in an environment where tribal expectations are diluted by an impinging economic world. The home-grown models that served rulers well for over two hundred years are now joined by a multitude of models with roots in other societies. Will the people of the UAE, especially Abu Dhabi, continue to defend their own ways or will they gradually incorporate other models into their repertoire? Will the coming generations accept leaders as father-figures or, for that matter, will younger leaders feel comfortable filling those roles? Can rulers create the same feeling of group spirit that suffused personal relations in the past or are more paternalistic models here to stay? Or, will relations become more impersonal as institutions and laws take over in the increasingly complex world of the UAE?

NOTES

Preface

1. Although scholars lament the lack of these studies, there are several notable books that take a similar approach including Robert Springborg on Egypt, Madawi al Rasheed on her tribe in Saudi Arabia, Rosemarie Zahlan on the Gulf, Peter Lienhardt on the Trucial States, and Fuad Khouri on a number of Arab countries.

2. Oral traditions are strong in the Gulf, but their accuracy diminishes with time. Even firsthand accounts tend to be inaccurate, reflecting the particular view of the speaker. Emiratis are quick to warn of this danger.

3. Both can be explained by cultural norms. The first places high value on consensus and goodwill—a corollary of the principle of creating social solidarities (see later chapters). The second reflects the desire to distinguish between private and public and to keep women's lives private.

4. For women, the privacy issue is becoming situational. Increasingly the names of rulers' wives are published in newspapers to report their respectable involvement in social, charitable, and humanitarian activities. Women readily exchange names among themselves and have no hesitation in letting female outsiders know the names of women. Newspapers announce and sometimes show pictures of girls who have graduated or achieved distinctions in school. The prohibition against naming women is mainly reserved for unmarried and younger married women whose reputations are at their most vulnerable, and the reluctance is mostly in conservative families.

5. Boot (nd 34) says that among the Bani Yas only the Nahyan who are the traditional leaders were given the title "Shaikh." The Hamid were also given the title not because they were heads of the Qubaisat but because they were close to the rulers. Heads of the Dhawahir are called "Shaikh" because they are a separate tribe from the Bani Yas. A religious personage may also be addressed as shaikh with a different connotation. These principles true to Abu Dhabi extend to royal family members and religious personages in other emirates, but not necessarily to other nations.

Emir, King, and Sultan are titles and terms of address used for rulers elsewhere in Arabia.

Chapter 1   The Economic and Political Context

1. Two emirates, RAK and Sharja, are ruled by separate branches of the Qawasim family.
2. In 2003, 97 percent of UAE girls attended primary school and 75 percent of university students were girls.
3. A main aim was to secure British rights to oil exploration over other westerners, but by the 1950s a number of foreign-owned companies were involved in exploration activities.
4. See Abdallah 1970 for more on the details of boundary definitions in the UAE.

Chapter 2   The Cultural Context

1. See Rugh A. (1997), for a description of how children are socialized to a cultural view in a Syrian village.
2. Anthropological literature is filled with examples of this tendency. The groups do not have to be hostile but often are. Some scholars dismiss this idea but I believe contrast serves as a good organizing device.
3. See Rugh 1986 for how dress marks sociopolitical distinctions in Egypt through contrastive styles.
4. The paramount chiefs of the Bani Yas were from the Bu Falah or later the Nahyans after descendents of Nahyan overcame other Bu Falah lineages. The reference to a Qawasim versus Bani Yas opposition is not exactly parallel since one is a family of related individuals and the other a confederation of tribes.
5. In the 1724 elections for the Imam in Oman, a Bani Ghafir candidate opposed a Bani Hina candidate. The Bani Ghafir were mostly Nizari (Adani) from central and northeastern Arabia, while the Bani Hina were Yamani (Qahtani) from southwest Arabia who conquered Oman in the ninth-century BC.
6. Female members of Abu Dhabi's royal family still keep up their relationships with royal Omani women.
7. Heard-Bey (1996) says years of constant strife between the two groups leave unresolved blood feuds that often take precedence over pragmatic interests in making alliances.
8. Wahhabism in the nineteenth century was a version of Islam initiated by the reformer Abdul Wahhab. He believed Muslims should return to the simplicity of the early faith of the Prophet with its one God.
9. The Qawasim at the time depended on goods captured from Omani ships and eventually from ships flying under the British flag. Some say their

conversion to Wahhabism made it easier to mistreat "infidel" groups, Christians, and Muslims of other sects that they captured (Heard-Bey 1996: 281).

10. These models are not unique to Arab societies, nor will they be exactly the same everywhere. The main caution is not to take them too literally. They help in understanding behavior but do not determine it.

11. Anthropological debate has focused not on whether segmentation as a concept exists but who the constituent members of a unit were likely to be— nuclear families, brothers and their families, in-laws. Empirical evidence shows that in real life units did not invariably coalesce on the basis of kinship but that blood relationship was one way to gauge affinity. Sisters might prevail on their husbands to travel together, even though prevailing ideology encouraged brothers and their families to combine forces.

12. The absence of women in this image is accurate. A tribal person would see women and children as extensions of the brothers.

13. A voluntary group in a tribal setting might include those who choose to follow a leader and frequent his audiences even though they have no structural obligation to do so.

14. Groups are influential in varying degree because of their numbers, their strategic locations, and their military or other advantages.

15. For example, Zaid, Shakhbut, and Hamdan are common names in the Nahyan family, while Saqr, Rashid, and Humaid are common among the Qawasim. Part of this comes from naming children after forebears.

16. Even where the stress is placed on older versus younger family members.

17. These descriptions and the ones that follow on outsider relations come from my long-term residence and fieldwork in several Arab countries.

18. Relationships based on these features contrast with those in the West. Western family relations are not well defined, people try to equalize them, they are tenuous, and optional. Briefly this means that family relations are not specified, they are what people make of them. People try to homogenize the roles of authority and obedience by bringing young children into family decision-making. Adults change partners easily, and children are mostly on their own after they become adults. Finally, individual families define their long-term relations.

19. This also helps explain Arabs' often uncritical acceptance of their heads of state. Their obligation to be respectful is stronger than their need to protest.

20. In Pashtun society in northern Pakistan, hospitality to foreigners is the "purest" form of generosity because there is no expectation of return.

21. National days were opportunities to show support in Abu Dhabi until security issues made these events invitation only.

22. These marriages are said to strengthen the husband's hand since those around him are his close kin. This contrasts with maternal kin marriage (MoSiCh or MoBrCh) where women are in a stronger position. Maternal kin marriages are common in ruling families where there have been earlier exogamous marriages to these families.

23. Another difference is that men can marry non-Muslim women, while Muslim women cannot.

Chapter 3   Early Leaders of Abu Dhabi

1. The Prophet Muhammad is also descended through Nizar. Another source (Rush 1991: 30) gives Zhelal, a descendent of Gharrem al Zeighee, as the antecedent of the Nahyans.

2. According to one source, the Sudan were the paramount sheikhs of the Bani Yas before the seventeenth century until the Bu Falah became more powerful (Butti 1992: 244).

3. Pearl Necklaces: the Days of the House of Saud in Oman; MS 1374/1955: 190.

4. Some of the descendents continue to call themselves al Falahi.

5. Some accounts say Nahyan had a son Isa ruling in the early-eighteenth century who was the first major Nahyan chief. He had three sons, Diab, Saqr, and Muhammad. Other accounts say Diab was the only son of Nahyan and that Shakhbut and Saqr were Diab's sons while Muhammad was the son of Saqr. Diab founded the first settlement on Abu Dhabi Island, but continued to reside in the Hamra plains north of Al Dhafra (Tammam 1983: 30).

6. Wilfred Thesiger 1950 (in Lienhardt 2001: 176) says Hazza ruled between 1793–1795 after he escaped a revolt, and Shakhbut came to power in 1795. Most other sources including Lorimer (1986) do not mention Hazza's rule.

7. This split is discussed in the first chapter. The Bani Yas were mainly Hinawi and usually not Wahhabi.

8. Reported by Lt. Hennell about 1831 in Bombay Selections XXIV, p. 464, appearing in Lorimer (1986), also Rush (1991: 31). Muhammad fled to Bahrain where with help from the Manasir he attacked Tahnun in 1823 but was repelled (Rush 1991: 32).

9. The estimate reported 18,000 residents of Abu Dhabi or about six members to each house.

10. Perhaps this is the Diab Isa who later killed Isa Khalid, murderer of Khalifa and Sultan, and restored the rule to the Shakhbut line. The fact that Khalifa sent him as an envoy shows he must have been part of Khalifa's trusted circle.

11. His full name showing the links to Falah was Isa Khalid Saqr Khalid Falah.

12. If that is the case, the name does not appear in official genealogical tables and therefore it is not possible to trace Diab Isa's exact connection either to Khalifa or Isa. It is possible that he may have been a son of Isa himself.

13. The Bani Qitab were an independent tribe whose support was courted because they occupied areas of the interior that had to be traversed to go from one coast to the other.

Chapter 4   Zaid the Great and the Consolidation of Abu Dhabi

1. To distinguish him from Zaid Sultan covered in the next chapter.
2. This was the section of the Naim that also ruled Ajman.
3. Heard-Bey (1996: 148) claims that Zaid did not have more than three wives at a time.
4. Birth dates tend to vary by a year or two from one source to another. Some of the inaccuracy comes from the 11-day difference per year in eastern and western calendars. Mainly though, local people pay little attention to birth dates.
5. Since there is no public record of rulers' marriages or of women in official genealogies, the information comes from oral comments or incidental mention in documents.
6. Heard-Bey (1996: 148) says Zaid had six wives (one Mansuri, two from the Bu Falah, one Bu Falasa, and two Naimi) but on p. 33 she mentions a seventh, a Suwaidi. This does not account for other marriages reported elsewhere. To Heard-Bey's list, Lorimer (1986) for example adds a Qassimi, but ignores the two Naimi women.
7. In 1887 Zaid went to war with the Dhawahir who resisted his efforts to own the area. (Heard-Bey 1996: 51).
8. There are of course other possibilities, that they remained married but no longer produced children, or that they produced only "invisible" girls.
9. Van Der Meulen (1997: 130), says Hamdan had a pregnant wife Shamsa Ahmad Utaiba when he was killed by Sultan in 1922. She fled with her three children Latifa, Saqr, and Miriam to Dubai where she sought the protection of Said Maktum, Ruler of Dubai, whose eldest son, Rashid, later married Latifa.
10. She later raised the second son of Zaid Sultan, her husband's brother.
11. Khalifa, the "king-maker," established a farm west of Hili near Al Ain called Masudi, where he dug the Masudi falaj system. This is the second area of Al Ain bought from the Dhawahir and developed by the Nahyan family.
12. Some reports say he was killed by his brother Hamdan but no details confirm this, and it is unlikely.
13. In the Lienhardt genealogy.
14. Tammam says Hamdan's "tolerance, clemency, and benevolence . . . won him great admiration and endearment among the tribes . . ." (1983: 42).
15. Other brothers were not involved in these conspiracies.
16. Diab said others received Saudi aid including the Qawasim and, some sections of the Bani Yas (Rush 1991: 212).
17. Tahnun had three sons who were students at the start of the twenty-first century, suggesting late marriage.
18. The classic example of a ruler who set out to build a royal lineage is Ibn Saud in Saudi Arabia who by 1953 had 43 sons and over 50 daughters through "an active strategy of polygamy and concubinage" (Al Rasheed 2002: 75).

19. Al Rasheed argues that in the absence of resources, Ibn Saud consolidated authority over conquered territories through marriages (2002: 9). In his case, marriage was a strategy to dominate and control other groups (2002: 80).

Chapter 5   The Bani Sultan and the Transformation of Abu Dhabi

1. The dates given as Zaid Sultan's birth vary from 1916 which seems the most common, to 1908 (Herb), to 1918 (from Tamman who says he was 8 at his father's death in 1926) to a source that says he was a babe in arms at his father's death.
2. The sequence of events and details surrounding Sultan's death and his sons' flight differ from one account to another.
3. He married the widow of Sultan's victim Hamdan.
4. Three of the daughters had no children. Only Aisha had children.
5. Rawda was married to Muhammad Khalid Sultan, Aisha to Mubarak Muhammad Khalifa, Quth to Khalifa Muhammad Khalifa, and Muza to Hamdan Muhammad Khalifa.
6. I am not certain these marriages are correct.
7. No marriages are allowed between aunt and nephew, uncle and niece, or to two sisters at the same time (Lienhardt 2001: 182–183).
8. In 1939 the Trucial Coast Petroleum Company obtained an exploration concession for 75 years from Shakhbut in offshore areas. But WWI broke out that year and exploration work was postponed until 1949 (Tamman 1983: 68).
9. He had no children, but his wife Miriam Hamdan Zaid I raised Zaid's son, Sultan, from 40 days of age.
10. He died in 1979 of liver/kidney disease. A section of Abu Dhabi is called Khalidiyya after him.
11. A year after Zaid's death, a map appeared on UAE's website showing its borders redrawn to pre-1974. Included were the 20 kilometer strip connecting with Qatar and a southern border that included much of Saudi Arabia's Shayba (Zarrara in Abu Dhabi) field, from which it pumps about 550,000 barrels a day.
12. Buraimi town and Hamasa, controlled by the Naim and the Al Bu Shamis, went to Muscat, and Al Ain to Abu Dhabi.
13. Hamad Mashghuni was an important pearl merchant.
14. Zaid had measles in 1952 which some claim may have accounted for 4 years with no births until Sultan in 1955.
15. Since he was still married to Hussa at the time, he may have exceeded the Islamic limit of four wives.
16. Awaida refers to a section of the Qubaisat; Shamsi to the Bu Shamis tribe. I have treated her as a Bu Khail.
17. Nahyan married Salama, Hazza to Muza, and Mansur to Aliya, all great granddaughters of Hamid Butti.

18. Only Zaid, Khalifa Zaid, and Muhammad Butti were said to know who owned land in Abu Dhabi to avoid conflicts over which tribe or family had been favored over others (Boot nd: 46).
19. One local view is that Khalifa and Muhammad had non-Nahyan mothers and therefore were less qualified to rule. This may be rationalization after the fact since several previous rulers had non-Nahyan mothers.
20. The position was called Prime Minister until 1974 when it became Chairman of the Executive Council.
21. Sultan born in 1965 and Muhammad, born around 1977.
22. Shamsa, born circa 1967, Muza and Aisha, circa 1969, Shamma, unknown, Salama, circa 1975, and Latifa in 1984.
23. Classifactory paternal cousins are paternal cousins one or more times removed.

Chapter 6   The Maktums (Al Bu Falasa) and the Development of Dubai

1. The Bu Falasa supported a cousin in the contest for the rule of Abu Dhabi, and Khalifa executed the ringleaders and expelled others to Sharja (Lienhardt 2001: 215).
2. Earlier Rush says "Dubai's first two rulers—the eponymous Maktum bin Buti (1833–1852) and his brother and successor, Said (1852–1859). . . ." (1991: xix).
3. The tensions that caused the exodus in 1833 have simmered until recently. Dubai acted as a refuge to opponents of the Abu Dhabi regime, supported the Thani Rulers of Qatar against them, and provided little support to Abu Dhabi in its disputes with Saudi Arabia over Buraimi. As recently as 1945 to 1948, there was open warfare between the two emirates.
4. Another version has him traveling to Abu Dhabi and on his return developing pleurisy from which he died.
5. The Bani Yas had 440 houses, Arabs from Bahrain, Kuwait and the Persian Coast had 400, 250 belonged to the Sudan, 250 to the Persians, 200 to the Baluchi and Indian British, and small numbers of others (Heard-Bey 1996: 242–243).
6. The Documentation Center Tables say Said was 28 (born in 1878), Juma was 15 (born in 1891), and Hashar was 7 (born in 1899). British reports say Said was only 18.
7. A prominent Dubai official, Khan Bahadur Esa, once noted that women of the Bani Yas tribes of Dubai and Abu Dhabi enjoyed an altogether exceptional position. "They are practically free from Purdah and consult freely and openly with their husbands and relatives" (Rush 1991: 303).
8. I know of only one other prominent wife who convened a public majlis attended by men: Shaikha Hussa Muhammad Khalifa, the wife of Shaikh Zaid of Abu Dhabi.

9. Zura was the island that Sultan Nasir Suaidi attempted to colonize with the support of Zaid I of Abu Dhabi.

10. The specifics of the complaints, according to the Residency Agent, were that Shaikh Said did not protect the Bani Yas from plundering Awamir Bedouin and when they came to town he provisioned them; that a slave was in charge of the receipts of Dubai; that he didn't recover claims for them against the people of Trucial Oman; and that his friendly relations with the Resident Agent caused him to meet the latter's demands without first asking the people (Rush 1991: 318).

11. Actually Rashid was the brother of Said's grandfather, and Butti the son of another brother, so in effect the quarrel was among the sons of three branches of the original Maktum.

12. The Manasir were also involved in the overthrow of Saqr Nahyan and restoration of the Bani Sultan to power.

13. Said is reputed to have put out the eyes of 5 of his opponents with hot irons.

14. The use of the term Al Bu Falasa here refers to the tribal section as a whole rather than directly to the ruling family itself. There is ambiguity about when "Maktum" became the name for the ruling subsection.

15. Latifa's mother came from the Sultan Mujrin line, a nonruling family of the Bu Falasa.

16. One source says Khalifa married Shamsa Suhail Maktum but others say Ahmad Said, Rashid's brother.

17. After expelling Juma, according to the Political Agent, Rashid became "a victim of Obaid bin Thani, Saif bin Chalban, Hamid bin Majid bin Fatim and Hamid bin Majid bin Ghurair" (Rush 1991: 401), merchants in Dubai.

18. At least four of the Mugrin women married Maktums.

19. Hamdan was assassinated by the father of Zaid Sultan. His family likely has feelings about the Nahyan rulers.

20. Hamdan's daughters also married well, Latifa to Shaikh Rashid of Dubai and Miriam to Hazza Sultan Nahyan, son of her father's murderer. When Latifa died in 1983, Miriam acted as surrogate mother for Latifa's children.

21. The exceptions were a Qassimi woman married to Zaid I and a granddaughter of Saqr Zaid, who married a Qassimi.

Chapter 7   Sharja and Ras al Khaima (RAK) During Early Qawasim Rule

1. There are a number of discrepancies reported in the relationships among the early Qawasim leaders. Lorimer (1986) says Matar's son was Rahma whose son was Matar with a son Rashid. Slot (1993) believes Rahma Matar was an Omani commander in the Gulf in 1718, and was succeeded in 1760 by his brother Rashid Matar. Slot (1993) believes Lorimer

mistook Rashid of Basidu for Rashid Matar. Lorimer says Rashid was Shaikh from 1747 until he resigned in 1777, while Slot believes otherwise. Lorimer says his wife was the daughter of the governor of Bandar Abbas, Mulla Ali Shah, whom he married to strengthen his alliances against enemies on the Arab main land. Slot says instead that this was Rashid of Basidu's wife, who fled to RAK after the death of her husband.

2. The population figures include foreign workers and therefore the numbers are greater in emirates where there are more employment opportunities. Independent estimates suggest that fewer than 10 percent are nationals.

3. The author's evidence comes from the same British Foreign Office records that serve as sources for other versions. My version is the conventional one, but readers may want to reserve judgment about whether the attacks were as the British portrayed them. Subsequent suppression of the Qawasim was certainly based on the official version.

4. During most of the nineteenth century, the positions of Imam and Sultan were held by different men, the Imam usually representing the inland sections and the Sultan the coastal areas of Oman.

5. This incident is described in more detail in the Nahyan chapters.

6. A nomadic subsection of the Bani Kaab.

7. The sons most often named are Saqr, Ahmad, Majid, Rashid, Muhammad, Ibrahim, Abdalla, Khalid, Salim, Jasim and Nasim. Some reports have a son Saif or Said, some have Muhammad missing, and some have Nasir instead of Nasim.

Chapter 8   Sharja and Ras al Khaima (RAK) Separate Under Qawasim Rule

1. The DC genealogy says instead that he is son of Rashid Matar Rahma Matar Kaid Qassimi.

2. This Qadhib may have been the son of Rashid Salim Qadhib—or grandson of the earlier Shaikh Qadhib of Linga.

3. I assume Ahmad and Salim were full brothers. Salim shows favoritism toward Ahmad which suggests closeness.

4. His father, Abdalla, administered Sharja under Sultan Saqr until he was killed at Hamriya in 1855.

5. Sources differ somewhat on these dates and the role of Muhammad.

6. The Qawasim are a section of the Huwala tribe, a name once applied to all coastal people engaged in maritime activities. Eventually in the eighteenth century, those located in RAK became known as Qawasim (Van Der Meulen 1997: 389).

7. It is not clear who Muhammad Khadim was or whether he acted on behalf of a specific Qassimi family.

8. Documentation Center trees report that Rashid was born in 1909, which would makes it impossible for him to take over in 1904.

9. Sultan reported five brothers—including Rashid, Abdul Aziz and Humaid which makes it six (Rush 2 1991: 157, 158, 162); Other reports say there were nine: Khalid, two Rashids, Sultan, Abdul Aziz, two Muhammads, Majid, and Humaid.

10. He wanted to reestablish Bu Shamis leadership that was displaced by the Kharaiban (Heard-Bey 1996: 214).

11. The Midfa are a big family that resides primarily in Dubai and Sharja. Although they have no tribal connection they had considerable influence on Qawasim finances. A Midfa was minister more than once in the UAE Cabinet.

12. Later Saqr appointed Hassan Abdalla, son of a former Shaikh of Jazirat al Hamra, as Wali of Kalba in place of Saif who he decided was weak. Saqr complained that the Sultan of Muscat claimed control over Wadi Madha near Kalba (Rush 2 1991: 265).

13. These are described in more detail in Rush 2 1991: 80.

14. Burke's Royal Families of the World contradicts Lorimer in some details. According to Burke, RAK was part of Sharja until 1869 when Humaid Abdalla Sultan declared himself the independent ruler of RAK. On his death in 1900, RAK was reunited with Sharja and did not gain final independence until 1921. After Salim Sultan (Sharja 1868–1883) was deposed he governed RAK until 1919.

Chapter 9   Preserving Ajman Independence Under Al Bu Khuraiban

1. The son, Ahmad Abdalla, became Shaikh of UAQ (1873–1904), succeeded by his son with the Ajmani wife.

2. See chapter 2 for the Ghafiri-Hinawi alignments. Often the distinction prevented alliances among tribes and rulers but not always.

3. Not to be confused with an earlier Abdul Aziz Rashid who deposed another Humaid Rashid Humaid in 1841.

4. A later report felt the case against Abdul Aziz had been overstated.

5. Debate persists over whether she and her brother Rashid were children of Sultan Saqr's daughter (Rush 1991: 480) or an Al Ali wife from UAQ. Since she later married an Al Ali, the latter seems more likely. On the other hand, the British warned the Ruler of Sharja not to be found meddling in this affair (Rush 1991: 292).

6. The full names are: Humaid Abdul Aziz Humaid Rashid Humaid Rashid and Sultan Muhammad Ali Humaid Khamis Rashid.

7. In 1926, the British sent Abdul Rahman to Aden because of his possible role in the murder of a cousin of the Residency Agent, although there was no clear evidence. He returned to Ajman in 1929 after Humaid had died.

8. This is another example of name repetition in families. The convention prohibits naming a child after his father before his death but frequently children are named after their grandfathers.

9. He was born in 1919 or 1920, and the first of his half brothers, Humaid, in 1930.
10. I believe these sons were not from Amna.

Chapter 10   Um al Qaiwain's (UAQ) Survival Under the Mualla

1. Their status however remained somewhat ambiguous well after that time.
2. There is some confusion among sources about the line of succession. I am using Documentation Center reports.
3. Rush 1991: 560 says Ahmad Abdalla had nine sons, but they may have meant Ahmad Rashid. The former, according to Documentation Center trees had only five: Rashid, Ibrahim, Said, Abdalla, and Abdul Rahman.
4. Nasir according to the DC tree was the son of Shaikh Ali (1853–1873) and not the son of Ahmad Abdalla (see above). His disputes with Rashid make sense if he were trying to regain the rule for Ali's branch. The argument for Ali being Nasir's father is strengthened by the fact that Nasir's mother was a slave in Ali's house.
5. The Political Resident was a British citizen stationed in Bushire who was assisted by a Residency Agent—a local Indian Government civil servant—residing in Sharja. In 1934, a British Political Agent in Bahrain supervised the local Agent. By 1948, the Political Agent was living in Sharja and in 1949, the Residency post was discontinued.
6. The fourth state to join the smaller emirates was Fujaira. Headman Muhammad Sharqi married the daughter of Rashid Humaid of Ajman (nephew to the Ruler of UAQ's wife) probably in the 1940s.
7. The Baluch emigrated from the Makran area of Pakistan and worked usually as servants, laborers, or military. The term Baluchi was also used to refer to immigrants from Persia. Rashid's wife may have been a servant in his household.

Chapter 11   The Sharqiyin and Pursuit of Fujairan Independence

1. From Lorimer 1986: 777. Except as noted Abu Dhabi Documentation tables are compatible.
2. He was called Hamad Majid by the Sultan of Oman and Hamad Abdulla Saif by Hellyer (1994) and Zahlan (1978).
3. There are references to him as Fujaira headman as early as 1879 when he may have been acting for his father.
4. Hamad was said to be chief from 1888–1932 in most sources: Rush 1991 however says he died in 1938.
5. He reportedly received about 2,000 dollars a year, mainly from dates and wheat.

6. Zaid I was then allied with UAQ and RAK, and Saqr may not have wanted to aggravate him.

7. Khalid was brother-in-law to Hamad, and related to Hamad's great-grandfather who was Khalid's uncle (FaBr). The Shaikh of Sharja supported him as Regent probably to keep him from trying to regain the Sharja rulership.

8. One report in the 1940s says Khalid Ahmad at 64 married and had four sons he hoped to install in Kalba.

9. Both were "Saqr Sultan," Saqr Sultan Saqr ruler of Sharja and Saqr Sultan Salim son of the ex-Ruler of RAK.

10. See Rush 2 1991: 234 for a negative report of Muhammad.

11. The terms of agreement are found in Rush 2 1991: 605–607 and are quite restrictive of his powers.

12. The words sound harsh in English, but in reality the admiration that accompanies the "risk-taker" who puts something over on a much bigger adversary seems to correct for any negative impression.

Chapter 12   The Political Culture of Leadership

1. Bellin (2004) credits coercive structures and the abundance of rent (in this case oil revenues) to pay for them as two of the conditions fostering robust authoritarianism in the Middle East and North Africa. A third is international support of its leaders. See note 5 below for the fourth.

2. Some have argued that Qawasim power might have declined anyway after the invention of the steamship with its greater gun power, metal hulls, and ability to navigate without wind-power.

3. The responsibilities may come from custom, but their moral quality may be attributed to religious sources.

4. Peterson (2001: 581) says a "traditional Arab" principle was that a ruler had no right to name his heir, but that has now become commonplace.

5. Bellin (2004) says patrimonialism (patronage) is a condition fostering robust authoritarianism in the Middle East since it allows a ruler to surround himself with supporters. And indeed the UAE is only now in 2006 beginning to institute a partial election of the Federal Council where candidates will still be vetted by the local rulers.

6. She was daughter of Saqr Sultan Saqr, Ruler of Sharja (1951–1965). He was deposed and exiled to Cairo.

7. Abu Dhabi is the main source of subsidies for RAK, one of the poorest of the emirates.

8. The Constitution says the President of the UAE appoints the ministers and therefore the announcement had to be made while he was alive or wait for the new president to make appointments.

9. An Awamir, Rakad Rakad, appeared in the last cabinet. During the Buraimi crisis his branch defected to the Saudis before submitting to the Nahyan. The Awamir, Manasir, and Dhawahir are Abu Dhabi loyalists.

10. See Rugh, W. 1997.
11. Khaldoun Muharak's father was assassinated while UAE's ambassador to Paris. The family is originally Saudi. This appointment has more to do with Khaldoun's competence than his political prominence.
12. Saudi Arabia's system of transferring the succession through brothers has help avoid open conflicts.

BIBLIOGRAPHY

Abdullah, Muhammad Morsy. 1978. *The United Arab Emirates: A Modern History*. London: Croom Helm.

Al-Nabeh, Najat. 1984. *United Arab Emirates (UAE): Regional and Global Dimensions*. Ph.D Dissertation. Claremont: University of Claremont.

Al-Qasimi, Sultan M. 1986. *The Myth of Piracy in the Gulf*. London: Croom Helm.

Al-Rasheed, Madawi. 1991. *Politics in an Arabian Oasis: The Rashidi Tribal Dynasty*. London and New York: I.B.Taurus and Co. Ltd.

———. 2002. *A History of Saudi Arabia*. Cambridge: University Press.

Anani, Ahmad and K. Wittingham. 1986. *The Early History of the Gulf Arabs*. London: Longman Group Limited. pp. 34–35.

Anthony, John Duke. 1975. *Arab States of the Lower Gulf*. Washington: The Middle East Institute.

Bellin, Eva. 2004. The Robustness of Authoritarianism in the Middle East: Exceptionalism in Comparative Perspective. *Comparative Politics*. Vol. 36, No. 2, January: 139–157.

Boot, Aernout. n.d. *Tribes and Families of Abu Dhabi* (manuscript).

Brynen, Rex, Korany Bahgat, and Paul Noble, editors. 1995. *Political Liberalization and Democratization in the Arab World. Theoretical Perspectives*. Vol. 1. Boulder: Lynne Rienner.

The Buraimi Memorials. United Kingdom. Vol. I and II. 1987. Slough, UK: Archive Editions.

Butti, Obaid A. 1992. *Imperialism, Tribal Structure, and the Development of Ruling Elites: A Socio-economic History of the Trucial States Between 1892 and 1939*. Ph.D. Dissertation. Washington, DC: Georgetown University.

Cole, Donald P. 1975. *Nomad of the Nomads: The Al Murrah Bedouin of the Empty Quarter*. Chicago: Aldine Publishing Company.

Crone, Patricia. 2004. *God's Rule: Government and Islam*. New York: Columbia University Press.

Geertz, Clifford. 1968. *Islam Observed*. Chicago: University of Chicago Press.

Hawley, Donald. 1970. *The Trucial States*. London: George Allen and Unwin, Ltd.

Heard-Bey, Frauke. 1996 edition. *From Trucial States to United Arab Emirates*. Essex: Longman.

———. 2004. Middle East Institute talk, Washington, DC, November 30, 2004.

Hellyer, Peter, 1994 edition. *Fujaira, An Arabian Jewel*. Dubai, Abu Dhabi, and London: Motivate Publishing.

Henderson, Edward. 1999. *Arabian Destiny: The Complete Autobiography*. London: Motivate Publishing.

———. 1988. *This Strange Eventful History: Memoirs of Earlier Days in the UAE and Oman*. London: Quartet Books.

Herb, Michael. 1997. *All in the Family: Ruling Dynasties, Regime Resilience and Democratic Prospects in the Middle Eastern Monarchies*. Ph.D Dissertation. Los Angeles: University of California.

Ibn Khaldun. 1967 edition. *The Muqaddimah: An Introduction to History*. Translated by Franz Rosenthal, edited and abridged by N.J. Dawood. Princeton: Princeton University Press.

Jabbour, Jibrail S. 1995. *The Bedouins and the Desert: Aspects of Nomadic Life in the Arab East*. Albany: State University of New York Press.

Kanafani, Aida S. 1983. *Aesthetics and Ritual in the United Arab Emirates: The Anthropology of Food and Personal Adornment Among Arabian Women*. Beirut: American University of Beirut.

Kelly, J. B. 1964. *Eastern Arabian Frontiers*. New York: Praeger.

Khuri, Fuad I. 1980. *Tribe and State in Bahrain. The Transformation of Social and Political Authority in an Arab State*. Chicago: University of Chicago Press.

———. 1990. *Tent and Pyramid: Games and Ideology in Arab Culture from Backgammon to Autocratic Rule*. London: Saqi Books.

Lancaster, William. 1997 edition. *The Rwala Bedouin Today*. London: Cambridge University Press.

Lienhardt, Peter. 2001. *Shaikhdoms of Eastern Arabia*. Ed. Ahmed Al-Shahi. Oxford: Palgrave.

———. 1975. The Authority of Shaykhs in the Gulf: An Essay in Nineteenth-Century History. In *Arabian Studies*. R.B. Serjeant and R.L. Bidwell, editors. London: C.Hurst and Company, The Middle East Centre, University of Cambridge. pp. 61–75.

Litwak, Robert. 1981. *Security in the Persian Gulf 2: Sources of Inter-State Conflict*. International Institute for Strategic Studies. London: Gower.

Lorimer, J.G. 1986 edition. *Gazetteer of the Persian Gulf, Oman and Central Arabia, Geographical, Statistical and Historical Edition*. Slough, UK: Archive Editions.

Maitra, Jayanti and Afra Al-Hajji. 2001. *Qasr Al-Hosn: The History of the Rulers of Abu Dhabi*. Abu Dhabi: Centre for Documentation and Research.

Malley, William 1998 edition. *Fundamentalism Reborn? Afghanistan and the Taliban*. New York: New York University Press.

Mayer, Ann Elizabeth. 1999. *Islamic Tradition and Politics of Human Rights*. Boulder, CO: Westview Press.

Onley, James. 2002. *The Infrastructure of Informal Empire in the Gulf: The Local Elite and the Pax Britannica in the 19th Century*. Paper presented at the Middle East Studies Association Conference, Washington, DC.

O'Shea, Raymond. 1947. *The Sand Kings of Oman*. London: Methuen and Co., Ltd.

Peterson, J.E. 2001. The Nature of Succession in the Gulf. *The Middle East Journal.* Vol. 55, No. 4, Autumn: 579–601.

Pope, M.T.G. 1994. *Businessman's Guide to the UAE.* Sharja: Dar al Fatah Printing and Publishing.

Rugh, Andrea B. 1984. *Family in Contemporary Egypt.* Syracuse: Syracuse University Press.

———. 1986. *Reveal and Conceal: Dress in Contemporary Egypt.* Syracuse: Syracuse University Press.

———. 1997. *Within the Circle: Parents and Children in an Arab Village.* New York: Columbia University Press.

Rugh, William. 1997. The United Arab Emirates: What are the Sources of its Stability? *Middle East Policy.* Vol. 5 No. 3. September: 14–24.

Rush, Alan de Lacy, editor. 1991. *Buraimi Memorial,* SA Memorial, Vol. 1: 31. Slough, UK: Archive Edition.

———. editor. 1991. *Ruling Families of Arabia: The United Arab Emirates.* Vol. 1 and 2. Slough, UK: Archive Editions.

Sanger, Richard H. 1954. *The Arabian Peninsula.* Binghamton, NY: Cornell University Press.

Serjeant, R.B. and R.L. Bidwell, editors. 1975. *Arabian Studies II.* London: The Middle East Centre, University of Cambridge.

Slot, B.J. 1993. *The Arabs of the Gulf-1602–1784: An Alternative Approach to the Early History of the Arab Gulf States and the Arab Peoples of the Gulf, Mainly Based on Sources of the Dutch East India Company.* Leidshendam, the Netherlands.

Tammam, Hamdi. 1983. *Zayid bin Sultan al-Nahyan: The Leader on the March.* Tokyo: Dai Nippon Printing Company, Ltd.

Taryam, A.O. 1987. *The Establishment of the United Arab Emirates 1950–85.* London: Croom Helm.

Tuson, Penelope, editor. Records of the Emirates 1820–1960, 12 volumes. Archive Editions.

UAE Ministry of Culture and Information. 2002. *UAE Yearbook 2001/2002.* Abu Dhabi.

———. 2001. *UAE Yearbook 2000/2001.* Abu Dhabi.

Van Der Meulen, Hendrik. 1997. *The Role of Tribal and Kinship Ties in the Politics of the United Arab Emirates.* Ph.D Dissertation. Medford: Fletcher School of Law and Diplomacy.

Zahlan, Rosemarie Said. 1978. *The Origins of the United Arab Emirates: A Political and Social History of the Trucial States.* London: The MacMillan Press, Ltd.

———. 1989. *The Making of the Modern Gulf States: Kuwait, Bahrain, Qatar, the United Arab Emirates and Oman.* London: Unwin Hyman.

INDEX OF LOCAL PEOPLE AND TRIBES

INDEX

Qawasim (RAK and Sharja), 123–63,
  80, 82, 123–63, 233–4
  borders, 100, 119, 155
  characteristics, 4, 39, 115,
    124–5
  economy, 8, 113, 124–5, 182
  education, 152–3
  empire, 123–5, 137, 139
  identities, 18
  influence on Shamaliya coast
  marriages, 126, 136, 143, 146, 151,
    153, 156, 159
  military forces, 45
  modern status, 124
  oil, 124, 137
  RAK independence, 159–60
  RAK succession crisis, 230–2
  refuge for other leaders, 43, 45,
    64–5, 73, 102–3, 110, 173–4
  relations between Sharja and RAK,
    57, 124, 129, 132, 144, 157–61
  relations with Abu Dhabi, 39–41,
    52, 102, 108, 133–4, 156
  relations with Ajman, 125, 131, 134,
    142, 156
  relations with the British, 126–32,
    138, 144, 146, 149, 159, 161
  relations with Dubai, 39–41, 43, 44,
    45, 101, 105, 136, 147, 148,
    155, 156
  relations with Fujaira, 199–201,
    See also Kalba
  relations with kin, 123–5, 134–5,
    138, 143–9, 150, 152, 154,
    159, 162
  relations with Oman, 125, 127–33,
    159–60
  relations with Persians, 123, 126,
    128, 131, 142, 161
  relations with tribes, 68, 84, 125,
    137–8, 143, 144–5, 147, 152,
    155, 160, 220
  relations with UAQ, 125, 131, 133,
    135, 136, 142, 146, 147
  relations with Wahhabis (Saudis),
    126–32, 134, 144, 152

  succession, 127, 138, 143–5, 146,
    150, 156, 163
  See also, Dibba, Fujaira, Hamriya,
    Kalba, Khaur Fakkan Zura
Qishim, 104
Qubaissat, 34, 40, 44, 47, 52–3, 61–3,
  68, 73, 77, 79, 102, 237, 242

raids (see military engagements)
Ras al Khaima, See Qawasim
Ras Musandam, 3, 7, 105, 198, 201,
  214
revenues, 6, 9, 13, 36, 45, 78, 84, 107,
  109, 114, 120, 124, 132, 162,
  175, 182, 191–2, 203, 207–8,
  215, 219

Saudi Arabia, 4, 12, 13, 54, 59, 64–6,
  68, 74, 76–7, 79–80, 83, 85, 87,
  111–13, 116, 118, 152, 154, 160,
  176, 208, 211, 226, 237, 240–1,
  243
  See also Wahhabis
Shaikh, used as title, 237
Shamaliya coast, 17, 136, 193, 195–8,
  200–3, 213–15
Sharja, See Qawasim
slavery, 7, 12, 104, 184, 207
  British influence, 7, 202
  slave routes, 7
  Treaty of 1839, 7
Sohar in Oman, 44–6, 54, 102, 127,
  197, 214
solidarities, 1, 10, 22, 24, 46, 48, 237
  allegiances, 22, 46, 47
  alliances, 22, 44–7, 58, 70, 120,
    130, 182, 221–3
  blood ties, 48, 137, 214, 220, 239
  See also marriages
study approach, ix, x, 220
study organization, xiii
study sources, x, xi, xii
succession, 89, 70, 89–93, 115, 142,
  145, 151, 220, 224
  assassination, 64, 87
  age order, 121, 138, 183, 225, 226